STRANGE HEAVENS

About the Author

Philip Imbrogno (Connecticut) is a recognized authority in the field of UFO research. He has been interviewed by the *New York Times* and *Coast to Coast AM*, has appeared on NBC's *The Today Show* and *The Oprah Winfrey Show*, and has been featured in documentaries on the History Channel, A&E, Lifetime, and HBO. Imbrogno worked closely with many top UFO investigators, including Dr. J. Allen Hynek and Bud Hopkins. He is a retired educator who spent thirty years teaching science.

To Write the Author

If you wish to contact the author or would like more information about this book, please write to the author in care of Llewellyn Worldwide, and we will forward your request. Both the author and publisher appreciate hearing from you and learning of your enjoyment of this book and how it has helped you. Llewellyn Worldwide cannot guarantee that every letter written to the author can be answered, but all will be forwarded. Please write to:

Philip J. Imbrogno
⅍ Llewellyn Worldwide
2143 Wooddale Drive
Woodbury, MN 55125-2989

Please enclose a self-addressed stamped envelope for reply, or $1.00 to cover costs. If outside the USA, enclose an international postal reply coupon.

PHILIP J. IMBROGNO

STRANGE HEAVENS

THE Celestial Sphere AND ITS Influence ON Mythology, Religion, AND Belief IN THE Paranormal

Llewellyn Worldwide
Woodbury, Minnesota

FIRST EDITION
First Printing, 2019

Book design by Bob Gaul
Cover design by Shira Atakpu
Interior art by Llewellyn art department

Llewellyn Publications is a registered trademark of Llewellyn Worldwide Ltd.

Library of Congress Cataloging-in-Publication Data (Pending)
ISBN: 978-0-7387-5604-2

Llewellyn Publications
A Division of Llewellyn Worldwide Ltd.
2143 Wooddale Drive
Woodbury, MN 55125-2989
www.llewellyn.com

Printed in the United States of America

Contents

To my mother and father, who gave me my first telescope.

Introduction

There is something about the infinite expanse of the starry night that has always and will forever capture the imagination of the human mind. The night's inky velvet, dappled with beautiful, colorful points of luminous effervescence, affects the human mind like no other spectacle of nature.

Throughout human existence these mysterious, beautiful, and sometimes frightening celestial spectacles of nature have influenced worldwide scientific theory, religious beliefs, mythology, history, and how we perceive and interpret paranormal events. In many cases the night sky also inspired classic literature and, in modern times, the motion picture industry.

Since the beginning of recorded time, earthly cultures have looked up to the night sky and wondered what the points of lights, which today we know to be stars and planets, could be. Ancient African and European nomadic tribes believed they were campfires of powerful beings that lived in the sky. As time progressed many ancient civilizations believed the sky was a dwelling place for powerful deities who had a direct influence on the destiny of all mortals below them.

In modern-day Christianity, the faithful still point to the sky beyond the clouds as the dwelling place of God, angels, and other powerful beings. Did the wonders of the heavens act as a catalyst to stimulate the minds of priests, mystics, and prophets, or are they based on real experiences our ancestors had with paranormal forces beyond their comprehension?

For centuries cultures in both the Eastern and Western Hemispheres told stories of contact with these supernatural beings from the fires in the sky. These tales were absorbed in their mythology and became part of their religious doctrine. Many of these myths are present today and have evolved into countless forms, creating a foundation for world-wide cultural beliefs.

When people of ancient cultures looked up to the night sky, they firmly believed the gods were always watching them. It is clear the constellations and brighter stars influenced not only our mythology but also modern religious beliefs. Some of these celestial manifestations that helped shape history were the appearance of comets, phases of the moon, lunar and solar eclipses, planetary alignments, and meteorite impacts, just to name a few.

Ancient myths from China, Japan, Africa, Babylon, Greece, Persia, and the Maya, Toltec, and Aztec nations of North and South America all tell stories of how magnificent godlike beings came down from the fires in the sky and interacted with them. The legends tell how these supernatural beings were responsible for teaching humans written language and science and set the foundations for civilization.

Celestial manifestations are mentioned in such classic works of literature as *The Iliad* and *The Odyssey* and religious books including the Bible, Qur'an, and Torah. It's clear from modern interpretation of these passages that events on the celestial sphere were attributed to signs from a power greater than man. These ancient dogmas were then carried throughout human history with their interpretations changed by wise men, priests, and modern-day scientists to suit the age and culture of their time. Today, despite our technological advances, we still look at the sky and wonder. We are not only influenced by the stories of old, but are creating new ones for the present and future.

In modern times what we call a paranormal experience often has its origin and a connection with the brightest stars and most prominent constellations. These same stars and constellations were also identified by Bronze Age and Iron Age civilizations as being the home of their deities and are frequently mentioned in their myths, sagas, and religious prayers. Is it just a coincidence that these stellar objects and configurations of stars are the brightest as seen from Earth? Could their prominence have influenced the oracles of long ago and people of today who claim contact with aliens and supernatural beings?

Some modern researchers view these ancient myths and modern paranormal experiences as proof of contact with an extraterrestrial civilization, while others say they are merely flights of fancy or stories used by cult leaders and priests to control the population and secure their own position in society.

As a result of these alleged contacts in both ancient and modern times, the human medium channels information not only of a spiritual nature, but—in rare cases—prophecy, symbols, technical scientific diagrams, and other information which cannot be easily dismissed by even the most skeptical. If we take into account that only a small percentage of these people had a real experience, then this leaves a respectable number of individuals who require further investigation. Yet, modern scientists turn a deaf ear and laugh while physicians suggest these individuals take medication to control their delusions. In extreme cases some of these people are placed in mental hospitals and are give a regiment of drugs.

Human history often repeats itself; what our ancestors have experienced in the past is still being reported today. The only difference is the language and terminology used to describe these otherworldly encounters has changed. At one time we referred to these beings from the stars as gods or spirits; today we are calling them aliens, extraterrestrials, or interdimensional entities.

After forty-plus years of studying astronomy and investigating claims of UFO encounters and other paranormal events, it's still a mystery to me. Although I have collected a great deal of information and learned more about the multidimensional universe, the unseen world still remains elusive. My case files are filled with people who claim their paranormal experience had a connection to a planet, star, or constellation.

This work is not a science book, and its purpose is not to support any extraterrestrial or spiritual origins of UFOs and other forms of paranormal phenomena. This study is the result of decades of research, presents the historical, physiological, psychological, and psychic connection we have with the heavens, and shows how events and various phenomena on the celestial sphere have influenced not only our scientific knowledge but also worldwide religious beliefs, mythology, history, and modern interpretations of the paranormal.[1]

My wish is that this book will inspire you to take a journey through the multiverse in a starship of the imagination—good voyage!

---

1   Although some may disagree with me, religion is a paranormal belief. The definition of paranormal relates to experiences outside of our normal physical existence.

1

The Alluring Night Sky

During a snowy Christmas morning in 1959, I woke up early to get a glimpse of the colorfully wrapped presents under the tree. Being careful not to wake my parents, and with only a faint night-light in the hall for illumination, I took a closer look and saw a very large box at the rear of the tree with my name on it. I wondered what this could be. It was the largest present under the tree, and I fought all temptation to pull it out and rip it open. I quietly tiptoed back to my room, climbed into my bed, and found it very difficult to fall back to sleep.

Just hours earlier, my father walked me over to the window and pointed to a bright star in the east and said it was "the Christmas Star" and was used "to help Santa Claus find his way home." Although I was only eight years old, it was obvious to me from watching science shows on television that stars were suns very far away and the reality of Santa Claus was questionable.

As the years went by, my thoughts would often go back to that Christmas Eve, and I'd wonder what the bright object in the crystal clear winter night sky could have been. To a child with a vivid imagination, it was a dazzling and mystifying sight.

During my late thirties I finally was able to get the answer to that Christmas Eve mystery by using a computer planetarium program.

By entering the exact date, time, and coordinates on the celestial sphere, my decades-old question was answered. What my father called the Christmas Star was actually the planet Jupiter! Although my curiosity was finally satisfied, I couldn't help feeling that a small portion of my childhood was lost by solving this mystery.

However, according to historical astronomical records and the Bible, there really was a starlike apparition in the sky sometime around the birth of Jesus. The possibility of the reality of this ancient celestial event would once again inspire my inquisitiveness to do research with the hope of finding the answer to two questions: Was there really a Christmas Star? And what was it?

Finally, as daylight arrived and the family gathered in the living room, my mother gave the OK to open up the large box that awaited me under the tree. To my delight it was a telescope! I had wanted one since I first became interested in astronomy. Although it was only a small astronomical telescope, to me at the time it was like the Hale telescope at Palomar Observatory in California.[2]

I could not wait to use it. Much to my excitement that very night was clear, and after setting up my new telescope, I pointed it out the window and began searching the night sky. It was a difficult task since my field of view was limited, plus the sky was glared out by the town's bright lights.

Despite all the restrictions I was able to get a good look at the rising moon. The sight of the lunar landscape at low power amazed me. I observed with wonder the famous "seas," craters, mountains, and many other physical surface features of our natural satellite. I had seen many pictures in library books of the lunar surface, but none compared with looking through the telescope and seeing it live!

---

2   The Hale Telescope at Mount Palomar just outside of Los Angeles was the largest telescope in the world at the time, with a mirror diameter of 200 inches.

The moon's surface features seemed incredibly clear, sharp, and close. In my spaceship of imagination, I was flying above the lunar surface. This was a decade before the first lunar landing and no one knew what mysteries our nearest neighbor in space hid from us. In the 1950s there were television programs and stories about aliens having a base on the moon, so with my telescope at a higher power, I meticulously searched the lunar surface. But to my dismay no alien bases were to be discovered that night.

Unlimited Horizons

In the spring we visited my aunt who lived in a more secluded part of town, far away from the bright street lights, and—more importantly—there was a clear, unobstructed view of most of the sky. I brought along my telescope and quickly set it up in the front yard, eagerly awaiting sunset. The crescent moon was used to align the telescope finder scope and would be my first target for the evening.

Observing at high and low magnification, despite some atmospheric turbulence, the lunar detail was incredible! My attention was then directed to a brilliant starlike object in the western sky. I turned the telescope toward the object and, after getting it directly in the center of the crosshairs of the finder scope, carefully focused the eyepiece. A crescent-like disk was visible that looked like a miniature moon; to my delight it was the planet Venus.

Many of my relatives as well as several neighbors who were also visiting came out to look through the telescope and seemed quite impressed. While looking at the moon, my great-aunt and uncle attached some type of supernatural and religious significance to what they were seeing.

That evening was magical for me. Later I entered a note in my observation book stating that it was my initiation day. From that day on my life would be dedicated to the study of the universe and perhaps contribute to helping solve the many mysteries that await us in the vastness of space.

A Planet of Mystery

Every clear night I would use my telescope and observe the wonders of the universe. Despite heavily light-polluted skies as the result of living near a populated area, I was undaunted. While observing the planet Mars when it was at a close approach to Earth, I wondered if there were living creatures on the red planet. The United States space program was at its infancy at the time and human beings had only gone ankle deep into the vast cosmic ocean.

I excitedly observed Mars, straining my vision with the hope of seeing something that would indicate intelligent life. Due to atmospheric turbulence, the image of the red planet faded in and out, but at times, just for a brief second, the planet would appear sharp, and one of its polar caps and definite dark surface markings stood out in contrast with the red-orange surface. To my dismay, after hours observing the red planet, no evidence could be seen to indicate that Mars was inhabited.

Evidence of Martian Life

During the end of the nineteenth century, while observing the red planet during a favorable opposition (close approach), Italian astronomer Giovanni Schiaparelli reported he observed a definite pattern of straight lines that formed a crisscross pattern on the Martian surface. In his report Dr. Schiaparelli called them *canali*, which is Italian for "channels." When the *New York Times* carried the story, the word was mistranslated into "canals." This mistake implied that the so-called Martian canali was artificial in nature and constructed by intelligent beings that possessed an advanced technology.

Inspired by Schiaparelli's observations of the Martian canals, a well-respected American astronomer named Percival Lowell,[3] using his own

---

3   Percival Lowell (March 13, 1855–November 12, 1916) was a mathematician and astronomer who supported speculation in favor of the existence of Martian canals. After his observations of Mars, Lowell began the search for Pluto, which was called Planet X at the time.

money, built an observatory on a mountaintop in Arizona with, initially, the primary purpose of observing Mars. He called the location of his new observatory Mars Hill. The observatory housed one of the largest refracting telescopes in the world and is still in use today.[4]

Lowell claimed he also saw the canals of Mars and was convinced they were the work of an intelligent race of beings trying to tap the last of their water from the Martian polar caps in a desperate attempt to save their dry, dying planet.

Having an art background, Lowell made detailed drawings in his observation book showing the surface of Mars crisscrossed with a network of complex canals and junctions. In 1895 Lowell published a book based on his observations of the red planet entitled *Mars*. His observations were never confirmed by other astronomers in the United States and Europe, and although photography was in use at the time, the so-called Martian canals were never imaged. It's clear from interviews that Lowell wanted very much to believe there was life on Mars—perhaps he wanted to believe too much!

In 1976 when the *Viking 1* and *2* spacecraft[5] gave us our first high-resolution images of Mars, the Valles Marineris (Mariner Valley)[6] was one of the first pictures transmitted back to Earth. The Valles Marineris is a vast canyon system that runs along the Martian equator 2500 miles long and 4 miles deep. It is visible under favorable conditions from Earth with a modest-sized telescope. Today science historians believe Lowell actually saw this giant Martian canyon and with some imagination wrongly perceived it as a network of canals.

---

4   A refracting telescope uses a large lens to gather the light and provide resolution. Lowell's telescope had a lens diameter of 24 inches, which in that period of time was a very large instrument.

5   NASA's Viking Project became the first US mission to land a spacecraft safely on the surface of Mars and return images of the surface.

6   Named after the *Mariner 9* spacecraft that first imaged it in 1971–1972 in lower resolution.

After his obsession with Mars subsided, Lowell began the search for a trans-Neptunian planet, which at the time was called Planet X.[7] Lowell never found the mysterious planet, and it was not until fourteen years after his death that Pluto was discovered. Many modern-day astronomers, including the discoverer of Pluto, Clyde Tombaugh, credited Lowell's early observations as a major factor in the discovery. The name "PLuto" was chosen for the new planet after the Roman god of the underworld with the first two letters often capitalized in honor of Percival Lowell.[8] In the late 1940s it was discovered that Pluto was much too small to cause the gravitational perturbations observed in Neptune's orbit, so the hunt for Planet X continued.

Barsoom

It was the telescopic observations of Mars and its alleged canals by Lowell at end of the nineteenth century that inspired writer H. G. Wells to write his classic story *The War of the Worlds*. In 1894 French astronomers observed "strange lights" on Mars and published their findings in the scientific journal *Nature* during August of that year.

Wells used the observation of the French astronomers to open the novel, imagining the unexplainable lights on Mars to be the ignition of rocket engines launching the Martian spaceships toward Earth. Wells used Lowell's idea that Mars was a dying planet with very little water. In his story the Martians invaded our planet to steal our water and save their race by wiping out all intelligent life on Earth.

The Martians that Lowell envisioned were a peaceful, almost godlike, highly technological society that was desperately trying to save their race, but Wells saw them as a race of monsters that would stop at nothing to secure the water of Earth to save their world.

---

7   The search for Planet X inspired the 1951 classic science fiction thriller *The Man from Planet X*.

8   Pluto was discovered in February of 1930. Today it is not considered a planet, but a dwarf planet, making the total number of planets in the solar system eight.

Think about it: had it not been for the observation of the Martian "canals" by Percival Lowell and Giovanni Schiaparelli, the literary classic the *The War of the Worlds* probably would have never been written, the film library in Hollywood would be minus four movies, and the studios would have never earned the hundreds of millions of dollars in profit that the films generated.

During my youth the possibility of life on Mars and elsewhere in the universe fascinated me. I began to read every book on astronomy and UFOs available to me. While other children my age went to the movies and played baseball on Saturday, my day would be spent at the library, reading. It was a magical time for me, one of wonder, discovery and great adventure.

At the library there were books and magazine articles about people who claimed to have had encounters with flying saucers and some even said they saw aliens. In several of these publications there were fantastic tales about people who claimed they were taken on a spaceship ride by extraterrestrials to visit Venus, Mars, Jupiter, and the moon. Although not one of these individuals offered proof of their incredible claims, I still wanted to believe the stories. But there was always a foundation of skepticism buried deep within my mind.

Among the many science fiction novels that influenced me during those young years were a series of adventure sagas by Edgar Rice Burroughs entitled *A Princess of Mars*, later changed to *John Carter of Mars*.[9]

In 1911, inspired by Lowell's book *Mars*, plus all the strange newspaper accounts concerning life on the red planet and, of course, the work of H. G. Wells, Burroughs wrote a series of short novels about a fictional character named John Carter who is transported to Mars.

---

9   Edgar Rice Burroughs (September 1, 1875–March 19, 1950) was an American author, best known for his creation of *Tarzan*. He had a great belief in the paranormal and would often back well-known spiritual mediums.

John Carter, a gentleman from Virginia, serves as a cavalry officer in the Civil War on the side of the Confederacy. At the end of the war, he travels to Arizona to look for gold and strikes it rich. He is then mortally wounded by hostile Apaches and hides in a cave waiting to die. Carter then leaves his body and somehow, through astral projection, is transported to Mars. He wakes up on the red planet and finds himself in a copy of his physical body and very much alive.

During Burroughs's time, the thought of traveling to Mars in a ship was considered out of the question. It seems his interest in the paranormal and spiritualism influenced him to come up with the idea of Carter traveling to Mars in his astral form and generating a new physical body.

Mars (called Barsoom by the inhabitants) was populated by several types of intelligent beings and a multitude of exotic animals. One race of Barsoomians looked human but had red skin, jet black hair, and large deep blue eyes—the Red Martians. They built fantastic palace-like cities and had flying machines that amazed Carter.

Despite their technology the planet was dying and water was scarce. In a monumental desperate attempt to save themselves, the inhabitants of Barsoom constructed a complex series of canals to tap the last of their water from the planet's north and south polar ice caps. Since water on Barsoom was in short supply, kingdoms went to war to possess it. The warlord who controlled the planet's remaining water would be master of all of Barsoom.

Since the gravity of Mars is one-third of that on Earth, Carter was able to run faster, jump three times higher, and had superior strength than the mightiest warriors on the planet. Carter finally tells the Barsoomians he was from Earth, the third planet from the sun (which they knew as Jasoom), and had no idea how he was transported to Mars. The people of Barsoom listened with amazement and envy as Carter told them that on Earth (Jasoom) they had vast oceans of water and great ships that sailed to far-off lands.

There was also another race of beings that lived in the mountains that were not humanoid: the Green Martians. They were warlike, green in color, ten feet tall, with four arms. After a great battle with Carter, they admire him for his fighting skills and come to be his allies. After many heroic deeds Carter is named leader of the armies and defeats the evil warlords of Barsoom. John Carter finally marries the beautiful but strong-willed Dejah Thoris, a princess of the great Kingdom of Helium. John Carter then has children with his beloved princess and, for a time, all is well.

After living many years in peace, a great evil returns and threatens to enslave all the people of Barsoom. Carter sacrifices his life to defeat the evil force. At the moment of his death on Mars, he is once again magically transported in his astral body back to Earth. As he awakes in his original body, he discovers only days have passed and not years. Carter then leaves the cave to spend the rest of his life living in a small cottage in a town called Catskill, New York, in the Hudson River Valley. For years he tries to return to Mars to be united with his wife and children, but cannot. He finally dies for the last time on March 8, 1886.

The amazing thing about this story is there really is a Catskill, New York, and while John Carter may be a common name, a real person with the same given name lived there until he passed away in 1886. There are local people of that New York town who believe this real John Carter spun a tall tale that came to the attention of Burroughs and was the foundation for the John Carter series.

In 2011 Walt Disney Pictures announced they were finishing a movie based on the Edgar Rice Burroughs classic sci-fi story. The movie was released on March 9, 2012. Coincidently enough, the preview was shown on March 8, 2012—the 126th anniversary of the fictional and real John Carter's death. But was it really a coincidence?

The movie did not do well from a financial point of view, since younger people had never heard of the John Carter saga. The tales of

John Carter on Mars were the Star Wars of my generation. While in the theater, I noticed many who attended were about my age and most likely were childhood fans of the novels. The movie was quite different from the books and this was disappointing. Perhaps the movie would have done much better if the writers stuck more to Edgar Rice Burroughs's original stories instead of depending on special effects and computer-generated images to compensate for a poorly written script and terrible acting.

For the PBS television series *Cosmos*, writer Dr. Carl Sagan said the John Carter saga inspired his interest in the planet Mars. Dr. Sagan tried to change the license plate on his car to "BARSOOM," but at that time only six letters or a combination of letters and numbers was allowed. Dr. Sagan was disappointed because as a young person he was enthralled with Burroughs's work. Sagan then had his car plates changed to "PHOBOS," which is a name of one of the two Martian moons. It was a compromise he was not happy with.

Recently, while doing research at the New York City Public Library's main branch, I made arrangements to read a rare second edition of the John Carter novel for the first time since my childhood. Since it was the original work of Burroughs it was exciting for me. It was surprising to see how different the story was when compared to the books and comics of the 1950s and '60s. Fans of John Carter should not blame Hollywood for bungling the story. Who knows what version they had?

Is Anyone Out There?

As a young person with a very active imagination, greatly influenced by the reports of UFOs and Edgar Rice Burroughs's stories of John Carter's adventures on Mars, I would often walk out to a field on a clear night and, while standing with my eyes closed and arms spread out wide, attempt to mentally send out messages to the alleged aliens in the UFOs, imploring them to appear and take me aboard their craft.

Also, reminiscent of John Carter, I would lie down on the grass while looking up, wishing to be magically transported to Mars—but it never happened.

Shortly before my twelfth birthday, while in the field on a cloudy night and looking up to the sky hoping to see something, without warning a burst of green, yellow, and red, bright, cloud-like lights appeared in the sky out of nowhere with no sound at all.

I was not expecting this and could feel my heart pounding in my chest. It was as if my calls for contact had been heard. I ran to a neighbor's home and asked them to come outside to witness the event. To my excitement and delight, the glowing clouds were still visible in the sky. It was evident from the expressions on the adults' faces they were surprised and shocked to see this apparition. As we watched, several more people came out of their homes to see what was going on.

There were other children about my age also present observing the strange lights. One young boy asked with a fearful voice, "What is that?"

After much hesitation, one of the adults said, "Oh, that's nothing but a plane going through air pockets." I found this answer puzzling and thought, *How does a plane create colors while traveling through an air pocket?* It was evident by their expressions my neighbors were quite amazed at what they were seeing, and in their voices was definite fear. An older woman started saying prayers in Italian and making the sign of the cross. After ten minutes the colorful clouds dissipated and my neighbors went back into their homes.

The next day I would discover the unusual event was seen by hundreds if not thousands in the southern New York area. In the days to follow, the military offered an official explanation. A statement made on ABC, NBC, and CBS television news said that the National Weather Service in Long Island launched a number of rockets with barium color gas to track air currents.

I still wonder to this day if this was the real cause of the strange glowing clouds. The local papers and television news carried accounts of people who saw the lights. Many thought it was either a Russian or alien invasion. Some thought the Chinese were testing atomic weapons in the upper atmosphere, and many people in my neighborhood believed it was a sign of the second coming of Jesus Christ. However, most did accept the explanation by the National Weather Service and the matter was put to rest and soon forgotten by the general populace.

That night showed me the powerful influence the heavens have on the human mind. We are used to seeing an unchanging sky, and when something out of place appears that we have no control over, it generates not only wonder but fear. The looks on the faces of my neighbors when they looked up to the sky and gazed at the unknown apparition is something I will never forget.

A Dead World

During November of 1964, NASA launched an unmanned space probe called *Mariner 4* to Mars. Although its computer and imaging system was primitive when compared to what we have in the twenty-first century, at the time it was the state of the art and was going to give us our first close-up pictures of the Martian surface.

For months I eagerly waited for information on the probe since previous attempts by the United States and Soviets were unsuccessful. In some cases the spacecraft mysteriously disappeared. Some people, including this wide-eyed teenager, believed that perhaps the Martians did not want their privacy violated by the hostile people of planet Earth.

It was difficult to get information in those days. In the early- to mid-sixties there was no internet. Radio, television, and newspapers were the main sources of acquiring information. Then one day in mid-July of 1965, I heard a radio newscast saying that *Mariner 4* had reached Mars, and the first pictures of the surface had been radioed back.

I collected a number of bottles for refund, cashed them in, and ran to the local stationary store to eagerly wait for the newspapers to be delivered. Although I only had to wait about an hour, to an impatient young person it seemed like days. Finally, when the paper was put on the stand, I saw the headline "*Mariner* Sends Back First Image of Mars." After giving the clerk my hard-earned ten cents, I went straight for the picture.

The image of Mars was black and white and very low resolution. It showed nothing but a desolate surface with craters. There were no fantastic cities, exotic beasts, or canals. The picture in the paper showed Mars as a barren dead planet much like our moon; it was one of the greatest disappointments of my life. Although this was a major setback, it did not hinder my interest in exploring the possibility that life did exist out there somewhere. After all, the universe is a very big place.

Years later my interest in the possibility of life on Mars would be rekindled when the *Viking 1* and *2* spacecraft imaged the planet with high-resolution cameras. There was evidence Mars once had oceans and rivers and the orbiters imaged a number of very strange features on the surface that appeared like the ruins of an ancient civilization.[10] It seems the earlier *Mariner* spacecraft only imaged a small part of the planet and the resolution was so low only the largest features were seen.

Greeting Old Friends

To get a clear, unobstructed view of the sky, on many a clear, moon-less night I would visit a local town park near my home and climb a fifty-foot pine tree close to the top. Here I would sit for hours at a time, watching the sky for meteors and looking at the constellations and vis-ible-eye planets. It was pretty spooky in the park, but my love for the stars was greater than my fear of the darkness of night.

---

10   NASA agrees the formations are strange, but follow-up imaging showed they are natural in origin. This led many government conspiracy theorists to accuse NASA of covering up the discovery that Mars once had an ancient civilization.

In 1969, near the height of the Vietnam War, I left home for the military and served in Vietnam and Thailand. No matter what country in Southeast Asia I found myself in, the constellations were the same as the ones back home. The only difference was that in Thailand, Cambodia, and South Vietnam, they were higher in the sky.

While stationed in Thailand I would often look up at the sky on clear nights to gaze at the constellations of Orion, Taurus, Auriga, the Pleiades, Canis Major, and Canis Minor. Seeing them in the sky was like greeting old friends and it gave me a feeling of home while being so far away in an unpopular war on the other side of the world. It's hard to explain, but just the sight of my celestial friends gave me a feeling of inner peace.

Just like their counterparts in the West, people of every country in Asia had a mythology and religious belief that connected them to the sky. In Thailand, after making a number of friends, I had a rare opportunity to talk with many Thai people about their legends of the night sky.

After returning to the United States, or getting "back in the world" as many soldiers called it, I attended a number of colleges that offered astronomy programs and made it very easy for military personnel to attend classes and use the facilities on campus.

Sometimes while in the observatory, instead of using the telescope, I would climb the ladder to the top of the observing platform, open the dome, and just watch the constellations as they paraded by as a result of Earth's rotation. There was always a feeling of peace, inner tranquility, and well-being during these sessions.

Others who accompanied me or used the telescope on their own also reported the same state of mind. To my surprise, while watching the PBS television science series *NOVA*, they interviewed an astronomer about his discovery during a night session at an observatory. During his dialogue the astronomer described the same feeling of inner peace. He told the interviewer in a very calm monotone voice why he enjoyed astronomy—because there is a tranquil feeling while using the telescope and observing the splendor of the universe from our tiny planet.

I had many discussions about this with a psychiatrist friend of mine who experienced the same feeling while my guest at the observatory. She told me it was nothing but the brain chemistry slightly changing, most likely caused by the late hour and darkness. She theorized that the mind thinks it should be asleep and the calmness is caused by the production of melatonin.

I agreed partially with her theory, but also suggested that we might be tuning in on a vast number of energies that are constantly flowing through us from every direction in space. My doctor friend then looked at me strangely and there was only silence.

Backbone of the Night Sky

Since there were no electric lights and a much smaller population, the sky was considerably darker in ancient times, and everything on the celestial sphere—whether their light be intrinsic or reflected—must have been much clearer and brighter and a beautiful sight.

On several occasions with a number of friends, we would camp out on the beach at Padre Island, Texas, and lie on the sand and look up. This was a time before the island became a popular location for spring break and there was not a soul around for miles. The nearest city, Corpus Christi, was just a small fishing town, so the skies at the beach were very dark.

I will never forget the sight of the Milky Way as its ghostly glow stretched across the sky from north to south. It's no wonder why the aborigines of Australia called it "the backbone of the night" and believed it supported the sky and kept it from falling. The Native Americans saw it as a path in which the spirits of those who have died walk to the afterlife. To the people of India and Southeast Asia, it was a great celestial river, which was used by supernatural beings to travel the universe. The ancient Greeks and Romans also have a story explaining how the Milky Way was created.

According to Greek mythology, it came into being when the goddess Hera (Juno), while breastfeeding the infant Hercules, spilled her milk across the heavens. It is this myth that gave the Milky Way its name.

The band of ghostly light we call the Milky Way is actually millions of stars and gas in the center of our galaxy, which from our point of view is located toward the constellation of Sagittarius. A galaxy is a collection of billions of stars, dust, gas, and most likely hundreds of millions of planets. Our galaxy is but one of more than 400 billion galaxies in the visible universe. Although there are many shapes to galaxies, ours is of the spiral type with a diameter of over 100,000 light-years. The sun and all the planets of our solar system are located about 27 thousand light-years[11] from the center.

The Milky Way's true nature was not known until the seventeenth century when Galileo first used his crude small telescope to look at the night sky. He was shocked to see the glowing mist of light resolve into countless stars. The church inquisitors did not believe his claim and even refused to look through his telescope, insisting it was a waste of time because what he claimed could not possibly exist. Galileo's observation of the Milky Way proved to those would listen that the universe was a great deal larger than anyone imagined.

That night on the beach at Padre Island, it was clear to me and my companions the mystical effect such a sight had on people long ago and why this feeling survived into the twenty-first century.

Star Therapy

A number of years ago it came to my attention that several therapists are now using astronomy to help their patience relax. "Star Therapy Groups" would meet at an open field on clear, warm evenings with

---

11   A light-year is the distance light will travel in 1 year, which is about 6 trillion miles.

little or no wind. The patients would bring a pillow and two blankets and lie down in the field on their backs in a circle looking up at the stars. The therapist stands in the middle of the circle and, using a green pen, points to the constellations and tells the legends on how each got its name. Many of the people who attended have reported that after the session they feel relaxed and refreshed and realize the universe is a much bigger place than they thought; many of their concerns seemed small when compared to the grand scale of the cosmos. After interviewing several of the people who attended these sessions, all said the feeling was "euphoric" in nature and made them feel happy.

I would often go out to a field on a clear night just to relax and look up at the stars. When you do this, after a while you seem to leave your earthly body and became one with the sky. The stars and constellations no longer seem like points of light at a great distance, but they now reveal their true nature to you as friends and companions that will never desert you. It is my belief we all need to reconnect with the universe.

Everything on this planet, including the basic materials of which our bodies are composed, was forged in the core of a giant star billions of years ago. This massive old star blew itself to bits, seeding the galaxy with the heavy elements that formed our sun, the planets, and eventually us! Although many have ignored this inner drive to reconnect with the universe, some of us now realize that we are all children of the stars looking upward, searching for our origins and the meaning of life. As the late Carl Sagan once said, "We are made of star stuff." [12] Perhaps because of this we feel a subconscious pull to reconnect to the night sky.

Today in this troubled world the majority of people are afraid to venture out to an isolated location in the dark. A psychologist friend explained to me it is a deep-rooted genetic fear in our subconscious that warns us of possible predators hunting and hiding in the shadowy

---

12   *Cosmos* documentary TV series by Dr. Carl Sagan, narrated by Dr. Carl Sagan, KCET and Carl Sagan Productions, 1980.

corners or behind bushes. This may have been so ten thousand years ago, and this genetic information could have been passed down from our human ancestors, but in this day and age the only predator we have to fear is another human being. Human beings are one of the few species in nature that preys upon itself. People of the twenty-first century would like to think we have evolved and become enlightened. Yes, we have come a long way, however, we are still very tribal and territorial and most of us still kill other animals and consume their flesh for food.

The human race is divided between having one foot in a cave and one foot in the stars. The question is: Shall we take that leap forward, up to the heavens, or fall back in the dark caverns from which we emerged?

It is very unfortunate that people hesitate to go out at night to look at the sky since it is part of who we are. As for me, I am reminded of a verse from a poem by English poet Sarah Williams that said, "I have loved the stars too fondly to be fearful of the night." [13] This simple short sentence is written on a plaque in my study next to one of my telescopes since it continues to inspire me even after many decades of stargazing.

A New Direction

It was my interest in astronomy that led to my passion investigating UFO sightings and other aspects of the paranormal. What is still of great interest to me are people who, after a paranormal experience, developed an obsessive interest in astronomy. This was especially true with those who claimed a close encounter with a UFO. These people would go to a lonely, isolated location on a clear night where they had an unobstructed view of the sky and stay for hours watching for the unexplainable to appear.

When this behavior was discussed with my psychologist friend, he was amazed and wondered what impulse was powerful enough to

---

13   Sarah Williams (December 1837–1868) was an English poet-novelist. Her best-known work is "The Old Astronomer."

suppress the fear of being alone in the dark that many of us have. This made him very interested and he often joined me on some of my investigations. He passed away in 2015 and left me his notes, which were very helpful in my research. During his last years he was convinced that some form of intelligent energy was flowing through the universe and all we had to do was condition our minds to receive and accept it. He believed by going to a peaceful place at night to look at the stars it may be possible to connect with this cosmic consciousness. His last note on the subject was that "star meditation" seemed to be similar to the psychological effect that the power of prayer has on the human mind.

2

A History of Discovery

If you stand in the middle of a large field with an unobstructed view of the horizon and look to the cardinal points on the compass, you will get the impression you are under a large blue dome encompassing the earth. This dome (the celestial sphere) from your prospective is 180 degrees, or half a circle. Looking toward the horizon it will appear as if there is an area of space where the dome of sky meets the ground. Of course we know today this effect is caused by the curvature of our planet, and no matter how far you walk, the point where the celestial sphere and the earth meet eludes you.

During the Bronze Age, people never went very far from their homes and their beliefs were based mostly on observation. From the viewpoint of these ancient peoples, the ground on which they stood and as far as they could see was flat. The mountains were elevated areas above the ground and were thought to be the home of beings that were more than human, but less than the gods of the heavens.

Natural forces that could not be explained were attributed to a celestial god, demigod, or other supernatural beings. Some of these gods and demigods they invented are still present in our media today in the form of superheroes and villains. Thor, Loki, Odin, Zeus, Ares, Hercules, and the Amazons are among them, just to name a few. Finally, what many people today don't know is a number of these ancient gods (Hecate for example) are still worshipped today.[14]

The Flat Earth

The flat Earth model is the oldest conception of our planet's shape. It was drawn as a two-dimensional flat disk. The stars, moon, planets, and sun were thought to be holes in the celestial sphere in which the ethereal fires of the cosmos can be seen. The known lands of the world were grouped together surrounded by ocean. It's clear from writings and paintings people living during this time actually believed that ships would fall off the earth if they sailed far enough from land.

Many ancient cultures assumed the earth was flat, including Greece until the classical period, Bronze Age and Iron Age civilizations in the Middle East until the Hellenistic period, and finally India and most of Asia until the seventeenth century.

The Native American tribes of both North and South America also believed in a flat Earth covered by an opaque firmament in the shape of an inverted bowl. As with the people of Europe and Asia, this belief was supported by observation and was common in prescientific societies for a great part of human history.

These early inhabitants in all parts of the world noticed the celestial sphere was filled with activity and motion. To them there seemed to be a purpose, and since the celestial objects moved in a predictable rhythm, they assumed it was not a natural occurrence, but the result of powerful beings.

Bronze Age civilizations of Europe, the Middle East, India, and China believed celestial movements were intertwined into the destiny of each individual and, if understood, could predict the future and control the fate of the human race. These early observations and interpretations

---

14   Hecate may have originated in Greece sometime around the eighth century BC. She was the goddess of magic, herbs, Witchcraft, and ghosts. Later, in Neopagan rituals, she was also associated with the moon and night.

of celestial events and cycles were viewed as divine communications to alert the populace of terrestrial events. For example, in ancient Egypt the flooding of the Nile River always took place when the star Sirius rose just before the sun.

The Druids used standing stones to mark the positions of the sun, moon, and bright stars at certain times of the year to predict seasons and eclipses. The Maya, Aztecs, and Chinese also developed systems for predicting terrestrial events from observations of the celestial sphere. This practice of observing and documenting the relationship between the celestial cycles and earthly events was to become the foundation for astrology and later astronomy in many parts of the world.

The ancient stargazers noticed that although the stars paraded across the celestial dome, their relative positions to each other remained the same year after year. They also observed that the moon and five bright stellar-like objects seemed to change position frequently when compared to the stars and patterns of stars known as constellations. These objects were called planets, from the Greek word *planetai*, which means "wandering ones."

When something new appeared in the sky, like a comet, nova, or even an unusually bright and dynamic meteor shower, it was thought to be a sign from a celestial supernatural entity. The meaning of these sky events would be interpreted by a priest or shaman who would inform the population of what they must do to appease the sky gods. In some cases human sacrifice was the remedy and we can assume it was usually a person the priest wanted to get rid of. It's obvious certain individuals obtained considerable power by claiming they were able to speak for the gods of the sky.

Believing the sun, moon, and planets were important, the Greeks assigned them to represent particular gods. The sun and moon were called Helios and Selene[15]; the planet Venus, since it was so beautiful in the sky, was sacred to Aphrodite, the goddess of love; Mars because of its red color was given to Ares, the god of war; Jupiter was sacred to Zeus; Saturn sacred to Cronus the Titan and father of Zeus; Mercury, because it moved quickly on the celestial sphere, was the representation of Hermes, the messenger of the gods. This custom of naming planets, moons, and other astronomical bodies after Greek and Roman deities continues into the twenty-first century.

The appearance of the planet Mars had a great effect on the ancient Greeks. The brightness of Mars changes considerably depending on its position in relation to Earth. When Mars is directly across from Earth, the distance between the two planets is considerably less and the red planet appears brighter than normal in the night sky. This planetary configuration is called an opposition and takes place about every two years. A favorable opposition of Mars takes place when Earth is at its farthest point from the sun (aphelion) and Mars is at its closest point to the sun (perihelion)—during this time the distance between the two planets is considerably less than a normal opposition. When this alignment takes place, Mars may outshine the planet Jupiter and appear blood red in the sky.

During the time of ancient Greece, the skies were pitch black at night and the sight of Mars during this special planetary configuration must have been an astonishing sight. The ancient Greeks saw it as an omen to go to war. Many of the major Greek conflicts from 1200 to 60 BC can be timed with a favorable opposition of Mars.[16]

---

15   Later in Greek mythology they were replaced by Apollo and Artemis. The Roman version of the moon goddess was Diana or Luna.

16   Robin Osborne, *Greece in the Making: 1200–60 BC* (London: Routledge Publishing, 1987).

The Geocentric Theory

The flat Earth theory placed our planet in the center of the universe and so did the geocentric theory. Geocentric is simply defined as relating to the Earth's center. The difference between the two theories was the geocentric model showed Earth being spherical and not a flat disk.

As knowledge was passed down from generation to generation and the population of Europe increased, people began traveling further from their homes, and noticed that as they went north or south stellar objects changed their declination (elevation) on the celestial sphere.

The earliest documented mention of the spherical Earth was in the fifth century BC. However, the idea was so contradictory to the flat Earth theory that is wasn't really accepted in ancient Greek philosophy until the third century BC. The most likely cause for this rejection was the spherical Earth theory challenged past ideas of religion, science, and literature. Teachers, priests, scientists, and educators at this time taught philosophies that were generated by the flat Earth idea. The people who were in power would not give in to new ideas since it would greatly jeopardize their positions in Greek society.

It's very difficult, even for people today, to be told everything you believe to hold true is wrong. This is one of the main reasons why the old Greek school rejected the spherical Earth and this new idea had to wait until the old professors and keepers of knowledge died out or lost power. We would see this flaw in human nature repeat often in history as the geocentric theory is replaced by the heliocentric theory and then once again as the human race entered the twentieth century with the unwillingness of the scientific establishment to even consider the reality of paranormal phenomena and the possibility of a multiverse.

There were many Greek mathematicians, geographers, and astrologer/astronomers who observed various motions on the celestial sphere that did not support a flat Earth, but pointed to a spherical Earth; these observations are listed below.

1. They noticed the sun on the same day at noon was at different angles over cities separated by at least 300 miles. If we lived on a flat Earth, the sun would always be at the same angle at noon no matter what your location. However, if Earth was curved it could account for the difference in the angle of the sun.

2. When ships with tall sails sailed out to sea, they seemed to slowly disappear. It appeared as if the sail was slowly sinking into the water. If the earth was flat, the entire ship would be visible until it was too far away to be seen by the human eye. If the earth was curved, the ship would slowly vanish from the bottom to the top of the sails as it followed the curve of the earth downward. The reverse was observed for a ship sailing to port from the sea.

3. "Naked eye" observations of the moon and sun implied it was not a flat disk, but a sphere.

4. These early great thinkers also discovered the further you travel south, the lower the stars in the north appear and stars in the south increased in elevation on the celestial sphere.

The observations above all supported the assumption that our Earth was spherical and not flat.

Finally, after 200 years of observations and debate, the concept of a spherical Earth displaced earlier beliefs of a flat Earth.

Although references to a spherical Earth were discovered in the works of Socrates (470–399 BC) and Plato (428–347 BC), early Greek philosophers credit Pythagoras for first suggesting it sometime in 500 BC.[17] The fact of the matter is we have no idea who first formally proposed the theory.

---

17   Pythagoras (570–495 BC) was a Greek philosopher, mathematician, and founder of the movement called Pythagoreanism, which appeared in 6 BC, centuries after his death. Most of the information about Pythagoras was written down centuries after he lived, so very little reliable information is known about him.

Finally, it was with the acceptance of the geocentric, spherical Earth that we see the earliest origins of astrology being accepted as a true science in Europe, the Middle East, and western Asia. Still, no one really knew just how large our world was. This problem was left to a Greek genius and head librarian at the Great Library in Alexandria by the name of Eratosthenes to solve.

Eratosthenes

Eratosthenes (276–195 BC) was born in Cyrene[18]; he studied mathematics in Athens and made a name for himself in many fields of science. Eventually, he caught the attention of the ruler of Egypt, Ptolemy III, who invited Eratosthenes to Alexandria to be the head librarian in what was at that time the largest library in the world.

Eratosthenes calculated the circumference of the earth by using the geometry that was available at his time. The story on how he made his discovery varies with the author, but his results are the same in all of these accounts.

While in Syene (today Aswan, Egypt) during the summer solstice, at noon, he noticed the sun was directly overhead. The next year at the same day and time Eratosthenes measured the sun's angle of elevation in Alexandria. He discovered there was about a 7 degree difference in the angle of the sun between the two cities. The Greeks knew a circle was 360 degrees and the difference turned out to be one-fifth of a circle.

He wondered how this could be. If the earth was flat, it would not matter where you went. The sun would be at the same angle in the sky at noon. However, if the earth was a sphere, then the angle of the sun would change in relation to your position because of the curve of the earth. He then divided 360 by 7 and got 50, and concluded the true circumference of Earth is 50 times the distance from Alexandria to Syene.

---

18   Cyrene was an ancient Greek city in present-day Libya. It was the oldest and most important of the five Greek cities in the region.

In one version of the story, Eratosthenes already knew the distance since he did considerable work for the Greeks in geography and cartography. In another version of the story he hired a man to walk from Alexandria to Syene and measure the distance.

The distance between the two cities in modern measurements was 500 miles. He simply multiplied 50 times 500 and got 25,000. The modern-day value for the circumference of our planet is 24,901 miles, an error less than 1 percent. To me this is very impressive since Eratosthenes didn't have a computer, laser measuring instruments, or satellites. Eratosthenes had only curiosity, determination to solve a problem, math, and brains.

When Eratosthenes published his work, his critics laughed and asked, "Where is the rest of the world?" During that time even 1,000 miles was a great distance, but to consider 25,000 miles was incredible to the Greeks. Of course they had no idea of how large the Atlantic and Pacific Oceans were and the existence of North and South America was unknown.

Seventeen hundred years later, Christopher Columbus also did not accept what Eratosthenes had written about the size of the earth, he chose to believe the circumference of our world was one-third smaller. Had Columbus set sail knowing that Eratosthenes' larger circumference value for the earth was more accurate, he would have known the place he made landfall was not Asia, but rather a large, unexplored area of the "new world." Also, more importantly, he would not have run out of food and fresh water.

The Great Ptolemy

Ptolemy (AD 100–168) was a mathematician, astronomer, and astrologer. He lived in the city of Alexandria, Egypt, and held Roman citizenship. When Rome was in power, for someone to say "I am a citizen of Rome" carried a great deal of weight. People paid attention when you spoke and took you very seriously. Also, during Ptolemy's time the Greeks were considered the most intellectual society in the known world. Although the ancient Romans had the biggest egos on the planet, the empire admitted to learning a great deal from the early Greeks. They even adopted their gods and utilized Greek science, engineering, and mathematics. Ptolemy claimed both Roman and Greek heritage, so when he said or wrote something, even the most educated listened. Today, it would be similar if someone claimed they graduated from Harvard, Yale, and Princeton, and have homes in Beverly Hills, California, and Greenwich, Connecticut.

Ptolemy's only surviving ancient book on astronomy is the *Almagest*. In the *Almagest* Ptolemy presented a useful means for astronomical calculations in tables, which contained all the data needed to determine the positions of the sun, moon, planets, the rising and setting of the stars, and finally and most importantly, eclipses of the sun and moon.

The *Almagest* also had a comprehensive star catalogue with detailed drawings of forty-eight constellations. Ptolemy's model of the cosmos was based on the geocentric idea and was used until the world accepted the sun-centered theory, which would not be for another 1,500 years.

Ptolemy's model went beyond the mathematical ideas of all previous works. He explained the motions of the celestial sphere using circular cycles and epicycles. One great mystery during his time is why certain planets appear to move backward then forward again in relation to the background stars. Ptolemy used his epicycles to explain this motion. After a number of modifications to fit the observations, he devised a complex system of multiple cycles within numerous compound epicycles. He should have known from his complex configurations that many of his ideas were wrong, but his ego got in the way of true science. This backward or retrograde motion of the planets would later be correctly explained using the heliocentric or sun-centered theory.

In AD 330, when the Romans adopted Christianity as the official religion of the empire, they liked Ptolemy's model of the universe because it placed Earth at the center. They had an influential belief over all of Europe and cited biblical reference that mankind was God's greatest creation and placed at the center of the known universe. However, many scholars did question the geocentric idea and visibly denounced this theory in favor of a sun-centered model. These people were severely dealt with and discredited by not only the established intellectuals of their time, but also by the church in Rome. The church not only supported the geocentric model, but fiercely defended it with all the power at their disposal. It would take over a thousand years for a new more accurate model to emerge and be accepted.

As for Ptolemy, many of his contributions did benefit the future of astronomy; however, his idea about a geocentric universe was incorrect. Having an impressive educational background and training doesn't mean everything you say or do is correct—in Ptolemy's case, he was dead wrong about the position of our planet in the universe.

The Heliocentric Theory

Unlike the geocentric theory, which placed Earth at the center of the universe, the heliocentric model placed the sun at the center. The conjecture that Earth revolved around the sun had been proposed as early as the third century BC by Aristarchus of Samos.[19] He not only placed the sun in the center, but also listed the five visible planets in their correct order from the sun. This was a remarkable accomplishment for his time.

There are some ancient astronaut proponents of the mid-twentieth century who believe Aristarchus had inside information from aliens who he might have considered as gods. Unfortunately, the astronomical theories of Aristarchus were considered much too radical, and his ideas were rejected by most scientists and philosophers of his time in favor of the geocentric theory and faded into oblivion for almost two thousand years.

---

19   Aristarchus of Samos (310–230 BC) was later credited by Copernicus for originating the heliocentric theory.

The heliocentric theory would not surface again until the sixteenth century, when Nicolaus Copernicus (1473–1543), a mathematician and astronomer in Renaissance Europe, once again proposed the sun was at the center of the universe and not Earth. The publication of Copernicus's book *On the Revolutions of the Celestial Spheres* took place just before his death in 1543. The belief today is Copernicus was cautious about publishing his research since there was considerable opposition to new ideas, especially in astronomy. The book was the beginning of a major scientific breakthrough.

Copernicus simply stated our Earth and the other five known planets revolve around a stationary sun, and our planet also rotates on an axis. This rotation gives us day and night as well as the impression that the celestial sphere is circling around a stationary Earth. Copernicus also stated Earth completes one revolution around the sun in a year or the number of days between each spring equinox.

The Copernican view of the universe was considered a radical idea, since for 1,500 years most of Europe held the geocentric model as the absolute truth. Today when we talk about a grand quick transformation in science or government it is still referred to as a "revolution," from the design of the Copernican universe and the effect it had on the people of Europe and later the world.

A Dark Time

In the Copernican heliocentric theory our planet lost its important position in creation and this was not taken lightly by the church in Rome. However, it would not be until several decades after the publication of the work of Copernicus that the church would take action and ban the book.

The church used the following passages from the Bible to oppose the heliocentric theory:

The world is firmly established, it cannot be moved. (Chronicles 16:30)

The Lord set the earth on its foundations; it can never be moved. (Psalms 104:5)

The sun rises and the sun sets; and hurries to the place where it rises again. (Ecclesiastes 1:5)

From a literal interpretation of these biblical passages, it was obvious to the religious leaders of the sixteenth and seventeenth centuries the supporters of the sun-centered theory must be wrong. The church firmly believed the Bible to be the word of God given to man, and it was to be taken literally without question. The pope and the cardinals also feared that if they were proven incorrect people might begin to question other doctrines of the faith, so they did their best to silence new ideas that conflicted with church doctrine.

The biblical passages mentioned above were used to charge many of the supporters of Copernicus with heresy. Although by the early seventeenth century there were a good number of astrologers, astronomers, and mathematicians who believed in the Copernican heliocentric model, only a few would go on record. This was because the new theory had very strong opposition from many powerful and feared leaders, including Cardinal Bellarmine, the church inquisitor.[20]

Despite efforts by the Roman Catholic Church to censor the work of Copernicus, a number of other great minds at the time were supporters of this new radical idea and spoke openly; they included Johannes Kepler, Galileo, and Giordano Bruno.

The most outspoken of the supporters of Copernicus was Giordano Bruno (1548–1600), a Dominican friar. Bruno was a philosopher, mathematician, and astrophysical theorist. His cosmological ideas expanded

---

20   Robert Bellarmine (1542–1621) was an Italian Jesuit and a cardinal of the Catholic Church. He was named Cardinal Inquisitor by Pope Clement VIII in 1599.

the Copernican model of the universe considerably. He proposed the stars were distant suns with planets circling them and perhaps some of these worlds harbored life. He also insisted that the universe was infinite and therefore has no center. When asked by the Inquisition where his ideas came from he responded, "God revealed to me the nature of the universe in a dream." [21]

His beliefs conflicted with church doctrine, and in 1593, Bruno was tried for heresy by the Roman Inquisition. The Inquisition found him guilty, and he was burned at the stake in Rome's Campo de' Fiori in 1600. Centuries after his death, modern scientists regard him as a martyr and a champion for free thought.

Galileo Galilee (1564–1642) was an astronomer, astrologer, and mathematician. He played a major role in supporting the Copernican heliocentric system in the seventeenth century through telescopic observations of objects on the celestial sphere. Galileo did not invent the telescope, as many think. He was historically credited as the first one in Europe to use it for astronomy.

His contributions to observational astronomy include the telescopic observation of the phases of Venus, as well as the discovery of the four largest satellites of Jupiter; the craters, mountains, and large basins of the moon (which he thought were oceans of water); sunspots; and the true nature of the Milky Way. It was his telescopic observations that finally helped prove the Copernican system.

Galileo observed that Venus and Jupiter were not points of light like the stars, but resolved into disks. They were worlds far away from Earth orbiting the sun. He observed Venus for an entire year and noticed it went through phases like the moon and at times it was not seen in the sky at all. He concluded from these observations that Venus was between Earth and the sun, which would account for its phases. Galileo

---

21   Giordano Bruno, *Fifth Dialogue*, translated by Jack Lindsay (Notre Dame: University of Notre Dame Press, 1962).

also concluded from his observations that when Venus was not visible in the sky, the planet was in front of the sun or behind it. Although he was cautious about revealing these new discoveries—the church hired investigators to watch Galileo closely.

In February 1633 Galileo was brought before inquisitor Vincenzo Maculani to be charged with supporting a heretical principle. Throughout his trial Galileo steadfastly maintained the observations of what was seen through his telescope speaks for itself. In July 1633, after being threatened with torture, he denounced the Copernican heliocentric theory on a written document, which also included a statement that his observations through the telescope were false.

The findings and sentencing of the Inquisition were delivered and Galileo was found guilty of heresy for having held the opinions that the sun lies motionless at the center of the universe and Earth is not at its center. The church officials believed that since the heliocentric idea was contrary to holy scripture, the writings and ideas of Galileo must be false. He was sentenced to formal imprisonment by the Inquisition. Since Galileo cooperated with the Inquisition, in an act of "leniency," the following day the sentence was changed to house arrest, which remained enforced until his death in 1642.

At the same time that Galileo was making his observations through the telescope, Johannes Kepler (1571–1630), a German mathematician, astronomer, and astrologer, and a firm supporter of the heliocentric theory, was working on a project that would combine Galileo's telescopic observations and Tycho Brahe's[22] star charts with mathematics.

Kepler and Galileo lived in a time when there was no clear division between astronomy and astrology. Many of the early astronomers were

---

22   Tycho Brahe (1546–1601) was a Danish nobleman known for his accurate observations of celestial objects without the use of a telescope. His observations of the retrograde motion of Mars helped Kepler formulate his laws of planetary motion.

commissioned to prepare astrological charts for the wealthy and royalty to advise on everything from politics to love.

Unlike Galileo, Kepler included religious arguments and reasoning in his work. He was motivated by the belief God created the universe according to a comprehensible plan that can be understood by man through the study of natural science.

Kepler was introduced to astronomy as a child of six in 1577, when his mother took him outside to see a bright comet. In 1580, at age nine, he witnessed a total lunar eclipse where the moon turned blood red during totality. From that day on the young Kepler loved astronomy and wanted to dedicate his life to finding out more about the wonders of the heavens.

By using observations of the five visible planets as they moved across the celestial sphere made earlier by Tycho Brahe and Galileo, Kepler discovered a mathematical sequence to the orbit of the planets and published his three planetary laws of motion that are still in use today.

Using this new form of math, which was to be the forerunner of calculus, Kepler was able to determine the distance from the sun for the planets Mercury, Venus, Mars, Jupiter, and Saturn. Kepler was convinced he had discovered God's geometrical design of the universe.

During October 1604, a bright new star, a nova,[23] appeared in the evening sky. The celestial sphere was considered to be unchanging so when something appeared out of nowhere, it was believed by all to be an important sign. Kepler began systematically observing the new star and was sure it was a sign that great changes were about to take place.

Astrologically, the end of 1603 marked the beginning of what astrologers called the "Fiery Trigon,"[24] the start of an 800-year cycle

---

23   A nova or supernova is a star that has flared up or exploded. When this takes place, one star may outshine every star in the galaxy.

24   A rare conjunction of Jupiter and Saturn while in opposition. In this conjunction, Jupiter and Saturn will apparently occupy the same position in the sky on three separate occasions over a period of a few months.

of prominent conjunctions of Jupiter and Saturn, which in the past astrologers associated with the rise of the emperor Charlemagne and the birth of Christ. Today, in the twenty-first century, we are supposedly still under the influence of the Fiery Trigon, and many astrologers, mystics, occultists, and paranormal researchers believe a sign will appear (or has already appeared) in the heavens to herald the emergence of the Antichrist.

Kepler would sit out on his balcony for hours during the night, staring at the stars. Friends and family who visited him during this time recall he was occasionally unresponsive, as if in some type of trance. When asked about this, Kepler would simply say meditation with the stars helped him connect to God, and the complexities of the universe would be simplified for him.

Sometime around 1609–1611, Kepler wrote a book entitled *Somnium*, which means "the dream." In a dream, Kepler is taken to another planet outside our solar system and shown by supernatural beings what the positions of stars and planets are like from another perspective in the universe. He is then taken to the moon, populated by exotic beings who have been watching humans on Earth for centuries. He is then returned to Earth and awakes on his balcony sitting in his chair.

The manuscript mysteriously disappeared shortly after Kepler allowed a number of people to read it. Historians of astronomy, including Dr. Carl Sagan, called it "the first science fiction story ever written"—or was it the first reported case of alien contact?

It was shortly after this experience that Kepler formulated his three laws of planetary motion. It's amazing to think his math is still used today to calculate the orbits of satellites, comets, planets, and other members of our solar system. Kepler was truly a man ahead of his time, but did this great breakthrough in math and science come from him or somewhere else?

Years later, a distorted version of *The Dream* surfaced and may have instigated an accusation of Witchcraft against his mother, saying she conjured a demon that took Kepler into space on its wings. After weeks in prison and threats of torture, she was finally released since there was no real evidence to condemn her as being a witch. Kepler believed the arrest of his mother was a plot to silence his work in astronomy.

A few years ago a group of UFO and ancient astronaut buffs invited me to one of their local meetings. Although I don't usually attend meetings and conferences or join clubs concerning this topic, I decided to go. During the discussion Kepler was brought up by one of the members and everyone was quite amazed at what this man was able to accomplish back in the seventeenth century. One of the group members pointed out that Kepler was very strange looking and the shape of his head and eyes resembled the gray aliens that are so prominent in UFO abduction stories. Some even proposed that Kepler was a hybrid and his insight to math and the complexities of the universe came from an extraterrestrial source. Although I agree that the early paintings of Kepler show a man who is not handsome, I pointed out to the group that we should not always look to aliens or angels to explain why people accomplish such amazing things. Perhaps they are just very intelligent human beings capable of extraordinary things.

A Modern View

At long last, the heliocentric theory was accepted in the last quarter of the seventeenth century. The majority of the works of Copernicus, Kepler, and Galileo were no longer banned by the church.[25] The Catholic Church in Rome also reviewed the trial of Galileo several times between the eighteenth and twentieth centuries and found him innocent of the charge of heresy.

---

25 The church finally approved Catholics to read all their books by the early nineteenth century.

In the late seventeenth century, astronomy and astrology split into two separate fields of study and astrology was no longer taught at the major universities. History tells us Isaac Newton at an early age was interested in astrology, alchemy, and theology, and it may have been the catalyst for his interest in science. As Newton grew older and became established in his field, he kept his interest in metaphysical topics confined to a few close friends.

By the nineteenth century astronomers discovered our sun is but one of billions of stars in an island universe called a galaxy. It wasn't until the early twentieth century, with the construction of larger telescopes and the application of photography, that astronomers discovered our galaxy is not the entire universe, but simply one of billions of other galaxies, each containing billions of stars and planets. Our view of creation was expanded greatly, and this had a direct effect on twentieth-century culture and the human mind as well.

A considerable number of twentieth-century astronomers were fans of science fiction literature as children. There is no doubt that many of the incredible theories of the universe being proposed today by these scientists were influenced by science fiction writers from 1950 to 1975. Television also had its impact since many scientists will tell you they got interested in astronomy and the other sciences from watching television shows like *The Outer Limits, One Step Beyond,* and of course the original *Star Trek* series.

The visualization of the universe that we have today is more complex than Galileo, Copernicus, Kepler, or even Bruno could have imagined. The simplest way to understand this modern theory is presented in a sequential form below.

1. Our sun and planetary system is one of billions of others in our galaxy.

2. In our bubble universe there are at least 400 billion other galaxies.

3. In our galaxy and in every galaxy in the universe, as well as in the space between, there are at least 11 dimensions or planes of other realities all separate from each other.

4. Our universe, which is about 20 billion light-years in size, is but one of a countless number of other bubble universes in the multiverse, each containing billions of galaxies, stars, planets and 11 dimensions.

5. Last but not least, each universe may have waves of time in which temporal displacement takes place and the past, present, and future all coexist.

6. WOW!!!

Recently, several new Earthlike planets has been discovered in our galaxy. The closest to us is about 3 light-years' distance, As stellar distance goes, this planet is nearby and knowledge of its existence has opened the door wider to the possibility that in the present day, or sometime in the past, our backwater planet may have been visited by a spacefaring race of extraterrestrial beings.

From very early times to our modern day, we continue to see the strong celestial connection we Earthlings have with the sky above. It has inspired us and helped humanity emerge out of the darkness and into the light by expanding our minds and allowing us to connect with the universe.

3

Myths of the Constellations

The late Joseph Campbell[26] was the foremost expert on mythology and how it influenced the cultural and spiritual development of ancient and modern civilizations. He set the foundations to show how legends of long ago influence us today. After studying Mr. Campbell's work in detail, I believe he would agree that the myths that have influenced a multitude of cultures the most are centered on the celestial sphere. In straightforward terms, the four basic effects that myth has on a society are listed below.

1. Inspiring a sense of wonder and respect for the mystery of the multiverse. This brings creativity, intensifies imagination, and binds a society together. It is also responsible for validating religious beliefs.

2. Mythological stories help prescientific societies explain the forces of nature and formation of the multiverse, making them

---

26 Joseph Campbell (1904–1987) was an American mythologist, writer, and lecturer, best known for his work in comparative mythology and the PBS presentation *The Power of Myth.*

less fearful. For prescientific societies, myth also functioned as explanations for the physical phenomena they did not understand, such as the change of seasons, weather phenomena, the celestial sphere, geologic forces, and the life cycles of people, animals, and plants.

3. Stabilize and establish the existing social order. In simple language, myth and religion help keep a society together and maintain cooperation among the people.

4. Guide the adolescent through the stages of life. Rites of passage give support to the young to make them feel they belong. Today we still have many tests, rituals, and challenges the young must go through to place themselves in a modern social structure. Myths help teach lessons to the young through imaginative stories that teach history and support proper social behavior.

Just before his passing, Mr. Campbell finished a series for PBS called *The Power of Myth*. This program is now available in book form and DVD. I highly recommend it to my readers who want to explore in greater detail the power mythology has on the social structure of a civilization.

Mythology and the Constellations

The scope of this book does not permit me to tell the star tales of all eighty-eight constellations. This chapter will present four constellations for each season and their mythology from a number of different cultures.

One of the many things I enjoyed about teaching science was taking my students to the observatory or planetarium for a session of evening stargazing. While pointing out the constellations to my students, at least one young person would make a comment like this: "Hey, I don't see a bear or a bull or a lion. All I see is a group of stars." Actually, some of the constellations do look like what they are supposed to represent; all you have to do is take a good look. If you have dark skies, an excellent imagination, and keen eyesight, the outline of their proper character will unfold.

The majority of the constellations and stars were named a very long time ago by cultures that had a direct connection with the night sky. In seafaring cultures the constellations were named to identify the locations of bright and important stars for navigation.[27] Ancient cultures also used the stars to tell the time of year, seasons, and religious holidays and to honor the gods. The ancient Greeks used the constellations as a focal point to tell stories that remember the exploits of their greatest heroes. Many of these stories were also used to teach lessons of good conduct to the young.

Ancient Greece had none of the many vehicles of entertainment we have today. A storyteller would travel from city to city and take the people out to a field during a clear moonless night and tell tales of monsters, heroes, gods, and great adventures using the stars and constellations as visual representation. If a bright meteor appeared while the audience was looking up, it was a bonus for the storyteller, since the event was explained as one of the gods taking part in the show.

On a clear moonless night, if you are far from the blinding lights of the city, you can count anywhere from six hundred to several thousand stars in the night sky with the unaided eye. At first it may seem like an impossible task to try to find a constellation out of the seemingly countless stars, but if you use the brightest stars in the constellation and the bright stars nearby as a guide, the character of the constellation will begin to stand out from the stellar background. The challenge now comes when you have to point out the stars of a constellation to another observer who is looking at the night sky for the first time.

Most people have heard of the Belt of Orion, Taurus, the bull, or the Big and Little Dippers, but very few know where to find them in

27 Before GPS, during WWII, pilots would use bright stars as guide points for navigation.

the sky. It's a known fact that because human population is growing and the cities are getting larger and starting to absorb the countryside, the artificial lights on planet Earth are getting brighter and the stars are appearing fainter. Because of this, very few people look up at the sky, and as a culture, we are slowly losing an important connection we once had with the celestial sphere. This is mainly because, besides the moon, bright planets, and some of the brighter stars, the night sky is too glared out by artificial lights. Light pollution is a serious problem for everyone from the novice stargazer to the professional astronomer.

Most ancient cultures did see pictures in the sky, and named them after objects, people, and animals that were common in their day. They also had a much greater imagination than we do today, since there was more mystery in the world. Looking at the starry night sky was a form of entertainment. Imagine how it must have been—centuries before artificial lighting, when these people of long ago stared at the dark celestial sphere above to see the brilliant stars against a dark velvet sky. Travelers, sailors, farmers, and wanderers of the Bronze Age would do this for hours since they did not have video games, cable, or the internet to keep them busy as we do today. As they watched, the stars would take on shapes, and just like viewing clouds, the stars would begin to resemble something they know, perhaps a character from a childhood story.

Just like our ancestors of long ago, people of the twenty-first century are also drawn to the sky. They don't understand the initial impulse to do so, but when their eyes catch the moon rising or the brilliance of the morning star, something stirs in not only the mind but throughout their soul, generating a feeling of peace, wonder, and euphoria. For a brief moment in time, they leave this world and are in harmony with the multiverse. However, things like bills, money, jobs, children, and preparing dinner slowly creep back into the mind and break the ethereal connection. It was as if some negative psychic force intervened and said that peace and tranquility is bad for our business—move on, human!

The earliest direct evidence we have from a culture that observed the constellations comes from inscribed stones and clay writing tablets dug up in Mesopotamia,[28] dating back six thousand years. These same groupings of stars appeared later as many of the classical Greek constellations, which still have the same names today. Constellations like Leo, Aries, Taurus, Auriga, Orion, and Ursa Major were well known by these people of early times. The first recognized Greek reference to the constellations can be found in the works of Homer,[29] which were written around the eighth century BC. Here I present book 18, verse 28 of the *Iliad*, paraphrased:

On it he made the earth, and sky and sea, the weariless sun and the moon waxing to full and all the constellations that crown the celestial sphere and heavens, Pleiades and Hyades, and the mighty Orion and the great bear. The great bear wheels around in the same place and watches for Orion and is the only one not to bathe in the ocean.

The above verse from the *Iliad* refers to the construction of the shield of Achilles by Hesperus who was the craftsman for the gods. During the time of Homer most of the constellations were not associated with legends; they were simply known as animals and things that were popular in ancient Greece.

Spring Constellations

Ursa Major

The most extensively known and oldest of the constellations is the Big Dipper, also called Ursa Major or the Big Bear. This constellation is

---

28   Modern Iraq

29   Homer is the name given by the ancient Greeks to the legendary author of the *Iliad* and the *Odyssey*. Very little is known about his life, and there may have been more than one Homer traveling Greece and telling stories.

visible throughout the year in the northern skies. It belongs to a group of constellations known as circumpolar, since from our viewpoint in the galaxy, they are apparently located near the North Star.

The Big Dipper was used to tell time during the night by many Native American tribes, since the constellation makes one turn around the North Star (Polaris) every twenty-four hours and is visible all night. They knew that its trip across the night sky represented a half of a day, or twelve hours of time.

The Big Dipper was known as the "Drinking Cup" to runaway slaves in the Confederate States of America and was used as a guide to travel north—to what they hoped was freedom.

Today we call this constellation the Big Dipper, but to the ancient Greeks and the Native Americans it was known as the Big Bear. How the Native Americans and the Greeks came up with the same name for this constellation remains one of the mysteries of astronomy, since the constellation looks nothing like a bear. To add to the mystery—both drew the constellation with a long tail and bears do not have long tails!

The Big Dipper is also known by other names. In England and France around the eighteenth century, it was called the "Wagon" or the "Plough." The Chinese called it the "Aristocrat" since they thought the pattern of stars looked like a politician standing on a platform, trying to persuade people to his political side. The Maya called it the "Parrot," and Egyptians thought it looked like a bull. To the people of Mesopotamia, it was known as the "Funeral Procession."

The two brightest stars that make up the bowl of the Big Dipper are called the "pointers," since they point to Polaris, the North Star. Polaris is the last star on the handle of Ursa Minor or the Little Dipper. For centuries Polaris was used as a navigation aid by ancient seafaring civilizations to help determine north. Since the angle of Polaris is equal to your latitude, observation of the star was essential in the eighteenth and nineteenth centuries to tell a ship's position north of the equator.

There are many stories that have been handed down to us about the Big Bear (Big Dipper). The two that are the most popular come to us from ancient Greece and the Native Americans, primarily the Cherokee Blackfoot.

The Greeks called the constellation "Arktos Megale," which translated to "Ursa Major" in Latin and "Big Bear" in English. According to the Greek legend, the Great Bear represents Callisto, one of the many mortal loves of Zeus, king of the gods. Callisto was fond of hunting and joined the cult of Artemis, the goddess of the hunt, to whom she swore a vow of chastity. On a visit to earth, Zeus saw Callisto sleeping in the woods and fell in love with her. Zeus approached her in the disguise of Artemis and when he embraced her the god revealed his true self. Despite Callisto's struggles and protests Zeus had his way with her and as a result of the encounter she became pregnant. Artemis became very angry and banished her from the huntress cult. Callisto gave birth to a son, whom she named Arcas. When he came of age, like his mother he also became a great hunter.

As a result of the romantic encounter with the king of the gods, Callisto became the target of Hera, the wife of Zeus and queen of the gods. The angry and resentful Hera changed Callisto into a great white bear. For many years Callisto wandered through the forest as a bear avoiding everyone, fearing she would be killed. This was the revenge of Hera—that the great huntress would now become the prey. One day she saw her son hunting in the woods and recognized him. She became so joyful that she forgot she was a bear and ran toward him. Arcas then raised his spear to slay the bear, and before he could release it, Zeus intervened. The king of the gods created a whirlwind, which lifted the bear and her son into the sky. He then changed Arcas into a smaller bear so that the two would be together forever and safe from the wrath of Hera.

In a slightly different version of the myth, Zeus grabbed the big and little bear by their stubby tails, and as he flung them into the heavens, the short tails were stretched. This is how the Greeks explained why the celestial bears have long tails. Today we know the two constellations as Ursa Major and Ursa Minor, or the Big Dipper and Little Dipper.

The Native Americans also have a tale centering on this group of stars. The story starts with the big and little bear coming out of their den in the spring. As they search for food, the hunter spots them and chases them around the North Star. Finally, the hunter catches up with them in the fall and fires his arrow, which wounds the big bear. The bear's blood then falls to earth and colors the leaves of the trees red and orange; this is how they explained the foliage color change of fall. The wounded bear then grabs her cub, runs away, and, by winter, reaches her den to heal. Here the bear and her cub stay in the den until spring, and then once again the cycle of the hunt is repeated.

The great hunter is represented by the constellation Boötes. In ancient Greece it was called "The Bear Driver." In some stories, both Greek and Native American, Bootes is the protector of Earth who chases the giant bear around the pole star to keep it from climbing down from the sky and destroying the world.

In 1998, while on a research project in Washington state, I was introduced to an elderly gentleman, a shaman of the Snoqualmie Tribe, who told a story about the Big Dipper, which was passed down verbally from generation to generation. No one seemed to know how long ago the myth originated, but it was informative, enchanting, and humorous.

One night there were five wolves, a dog, and a coyote looking at two animals in the sky that were walking with the stars. The dog and the five wolves were hungry and, since they only had a small rabbit to share, the two animals in the sky looked like easy game. The coyote said let's go get them, but one wolf said they were too high. The coyote took his bow and shot an arrow into the sky where it stuck. He shot another arrow, which stuck into the first arrow, then another and another until a ladder of arrows reached the ground.

The five wolves, the dog, and the coyote climbed the arrows up into the sky and saw that the animals were giant bears. The wolves and the dog sat near the bears and watched them, and the bears looked back. Seeing that they were distracted, the coyote climbed back down to the ground and removed his arrow ladder. He looked up at the five wolves and dog and laughed and said, "Now I will have the rabbit all to myself." Coyote left them stranded in the sky and had his dinner.

The three stars of the handle of the Big Dipper and the two stars of the bowl near the handle are the wolves. The two stars on the front of the bowl are the bears. The tiny star in the middle of the handle is the dog.[30]

If you take a close look at the second star in the handle of the Big Dipper, you might notice something strange. The star will look like one bright star when in reality it is two stars apparently very close together. If you have 20/20 vision, and it is a clear night, you will be able to see it as two stars rather than one. These two stars, which are called Alcor and Mizar, were used as a test for excellent eyesight during the eighteenth century.

Twenty years ago a bizarre case of contact and psychic photography involving this constellation came to my attention. This case study is presented for the first time in chapter 4.

Leo

Leo represents the Nemean lion slain by Hercules as the first of his twelve labors. The beast lived in a huge cave near the town of Nema and was no common lion. According to Greek mythology the lion was the spawn of the terrible monster Typhoon (Draco or Cetus) who fell from the sky to Earth in order to bring plague to both the gods and mortals. Leo was a monstrous animal with a hide stronger than any armor that

---

30 This is most likely the apparent double star of Alcor and Mizar. Mizar, the brighter one, is the wolf, while Alcor is the dog, but whoever originated the story had good vision since they are apparently close together but actually separated by 75 trillion miles.

could not be pierced by any weapon. The countryside lived in terror for years, and even the gods themselves would not confront the beast. Desperate to rid the world of the monster, Zeus sent his favorite and most powerful son, Hercules, to slay it.

Hercules fought the monster for months. Finally Hercules was able to grab the lion by the back of the neck and strangle it to death. Hercules then used the lion's claws to cut off the animal's hide to make an armored cloak. Zeus placed the body of the lion in the sky as a reminder of the deed of Hercules.

The brightest star in Leo is called Regulus, a yellowish star about 85 light-years from Earth. Regulus was known as the star of kings, mainly because the lion was considered the king of all beasts. The ancient people of the Middle East and southern Europe believed that any person born at the exact time of the rising of Regulus was destined to be a great leader.

During the dry season in ancient Egypt, the lions came to the Nile to drink. This usually took place when the sun was in the constellation of Leo. Some astronomy historians today speculate this is how this group of stars got its name. The Hebrews, Sumerians, Persians, Syrians, Greeks, Romans, and Egyptians of the Bronze Age all identified this constellation with a majestic lion. In Babylonian astronomy, sometime around one-thousand BC, the constellation was also identified as Great Lion; the bright star Regulus was known as "the star at the lion's breast."

The stars of Leo were mapped by the Chinese around 300 BC. They saw them as representing a great yellow dragon who was slowly walking up the steps to heaven. To the Chinese people a dragon was a symbol of fruitfulness brought by water. The months of June and July were times of drought in China; the people would make clay dragons then take them out at night and pray to the star Regulus for rain. The people of Thailand (Siam) thought Leo was the place where the spirit of the tiger went after death.

The stars of Leo actually look like a lion that is crouching or resting. The front section of the celestial lion is represented by several stars in the shape of a backward question mark. This is called the sickle of Leo. We shall see later how the constellation of Leo the Lion may have played an important part in the birth of Jesus and the Star of Bethlehem, or the so-called Christmas Star.

Virgo

The constellation of Virgo was named after Demeter, the Greek goddess of the earth. The fabled story of Virgo has been passed down to us from Greek and Roman mythology and is as follows.

Hades, the god of the underworld, fell in love with the goddess Persephone, who was the youngest daughter of Demeter. He promised her that if she married him, the god would make her queen of the underworld. However, Demeter did not like the idea and would not bless the wedding. Hades, despite the opposition of Demeter, was intent on making Persephone his bride, so the god sent a chariot with black horses to earth to kidnap her. Demeter began to worry when she could not locate her daughter, so she searched the earth for days without food or rest. The result of this was a great drought that encompassed the earth. The mortal inhabitants began to starve, since all their crops were dying, so they prayed to Zeus for help.

Zeus, the king of the gods, finally summoned Demeter to Mount Olympus and told the goddess her daughter was the guest of Hades and there was nothing she or even he could do to get her back. Demeter refused to take care of the earth unless her daughter was returned. As a result of her grief and anger, the crops and all plant life slowly withered and the earthly people were starving to death. Zeus knew he had to do something to stop this great disaster before the entire human race vanished from the face of the planet and there would be no one left to worship the gods.

Zeus then sent Hermes, the messenger of the gods, to the underworld to warn Hades that if he did not give up Persephone it could start a civil war between the gods of the underworld and the heavens. Hades knew that his brother Zeus was more powerful and would in time surely win the war, so he asked that for six months of the year Persephone be allowed to stay with him in the underworld, and for the remaining six months of the year she would stay with her mother, Demeter, on earth. Zeus agreed to the terms and although Demeter still did not like the idea of her daughter being away, she had no choice but to accept the agreement.

Legend tells us that when Persephone is with her mother for six months, Demeter is so joyful that land blooms with beautiful flowers and the crops grow, but while she is away in the underworld for six months with Hades, the earth turns cold and the plants and flowers wither and decay. This is how the ancient Greeks explained the seasons.

The constellation of Virgo has always been associated with the arrival of spring, when it appears in the eastern sky before sunrise, and the fall, when it is visible in the western sky just after sunset. The farmers of long ago used the constellation and its position in the sky to help determine the best times to plant and reap their crops.

It's fascinating to note the constellation was also identified with fertility, growing, and the harvest throughout the Middle and Near East, North Africa, and the Mediterranean. The Egyptians knew Virgo as Isis, the goddess of fertility of the earth. The Babylonians named the constellation "Ishtar, the mother of earth," the Hindus called her the "Maiden" who brings life to the earth, while the Persians called her the "Lady of the Harvest," and finally the early Sumerians called the constellation the "Queen of the Heavens and the Bringer of Life."

Between the years 1993 and 2009, my research centered on mysterious stone chambers, standing stones, and carved rocks in the Northeast

United States.[31] An important part of my investigations was putting together a history of the structures by discovering how far back in time their oral and written legends originated. A very good source for any type of research like this is talking to elders of Native American tribes. I had the fortunate luck to be introduced to a community of Algonquians in Northwest Connecticut.

One evening in June, while sitting outside and discussing the stone chambers with a medicine man and a number of council members, I noticed at least eight men and women bringing baskets of flowers, fruit, and plants to an open area, placing them down on the ground, and beginning to chant. My curious nature got the best of me and I asked what was going on. An older councilwoman told me they were giving an offering to the mother goddess as she rises in the sky, asking for rain and protection so their farms could have a good harvest. I asked the council members if they really believed it would make a difference, and the answer kind of caught me by surprise. The medicine man told me it doesn't matter if the goddess is real or not, the community act of the ritual under the stars gives out positive energy, which helps the earth and the plants become happy and grow. To make a long story short, the star they identified with the mother goddess was Spica in the constellation of—yes, you guessed it—Virgo!

Spica is the brightest star in Virgo. It is a Latin word which means "ear of wheat." The constellation represents the goddess Demeter holding wheat in her right hand. Spica is a prominent star in the late summer and early fall evening sky. Spica is a blue-white star twice the size of our sun and over 2000 times brighter. The star is 260 light-years from us and the sixteenth brightest star on the celestial sphere as seen from Earth.

---

31 This research is documented in my books *Celtic Mysteries in New England* and *Celtic Mysteries: Windows to Another Dimension in America's Northeast*.

Corona Borealis

Corona Borealis is a small but very beautiful constellation that appears like a half circle. The constellation always reminded me of the vanishing Cheshire cat's smile from *Alice in Wonderland*. Many ancient cultures found this pattern in the heavens to suggest a crown or fairy ring in the sky.

In Celtic folklore this group of stars was said to be six fairies that move across the sky looking for a place to enter our reality and enjoy the pleasures of Earth. To be standing under them when they descend was considered to be dangerous and foolhardy, since it was believed the ethereal beings would take you to their world, from which no mortal can return.

The Pawnee Native Americans of the Great Plains believe it was a circle of celestial chiefs. On a clear night, when the constellation is directly overhead, tribal chiefs spanning many generations would chant and pray to the great celestial circle of chiefs for guidance to help solve problems and make decisions. The legend states that if the trouble was great, a celestial chief would come down from the sky, sit with the earthly chief, and talk for hours in many different languages, giving him advice and sometimes power to handle the dilemma.

It is said the celestial chiefs are tall and glow gold and blue and their headdress is made up of stars of many colors, which sometimes shoot up or down into the sky. This was an interesting comment since there is a yearly meteor shower that radiates close to this constellation.

Although I personally have never seen the celestial chiefs come down from the sky over the years, I have had conversations with Native Americans from many different tribes in the Northeast and Southeast United States who claim to have interacted with them.

Native American tribes of the Northwest looked upon Corona Borealis as an opening to a cave where the Great Bear hibernated all winter. However, the Blackfoot Tribe of Montana say Corona Borealis is a spider that sits in his starry web (the constellation of Hercules), watches over the earth, and sometimes climbs down the Milky Way to hunt. The aboriginal Australians thought it was a boomerang of a powerful spirit, while a classical Greek myth saw it as the crown of the daughter of Minos.

Summer Constellations

Normally, constellations keep their individual borders and identities on the celestial sphere. However, sometimes several constellations may be united together to make one huge assemblage of stars. The constellations involved in this scenario are all birds; they include Aquila (the eagle), Lyra (the vulture or the lyre), and Cygnus (the swan). The three brightest stars in these constellations—Altair, Vega, and Deneb, respectfully—make up a super constellation called the "summer triangle" or "pyramid."

Lyra

The western corner of the summer triangle is marked by the bright star Vega in the constellation of Lyra, the lyre. The lyre was the musical instrument of Orpheus, which was originally made by the god Hermes. Hermes traded the lyre for a magical staff owned by his brother Apollo. Apollo then gave the lyre to Orpheus to take on his adventure with Jason and the Argonauts to help keep their spirits up throughout the long and dangerous voyage.

The music of Orpheus was so beautiful it could charm and quiet angry people and tame the wild beasts of the forest. Legend tells us his music was so wonderful that the oak trees migrated to the shores of Thrace just so they could hear the music clearer.

When he returned home from his adventure with the Argonauts, Orpheus lost his wife when she was bitten by a poisonous snake. Orpheus, himself, later died of heartbreak since he could not bear the thought of living without his beloved. Zeus sent a vulture to retrieve the

Lyre, which was set into the stars so that all mortals would remember the beautiful music that Orpheus played.

Vega is a brilliant blue star in the constellation of Lyra. Vega is an Arabic word, which translates into English as "the swooping vulture." It was also known as the "Vulture Star" during ancient times in the Middle East and India. In Asia it was called the "Weaving Princess Star." Vega is a star about 3 times the size of our sun and 26 light-years from Earth. Recently, a cloud of dust was discovered circling the star; to astronomers this indicates that Vega may be in the early stages of planetary formation.

The constellation of Lyra with its bright star Vega has always been a favorite point of alleged alien origin from people who claim contact with extraterrestrials. Is it because the aliens are really from this area in space or is the contactee just living out a fantasy to escape the reality of their otherwise dull or troubled life? It is possible Vega was selected by these people since it is one of the brightest stars on the celestial sphere.

Over the years I have interviewed six people who say they had an alien contact experience after claiming they were drawn to stare hypnotically at a number of bright stars in the night sky. After a considerable time in a so-called trance, the individual would retire to their bedroom, go to sleep and wake up in a ship of some sort or even on another planet.

This I really envy since it sounds like being teleported just like John Carter to Barsoom, something I wished for as a child, but it never happened to me. We have to consider that perhaps the sight of the celestial sphere triggers something in the brain in certain people which results in a lucid dream centered on the experiences described above.

Cygnus

The constellation of Cygnus the swan marks the eastern corner of the summer triangle. The constellation looks like a blazing cross on a dark night, so it is often called the "Northern Cross." During Christmas Eve the "cross" can be seen standing upright in the northwestern part of the celestial sphere. The bright star Deneb marks the top of the cross.

During the nineteenth century Baptist ministers in the United States would have their Christmas Eve mass out in a field. The ministers would position themselves with the starry cross behind them just above their head. I am told this practice is still done today in the Northeast United States by a number of different congregations. It must be very cool!

Cygnus has many stories from Greek and Native American mythology. In a Greek myth, the swan is the god Zeus in disguise flying off undetected from his wife Hera to Earth to seduce mortal women. In another story the swan represents the fallen son of the god Apollo. The Wappinger Native Americans of New York say it is a great bird who takes souls to heaven along the celestial path (The Milky Way).

Deneb is a bright star, which in Arabic means "the hen's tail"; it is a white supergiant star at a distance of 1600 light-years from Earth. It is 60,000 times brighter than our sun and is one of the most distant stars visible in the sky from our section of the galaxy.

Aquila

The most southern part of the triangle is marked by the star Altair. Aquila, according to Greek mythology, was the great eagle who was the servant of Zeus and carried his thunderbolts.

In another myth from ancient Greece, Aquila is assigned the task to bring the mortal Ganymede to Mount Olympus to serve the gods as the new cupbearer. One day, Zeus, king of the gods, saw Ganymede and was so taken by his good looks that he sent the great eagle Aquila to swoop down on him and bring him to Olympus. Zeus told Ganymede that he was to be the new servant of the gods, a position that all mortals longed for. However, at that time the position was already filled by Hebe, the daughter of Hera, queen of the gods.

There was furious competition between Hebe and Ganymede for the honor of serving the gods. After many years Ganymede won the job and eventually became the beloved cupbearer for all the Olympian deities. To honor the events surrounding the elevation of Ganymede, Zeus placed the shape of an eagle in the sky and next to it placed the constellation of Aquarius to immortalize Ganymede.

Aquila was very important to the countries of the Near East and Southeast Asia. The constellation represented the Garuda, a humanoid birdlike creature that is prominent in Hindu and Buddhist mythology. The phoenix is thought to be the European version of this creature. The Garuda are believed to be the servants of the god Vishnu and protect the earth from the dreaded snake people called the Naga. There will be more information about this being, race, and myth in the next chapter.

Altair is a white supergiant star 17 light-years from us and almost 100 times brighter than our sun. It is easy to spot since it is the brightest star in the lower southern section of the sky. In the 1950s movie *Forbidden Planet,* a future spacecraft from Earth, which looks like a flying saucer, lands on a planet in the Altair system to rescue the last survivors of a colony. The planet is the home of a very malevolent, indestructible, and invisible energy monster that starts killing off the crew one by one.

When I first saw *Forbidden Planet* back in the '50s, it really scared me! Besides the monster and a very young and beautiful Anne Francis, the best part of the movie is the flying saucer ship, which was influenced by the many sightings of flying disks or saucers in the 1950s. The movie stared Leslie Nielsen and Walter Pidgeon. This classic film introduced the biggest star of the 1950s science fiction scene, Robbie the Robot.

Scorpius

One of the most interesting constellations in the summer sky is Scorpius, the scorpion. Although it is located a little low in the south, most of the stars of the constellation are well above the horizon and stand out in the night sky.

The constellation's brightest member is called Antares, which means "the rival [or enemy] of Ares." Ares is the Greek name for the planet Mars, which, like Antares, appears red in the sky; this is where Antares got its similar name. Several summers ago, when Mars was at a close approach to Earth, Mars was a very bright object in the summer sky. During these few weeks Mars was located in Scorpius, near its rival Antares. I must admit the two looked very strange in the sky, and although Mars was the brighter and redder of the two, they looked like two red eyes on the celestial scorpion looking down at earth, hoping to catch prey.

Scorpius is one of the constellations of the zodiac, and if you were born when the sun was in this constellation, then you are considered to be a Scorpio. This takes place in late October and November, and although the position of the sun has shifted in respect to the constellations in the zodiac since ancient times, we still say November is the month of Scorpius.

The scorpion lies between Libra (the scale) and to the west of Sagittarius (the archer) near the center of the Milky Way. At one time Libra was considered to be a part of Scorpius and was called the "Claws of the Scorpion" by the ancient Greeks. The Romans later thought the constellation was too large, so they invented Libra to represent the scales of justice.

The celestial scorpion is a very old constellation, and there are myths about it from many cultures throughout human history. According to the Greek legend, it represents the scorpion sent by the goddess Artemis to punish the mighty hunter Orion for boasting that he was a greater hunter than even the goddess of the hunt.

The Chinese called Scorpius "Peaceful Dragon," a powerful, but peaceful creature who protected our planet from the other evil dragons in the sky and on Earth. The Chinese and Thai astrologers called the star Antares the "Fire Star" since they thought when it appeared in the sky it triggered fires on Earth. This would make sense since you would expect fires in the dry summer and this is when the star is at its highest point on the celestial sphere, displaying its brightest red. The Babylonians knew the constellation as the "Eagle" while the Egyptians, and coincidently enough, the Native American of the Great Plains, saw it as a snake.

In Hawaii the Scorpion was known as the "Fish Hook" of the god Maui who, while fishing one day, accidentally pulled up land from the bottom of the ocean. This land became the Hawaiian Islands, and the fish hook was placed in the stars to remind the people where their homeland came from. The people of New Zealand also have a similar story of how a powerful god was fishing one day, hooked the bottom of the ocean, and pulled it up, creating the islands of New Zealand.

Fall Constellations

The constellations of fall are rich in mythology and superstitious beliefs. Six of the most prominent constellations—Perseus, Andromeda, Cassiopeia, Cepheus, Pegasus, and Cetus—all belong to the same Greek myth. This legend was made famous in modern times by Hollywood in the movie *Clash of the Titans*.

In the latest version of the film, actor Liam Neeson played Zeus. At the time, I was still teaching, and his son was in my science class. During a parent-teacher conference, I found out about the movie and got some inside information. The Perseus legend is one of my favorites from Greek mythology and was happy to hear that a major motion picture was planned. Mr. Neeson did considerable research of his own before filming the movie and, although the script was only based on the Greek legend, it is my opinion that Mr. Neeson gave a fantastic performance as Zeus.

The constellations from the *Clash of Titans* saga that I mention here are Perseus, Andromeda, and Pegasus.[32] The additional two constellations presented in this section include Aquarius and Aries—both important signs of the zodiac and vital for this book.

Perseus

The constellation of Perseus is a prominent fall constellation. Perseus was one of the many sons of Zeus and is known as the celestial hero. The hero is seen in the sky stirring up the dust of heaven (the Milky Way) as he rushes to save the fair Andromeda from a sea monster called the "kraken."[33] Perseus is holding the head of the dreaded gorgon Medusa, a monster so ugly that any living creature that looked into its eyes would turn to stone. He then positions himself in front of the kraken, making the beast look directly into the eyes of Medusa, the sea monster turns into stone, and then, striking it with his magic sword, the beast crumbles into the sea.

The Hopi Native Americans called the constellation Perseus "The Gateway to Heaven" since they saw the stars as an entrance or door to the spirit world (The Milky Way).

One remarkable star located in Perseus is Algol. "Algol" is an Arabic word that originated from al ghul, which, when translated into to English, means "the demon." However in this case, al ghul means "the djinn." Al ghul is a type of malevolent djinn prominent in Arabic mythology, in the western world we know the djinn as "jinn" or "genie."

To the ancient Greeks, Algol represents the blinking eyes in the head of Medusa, and for many centuries it was thought if one gazed upon the star while it was high in the sky, you would have ten hours of

---

32   Andromeda and Pegasus are two different constellations that are joined together. Because of this they are presented as one.

33   The constellation of Cetus, the whale, was identified as the kraken.

bad luck. Because of this superstition, people of southern Europe would shield their eyes from the star when looking at the northern sky.

For centuries it was noted the star would appear to fade and grow bright in a predictable cycle, giving the impression that it is blinking and because of this the Persians called Algol "The Winking Eye of the Demon." The Egyptians thought it was the eye of Ra, the sun god, while the stargazers of ancient Mesopotamia called it "The Eye of Bel." The early Christians called the star "Satan's Eye," while the people of Southeast Asia called it "The Corpse." There is no reference in any Native American myths regarding the winking of Algol. I could be wrong, but years of research have not uncovered a single revelation that the indigenous people of North and South America considered the star unusual.

Algol is a bluish star with a surface temperature of about 13,000°F, like the sun. It is a main sequence star,[34] but is has twice the mass and is 100 times more luminous. Algol is located 93 light-years from Earth and has a very unusual feature. For centuries astrologers and astronomers have noticed that Algol changes in brightness considerably over a period of 2.8 days.

In the nineteenth century, astronomers solved the mystery of Algol. They discovered that Algol is actually two stars orbiting each other, with one being brighter than the other. As the fainter star moves in front of the brighter star, Algol seems to fade; when the two stars are side by side the Algol system appears as its brightest. Recent findings by astronomers indicate the Algol system may be ternary in nature. If this is true, it could contradict our current ideas of stellar evolution.

Andromeda

Andromeda was the daughter of the Ethiopian king Cepheus and his queen, Cassiopeia. One day Cassiopeia boasted that her beauty was

---

34   Stars close to the same size and surface temperature as our sun, with energy output that is stable over long periods of time.

greater than the sea nymphs. The sea nymphs went to their father Poseidon, the god of the sea and horses, and asked for revenge. The angry god then sent a giant sea creature to destroy the Ethiopian coast. The only way to stop the monster and end the curse was for Cepheus to sacrifice his beautiful daughter, the princess Andromeda, to the monster.

After a long debate, the parents decided to chain Andromeda to a rock in the ocean. As the monster approached, the great hero Perseus, who was also Andromeda's lover, came to the rescue, flying on the winged stallion Pegasus. Perseus was able to rescue her by making the monster look into the eyes of the severed head of the gorgon Medusa.

As a reward for killing the monster and saving the princess, Perseus demanded that Cepheus give him his daughter's hand in marriage and a kingdom of his own. However, Queen Cassiopeia thought Perseus was not good enough for her daughter and was against the marriage. One night Perseus and Andromeda slipped away and established a kingdom of their own.[35] Perseus and Andromeda lived happily ever after, and it was said that the gods were so pleased with this drama that they granted all the players a place in the stars.

Pegasus

Pegasus is a prominent northern constellation, and although it does not contain very bright stars, it is easy to spot because the stars form a giant square. The Arabs of the Middle Ages called this part of the constellation "The Great Diamond," modern astronomers call this pattern of stars "The Great Square of Pegasus."

The story of Pegasus comes to us from Greek mythology. His mother was the beautiful Medusa (before she was changed into a gorgon by Hera) and the god Poseidon, the Greek god of the seas and horses. After helping Perseus destroy the kraken, Pegasus became the horse of the

---

35 The Persians of 400 BC claimed they were descendents of Perseus and Andromeda. They called themselves "Persians" after Perseus.

hero Bellerophon, who would fly on his back to the top of Mount Olympus. For his arrogance Zeus hit him with a lighting bolt and knocked him off Pegasus, making Bellerophon fall to his death. Although Bellerophon was killed for trying to make himself an equal with the gods, Pegasus was rewarded by being placed in the sky.

Another Greek myth of Pegasus begins with the Muses holding a contest of who can sing with the most beautiful voice. During the competition, their singing was so wonderful that it made the streams of Mount Helicon start to rise to the heavens. The god Poseidon ordered Pegasus to stop the waters ascent by striking the mountain with his hoof. The vibrations caused the waters to fall creating a great fountain. The fountain became a magical place since whom ever drank from it was inspired to write music and poetry. The modern-day saying "a fountain of inspiration" came from this myth of ancient Greece. The stars in Pegasus have been recognized as a flying horse since the days of the ancient civilizations of Mesopotamia. In Rome the constellation was known as "Equus Ales," or the "flying winged horse."

Aries

In Greek mythology Aries was a ram with a golden fleece, not to be confused with Ares, the god of war associated with Mars. The god Hermes skinned the fleece off the ram and gave it as a gift to a beautiful mortal woman. The golden fleece had great power and could not be trusted in the hands of man, so the gods hid it in a faraway land guarded by a fierce monster.[36]

In order to regain his kingdom, the dethroned prince Jason was told he had to acquire the fleece. Jason put together a team of heroes which included the mighty Hercules, the Gemini twins Pollux and Castor, Atlanta the huntress, and the musician Orpheus. After great battles

---

36   It is possible the faraway land was North America and Jason and his crew sailed across the Atlantic Ocean. There are mysterious artifacts in New England that are European in origin and are thought to predate the Vikings by over a thousand years.

with demigods and monsters, they were able to retrieve the fleece, and Jason used its power to reclaim his kingdom.

The fleece was kept safe in a special secure chamber; however, one morning when Jason went to check on it, the fleece was gone. He was told by an oracle that the gods did not trust anyone with such great power, so Zeus took the fleece and placed it in the heavens so it would always be out of the reach of mortals.

In the 1960s Hollywood made the story of Jason and his band of heroes (called the Argonauts) into a movie. It is one of the classics of Hollywood, but the movie does not end. It seems the studio was planning a part two but never completed it since the cost of the special effects was much too high. One has to remember the movie was filmed before computer imaging. If the film was done again today, it would be spectacular and most likely a big hit as long as the writers didn't stray too far from the original Greek myth.

Aries is a very faint constellation and unless you are familiar with the celestial sphere it is difficult to find. It has been, however, a very important group of stars to astrologers—since 2000 years ago, during the first day of spring, and the sun was located in Aries. This point in time was known as the Age of Aries. The Ram is the first of all the constellations of the zodiac, and today is still called "the first point of Aries" by astrologers.

As a result of a wobbling movement as our planet spins on its axis, called procession of the equinoxes,[37] during the beginning of spring, the sun is now in the constellation of Pisces, the fish. We are now officially in the Age of Pisces. Six hundred years from now, the sun will be in the constellation of Aquarius during the vernal equinox, and we will be in

---

37 Imagine a top spinning; while it spins it wobbles, causing the top to point to different directions. The complete cycle for this wobbling effect for Earth is about 26,000 years.

the famous Age of Aquarius.[38] Whether or not there will be peace and harmony in the world at that time remains to be seen. There are some astrologers who believe the Age of Aquarius began in 2012. If this is so, then the mystical age is not living up to its promise.

Aquarius

There are many legends from ancient civilizations that tell us a great flood once engulfed the earth, killing every living thing except for a few chosen ones selected by the gods. These gods included the Christian/Judean/Islamic god, the gods of the Sumerians, the gods of the Chinese, the Great Spirit of the people of the Americas, and Zeus or Jupiter, the king of the Greek and Roman gods.

Science has proven that there was a great deluge long ago and water covered a large portion of the populated surface of Earth. The Aztecs of central Mexico and Toltec people of Central America believed we live in the fifth world, and the previous one was destroyed by the gods of heaven because people became corrupt and evil. They believed this previous fourth world was destroyed when a great spirit poured water down to Earth from the stars. Finally, legend tells us Atlantis was destroyed by gods from the stars with a great flood after its people became corrupt and enslaved the world.

In many cases this historical great flood was associated with the constellation of Aquarius, the water bearer. He is seen in the sky as holding a great vase of water and pouring it down to the surface of Earth. Aquarius became known as the taker and giver of life, since when the water is poured from the heavens in small amounts the crops grow, but large amounts bring floods and death.

Aquarius is a very old constellation and, although it is not very bright, this group of stars was considered important because when it

---

38   Made famous by the play and movie *Hair*, this introduced the song "Aquarius" in the 1960s.

rose just before sunrise it meant the start of the rainy season for many countries around the world.

Aquarius was known as the bringer or bearer of water by the Greeks, Romans, Sumerians, and Babylonians. Carved tablet stones that date back over five thousand years show the constellation in the sky as being the giver of life and death to the people of Mesopotamia.

Aquarius was considered to be the god of the waters by the people of North Africa; they saw him as being both a good and evil deity, who when angered threatened to destroy the human race. When the sun rose with Aquarius, the Egyptians referred to that time of year as the "days of cursed rain" and believed Aquarius poured water from the sky, which caused the Nile River to flood. It was very important to these ancient people that court astrologers or priests watch the position of Aquarius on the celestial sphere to advise the kingdom when this flooding was about to take place.

In ancient Greece, Aquarius was identified as a stellar being who was told by Zeus to destroy all life with a great flood because it became too corrupt. However, before the flood Zeus told several people in a dream, who were worthy in the eyes of the gods, to build a great ship and only allow those people on board who have a glow above their head. Zeus also told them to carry livestock and different animals since they would need them after the flood is over.

Aquarius then poured his water onto Earth, flooding the entire planet and killing everyone. However, the chosen ones were safe on the ship and wandered around the ocean for forty days and nights. Eventually the water resided and the ship ran aground on Mount Parnassus,[39] where the survivors disembarked and started a new world.

This myth sounds a great deal like the story of Noah's ark, and similar legends are found in quite a number of cultures. It is speculated by

---

39   Mount Parnassus is a mountain in central Greece north of the Gulf of Corinth. Its
      elevation is just above 8,000 feet.

ancient astronaut enthusiasts the message did not come from God or the gods, but an alien race who was trying to save a few chosen human beings and animals from a global catastrophe.

Aquarius is located along with other watery constellations which include Pisces, Cetus, and Capricorn. These are considered the water constellations because the sun passes through them during the rainy season for many Mediterranean and Middle Eastern cultures.

Winter Constellations

The constellations of winter have always been a favorite of mine, since they contain the brightest stars in the Northern Hemisphere. Although it is much colder, the nights are a great deal clearer with little haze. The constellations presented below include Orion, Gemini, Taurus, and Auriga. Canis Major, which contains Sirius, the brightest star in the sky as seen from Earth, is not included, since a lengthy chapter has been dedicated to this one star and its constellation of which has always been shrouded in mystery.

Orion

One of the brightest and largest constellations in the sky is Orion, the hunter. The constellation has several bright stellar members and is easily recognized due to its famous belt with three diagonal stars. Orion is perhaps one of the oldest constellations known to man, since records indicate it was meticulously observed by many different people as far back as four thousand years ago.

According to the Greek myth, Orion often boasted that he was a greater hunter than the goddess Artemis. Finally, Artemis just got tired of hearing him brag and arranged for Orion to meet his doom in a most embarrassing manner.

One day while Orion was hunting, Artemis sent a tiny scorpion to follow him. Orion had no idea that he was being hunted by the tiny creature. That night, after Orion made camp and went to sleep, the scorpion finally caught up to him, found him helpless in a deep sleep, and stung him in the neck. Orion quickly died from the poison. How ironic, for the greatest of all hunters to be hunted and killed by one of nature's smallest creatures.

The anger of Artemis was satisfied. She then decided to use Orion's death as an example to all mortals who try to put themselves as equals or above the gods. She asked her father, Zeus, to place Orion in the sky and place the scorpion alongside him. Zeus had great respect for Orion and his abilities as a hunter and warrior. Zeus then said to Artemis "I will place Orion in the sky and the scorpion; however, they will be placed very far apart so that they are not in the sky at the same time." Although Artemis was furious, there was nothing she could do since Zeus was not only her father, but also king of the gods. In reality, Orion and Scorpius are in never in the sky together. As seen from Earth, they are on opposite sides of the sun, which means when one rises in the east, the other is setting in the west.

In another Greek myth, Orion fell in love with all seven sisters of the Pleiades. The story has it that Zeus snatched up the seven sisters and placed them in the sky where to this day Orion still pursues them. Zeus then took the powerful Cretan bull, Taurus, and placed him between the seven sisters and Orion. They can still be seen doing battle in the sky, but according to the myth, the bull is losing the battle. The reason why the ancient Greeks believed this is because one of the stars that represent the eyes of Taurus is fainter than the other, giving the impression that the bull has been injured in the fight.

The native people of the American Northwest saw Orion as a large and small canoe in a race to the Milky Way. The Wappinger tribe of the Northeast United States feared Orion, thinking it was a giant ready to pounce on the earth if the people disobeyed the laws of nature.

The brightest star in Orion is Rigel, which in Arabic means "left foot." Rigel is 864 light-years from us and a very brilliant, white-hot star over 50 times brighter than our sun. The second brightest star in Orion is called Betelgeuse, an Arabic word meaning "armpit," since it marks the hunter's shoulder. This star is a red giant 643 light-years from Earth. Betelgeuse is so huge that if it was placed in the center of our solar system, the star would reach past Jupiter. It is a dying star, and in 100,000 years or so, it will have a spectacular death and become a supernova. When this occurs, the star will become so bright it may outshine the full moon.

It is very interesting to note that so many cultures saw Orion as a giant. We see that this belief was carried down in legend throughout the ages with a frightening prophecy that is meant for our time.

Gemini

The constellation of Gemini represents Castor and Pollux, who were twin brothers. Their mother was Queen Leda of Sparta and their father was Zeus. According to Greek mythology, Zeus seduced Leda as he approached her in the form of a beautiful swan. As a result she had two children who were identical twins that she named Castor and Pollux. Since their mother was a mortal and their father a god, one twin, Castor, was a mortal while his brother, Pollux, was immortal. Castor and Pollux were devoted to each other. Both were great hunters and warriors and they often used their talents to right a wrong and overthrow tyranny in ancient Greece. Pollux was a champion wrestler and boxer, while Castor became a skilled horseman. Both twins were also skilled with the use of the sword and were instructed by Hercules in the art of war.

The twins sailed with Jason and the Argonauts in search of the golden fleece and had many adventures together. During a battle, Castor was killed and Pollux grieved for his lost brother. He cried for days over Castor's dead body and prayed to their father, Zeus, to allow his own life to end so that he could join his twin brother. Zeus took pity on him and placed them both in the sky for all eternity as the constellation of Gemini.

Since the twins' loyalty to each other was legendary, when giving one's word or making a contract, people from ancient Greece up to the twentieth century would swear an oath to the twins. The saying "By Gemini" later turned into "By Jiminy" and was used when one person swore they were telling the truth.

Gemini is considered to be very important to astrologers since it is not only a sign of the zodiac, but more importantly, when the sun is in this constellation it marks the day of the summer solstice and the longest day of the year. Castor is actually six stars close together, 52 light-years in distance, and from Earth they appear as a single blue-white star to the unaided eye. Pollux is an orange-hued giant star 34 light-years from Earth; recently an extra-solar planet was discovered revolving around it.

Taurus

The bull is associated with a number of stories from Greek mythology. The most common tells a tale of how Zeus took the form of a bull to abduct Europa, the beautiful daughter of the king of Phoenicia, as she was swimming with her friends at the beach.

The princess, who was an animal lover, was so charmed by the bull that she climbed upon its back. The bull then ran into the water and swam with the girl to the island of Crete. There the bull revealed himself as the god Zeus and seduced the princess. The son that was born from that union became King Minos of Crete.

Taurus is a very large and brilliant constellation. The bright orange star Aldebaran easily identifies it. If you look to the right of Aldebaran, you will notice a V-shaped group of stars that form the front face and nose of the bull. This group of stars is known as the Hyades and, according to Greek mythology, they were the daughters of the Titan Atlas and the female Titan of the oceans, Aethra. They were also the older sisters of the Pleiades.

The sisters had an elder brother whose name was Hyas. One day while on the hunt, Hyas was killed by a giant fierce lion. His sisters loved him so dearly that they could not get over his death. Having mercy on their grief and impressed at their dedication and love for their brother, the gods placed them among the stars. Later Zeus placed their brother Hyas in the center of them so they could be together forever.

In another story that has its origin much later, the Hyades are identified with the nymphs, who nursed the baby Dionysius, in a cave located somewhere on a great mountain. Since the nymphs nurtured him with the juice from grapes, Dionysius became the Greek god of wine.

Auriga

To the north of Taurus there is a very bright yellow-white star. This star is called Capella and is the alpha star in the constellation Auriga, the charioteer. There are several stories from Greek Mythology telling how the charioteer got into the heavens; they are mentioned below according to their popularity.

The first story identifies the charioteer as the crippled king of Athens, Erichthonius. He was the son of the Greek god of fire, Hephaestus (the Romans called this god "Vulcan," from which we get the word volcano). Like his father, Erichthonius was born lame and had extreme trouble getting around. One day he took two horses and attached them to a platform on wheels and was able to travel easily from place to place. This new invention was called the chariot. For this great deed Zeus honored him by placing him among the stars so that all mortals can remember him forever.

The second story comes from Crete, where the charioteer represents Hippolytus, the son of Theseus—the legendary hero and friend of Hercules who slew a creature called the minotaur that was half man and half bull.

According to the Greek tale, as Hippolytus drove his chariot, he desecrated the sacred areas of Poseidon, the god of the sea. To punish him and make an example of him, the angry god caused a great wave that washed over the shore and took Hippolytus out to sea where he drowned. Poseidon then placed him in the sky for all to see as a warning not to defile his holy ground.

The third story identifies the charioteer with Myrtilus, a son of the god Hermes, and the chariot driver of King Oenomaus of the Greek kingdom Elis.[40] The king had a beautiful daughter whose name was Hippodamia, and there were many suitors for her hand. The king decreed that in order to marry his daughter, a suitor would have to first win a chariot race against Myrtilus. If he won he would be allowed to court his daughter, if he lost he would be executed.

Hippodamia's chances of marriage did not look good since Myrtilus was the son of Hermes, the messenger of the gods, and just as swift as his father. She was deeply in love with a young man by the name of Pelops, who was not much of a chariot racer.

Hippodamia arranged that Myrtilus would lose the race by sabotaging his chariot. As the race began, she was surprised to find out that the king, her father, was going to ride with Myrtilus against her love Pelops. Shorty after the race began, the wheel of the king's chariot fell off, and he and Myritilus were thrown into the sea where they drowned. Hermes memorialized his drowned son by putting his image among the stars.

The fourth story, which is my favorite, comes from the people of northeastern ancient Greece and parts of the Middle East where Auriga was known as the "Goat Herder." As a matter of fact, Capella, the brightest star in the constellation, is an Arabic word that translates to English as "she-goat." The gentle animal lover is shown holding three small baby goats, represented by three fainter stars in his left hand called "The Kids."

The Pawnee of the Great Plains of the United States saw Auriga as a celestial cougar in the sky that guarded the evening star from unfriendly forces of the heavens. The Wappinger of New York saw it as a great mountain lion that was slowly stalking prey on the earth below.

---

40   Elis is an ancient district in southern Greece on the Peloponnesus peninsula.

I have talked with the descendants of the Wappinger tribe, and some are still afraid to stand under this constellation at night for fear of something sweeping down from above and whisking them away. There are UFO investigators in the Northeast who speculate that what these tribal people really fear is an alien abduction.

Name Game

For thousands of years, the names of the constellations and their stars remained the same, then in the year 1629, the Catholic Church tried unsuccessfully to change all the Greek and Arabic names of the constellations and stars to Christian ones.

For a short time, the constellation of Andromeda (the chained princess) was known as "The Grave of Christ," Orion (the hunter) was called "The Good Shepherd," Leo (the lion) was changed to "Christ Praying," Cygnus the swan was called "The Cross of Christ," and Canis Major (the big dog) with the bright star Sirius was called "The Light of God." When the church lost its political power in Europe, the names of the constellations and stars were once again changed back to their original Greek, Latin, and Arabic origins.

I have always found it extraordinary that dissimilar cultures at different points in human history recognized many of the brighter constellations in a similar way, especially the myths. We can explain some of this by the infusion of ideas from countries connected by land, but what about cultures separated by oceans? Is it possible when human beings stare at the celestial sphere in awe at the beauty and mystery of the universe, some dormant psychic part of our nature is activated? Perhaps during this altered state of consciousness we subconsciously communicate with other people in the world, and perhaps the entire multiverse!

4

Apparitions of the Celestial Sphere

For several months in 1971, during the height of the Vietnam Conflict, I was stationed in Thailand close to the Cambodian border at a field hospital and aerovac unit.[41] My job was to run a treatment room, provide medical care, and stabilize wounded soldiers who would not need extensive surgery or could wait until one of our two surgeons could get to them. We would often receive wounded not only from South Vietnam, but also from Cambodia and Laos. It was customary to work alongside a Thai medic, since we would get wounded Thai marines and occasional civilians from several bordering countries.

Most of the time the night shift was quiet with very little to do, and since we were not allowed to sleep, play card games, or listen to music, each passing hour seemed like days. The field hospital and the helicopter landing pads were near the base perimeter. This area was sprayed often with the defoliant Agent Orange so security patrols could see

---

41   The 31st field hospital and aeromedical evacuation unit was a US Army medical unit on a Thai base. Note military designation of units is always done by number.

movement at considerable distance. The base was hit twice from small communist strike cells centered in Cambodia.

I would often walk outside with binoculars to look at the constellations. Many times some of the other soldiers working with me or those on perimeter duty would join me. I would point out the constellations and tell the mythological legends behind them. They all seemed to enjoy the stories and it sure made the night pass more quickly for everyone.

During one very quiet night, my Thai friend and I began talking about paranormal phenomena and UFOs. He had a great interest in the subject and told me a few UFO experiences that he heard from soldiers. The conversation was so interesting that, before we knew it, the light from the rising sun was visible in the east. Since the foliage was cleared, we could see a great distance. That morning the sky was pink and red with shades of purple; it was the most beautiful sunrise that I have ever seen. It was more than beautiful; the sight was magical.

In the distance the sky appeared to blend in with the ground, giving an impression there was some type of a red desert with mountains in the distance. It really looked like you could walk out there and enter some mystical land.

My Thai medic friend also saw this and said, "My grandfather told me sometimes that when everything is perfect, you can walk to the end of the sky, pass through it, and enter a hidden world." I questioned this and told him that what we were seeing was an optical illusion created by the low angle of the sun reflecting off dust and water vapor in the lower atmosphere, then projecting an image just above the ground. He began to tell me the following story how his grandfather walked through the "end of the sky" and entered another plane of existence.

A Parallel World

Although the story was told to me over forty-five years ago, it is still clear in my memory. Like a good researcher, I took notes that night, and one of my strengths is saving all of my information, so I still have those notes today. The event took place sometime in the summer of 1909 or 1910 when his grandfather was twelve years old.

On a morning after a violent thunderstorm, his father told him to walk out in the field to see how much damage was done to the crops they recently planted. As the young boy left the house and walked in the field, he noticed that the sky was a deep blue and, just ahead, it seemed to bend inwards where the color changed to a deep red. In the red he could make out what seemed to be "homes in the sky surrounded by ghostly trees." The images seemed to flicker and were distorted by what he described as "waves." He was very curious and slowly walked to the strange area to get a better look.

As he got closer he began to feel like "bugs" were crawling up and down his chest, arms, and back. It was so bad that he took of his shirt and began scratching his skin until he started bleeding. He continued to approach the unusual section of sky and began to hear a buzzing sound that got louder, but the unpleasant feeling on his skin stopped.

The boy noticed that in front of him was a red beam of light that curved from the sky to the ground. The closer to the ground it got, the deeper the red color. He put his hand into the glowing red sky and watched it apparently vanish. It was then he felt something grab his hand and pull him into the light. He tried to get away but the force was much too strong. As he went through the barrier he entered another world; the sky was a very light green and the grass was deep blue with hills in the distance and no trees. He knew he was somewhere else and definitely not in the field outside his home.

As he stood there, frozen with fear, a man dressed in a blue robe and a woman in a gold robe with long black hair came out of nowhere and tried to talk to him, but it was a language he didn't understand. The man and woman started talking to each other. He thought they were deciding what to do with him. Every time they talked he felt pain inside his ears. Finally the woman walked up to him and looked in his eyes, smiled, and placed her hands on the boy's chest and pushed gently.

The next thing he knew he was on the ground in his field and the "red sky that reached the ground" was gone. He then ran home and was told his parents were looking for him for six hours, yet he was sure only a short time had passed. His parents asked him where he was all that time—they were fearful something bad happened to him. When he told the story of the red sky and the encounter with the man and woman in the strange land, his parents went silent. It seemed they believed him and took him to see a Buddhist priest they knew at a nearby temple.

The priest told the boy and his parents that the reality in which we exist is simply one place in many. The other places are different, but most of the time the people look the same as us. He was told that when the conditions are just right, a very special person is able to walk into the next world through the "dome of the sky."

After the explanation the young man was no longer fearful and they went home. On many occasions he would return to the location where the sky met the ground, but never again found a passage to this other reality.

A wood painting that dates as recently as 1888 called the "Flammarion engraving" depicts a traveler who arrives to the end of a flat Earth and sticks his head through the domed firmament to view a strange world outside our normal reality. The Flammarion engraving is by an unknown artist, so named because its first documented appearance is in Camille Flammarion's [42] 1888 book *The Atmosphere: Popular Meteorology*. It has been used to represent a medieval belief of a flat Earth bounded by an opaque sky or firmament. The engraving seems also to be an illustration of a mystical quest for knowledge and understanding of the true nature of the universe.

---

42   Camille Flammarion (February 1842–June 1925) was a French astronomer and author of many books on meteorology and astronomy. He had a great interest in metaphysics and published a number of papers on the paranormal.

The Flammarion engraving describes what my Thai friend's grandfather may have experienced. The engraving could also be an attempt to record a true experience by the artist who wished to remain anonymous. I was to find out later, after considerable research, that throughout recorded history there have been others who claimed the same experience, several in the twentieth and twenty-first centuries.

Did his grandfather stumble into a parallel world? There are quite a few stories in which multiple witnesses are said to have seen phantom images on the celestial sphere or accidently entered another reality while out walking. If this is true, does the door swing both ways? Can people and creatures from these other dimensions enter our world? This might explain transient sightings of strange monsters, humanoid beings, unusual people, and some aspects of the UFO phenomena.

Many cultures like the Celts, Native Americans, and Chinese and people from the Near East and Southeast Asia have stories of other realities that exist in a place where the sky meets the ground. These stories or myths became part of their religion and tell of a race of supernatural beings that exist just outside our perception.

People from all over the world continue to see images on the celestial sphere in both the day and night. These apparitions include religious figures, cities, mountains, armies of men marching, and sometimes even giant, monsterlike creatures. Are we viewing the images of real things that are seeping through the barriers that separate realities, or are they nothing but mirages? The answer to this question depends on who is giving the explanation.

Phantoms

People have been reporting strange paranormal manifestations on the celestial sphere since recorded history. One of the most famous is the Roman emperor Constantine's vision of a blazing cross above the sun just before the battle of Milvian Bridge in AD 312. Although many historians think it was caused by a phenomenon called "a sun dog," [43] Christian scholars believe it was a sign from God. Knowing of the vision gave his soldiers hope, believing God was on their side. One can debate the cause of the manifestation, but it's clear its appearance gave his army a definite psychological advantage.

Constantine's victory allowed him total control of the Western Roman Empire, thus preparing the way for Christianity to become the prevailing religion for the empire and eventually for Europe. If Constantine had lost the battle, then there would have been a good chance that Christianity would not be as widespread as it is today. Think about it; one phantom event on the celestial sphere interpreted as a sign from God changed the course of human history.

The cross was once a symbol of Roman capital punishment that was feared by all who were under the rule of the empire. Today it is a symbol of hope and holiness. On the other hand, the swastika was once a symbol of good and was used by many pre-twentieth-century cultures to ward off evil. Today it is seen as a representation of evil, since many still associate it with the Nazi regime. The results of my research show there have been no swastikas seen in the sky, only the cross and ancient Celtic symbols.

Recently there has been a big craze to photograph angels in the sky. I have looked at many of the videos and still images and, in my opinion, they are sun and moon dogs. If one uses their imagination, you can make out the so-called wings of the angels in the images. The only reason we think angels should have wings is because it was handed down to us through paintings and sculpture from the early church in Rome. The founding church fathers were also influenced by winged angelic beings represented in Persian Zoroastrianism. [44]

---

43   A sun dog is caused by ice crystals in the atmosphere that glow by reflecting the light of the sun or moon. They can take on many shapes and a rainbowlike color. They appear to follow the sun or moon as it moves across the sky.

44   Zoroastrianism is one of the world's oldest monotheistic religions. It dates back to the fifth century BC and supports the existence of one god and angelic beings.

The early Christians believed firmly the sky above the clouds was the location of heaven and this was the abode of angels. The "great thinkers" of the early church reasoned that if these angels are in the sky, then they must be able to fly like birds.

The popes and cardinals of the Middle Ages commissioned painters to create large frescos in the churches, giving them clear and strict instructions on how angels, God, Jesus, and the saints should look. This representation of these ethereal beings is still used in the modern Roman Catholic Church.

The ancient Greeks and Romans believed their gods were watching over them from the celestial sphere. This gave the people a sense of security in an uncertain world; it made them feel like a child being protected by strong, loving parents. Today, with all the problems and fears in the world, we would still like to believe that powerful beings are in the sky watching over us. Since we no longer believe in the Olympian gods, we have substituted them with angels, saints, and other supernatural beings.

Supernatural entities we call angels are very real. They seem to be a higher order of ascended beings who exist outside the physical multiverse and have very little interaction with humans or any other corporeal beings in the material universe.

There are, however, many accounts from people who believe they have been saved by an angel. It is possible the entity they encountered was an ascended human rather than an angel. An ascended human is a person who has evolved beyond the need of a physical form and exists in a higher plane of existence that lies beyond the material multiverse.

In Nepal it is said that once they reach a higher stage of enlightenment, great masters of the mystic arts move on by shedding their physical body to become a bright glowing cloud of light that ascends to the heavens. In the television series *Stargate SG-1*, this method of ascension was used when the dying hero Daniel Jackson is elevated to a higher plane of existence after performing an act of bravery that saved thousands. It seems television writers really do their homework when preparing a science fiction script. It is logical to assume that if intelligent life exists elsewhere in the universe, there could also be ascended aliens.

Ghost Cities in the Sky

In 2011 residents in the Chinese city Huanshan were frightened when a giant "ghost city" appeared in the sky after a terrible electrical storm and heavy rainfall the night before. Witnesses reported they saw mountains, trees, and even a waterfall accompany the phantom city. The phantom city looked like it belonged to an ancient civilization and the construction was like nothing in the world today.

One witness said it was like a scene in a science fiction/fantasy movie. This sighting was not unique; similar manifestations have been reported previously in China over the past decade. However, the 2011 manifestation was said to be the clearest ever seen.[45]

In 2015 a floating city appeared in the sky in Hastings, England; once again the architecture of the phantom buildings looked like nothing on Earth today. This was the third time a ghostly image appeared in the heavens during the day in southern England. People who saw the city became so frightened they went to the church to pray because they thought it was a sign from God.[46]

There is a northwestern Native American legend of a city appearing in the sky each summer on the Alaska-Yukon border. A number of miners saw the vision in 1887 and described it as a scene that was tropical with bright flowers and castle-like buildings.

Manifestations on the celestial sphere have also been seen in Ireland. The *feadhreagh*, or "fairy castles," have been reported since the

---

45   *China Daily*, English-language version, September 2011.

46   *Sunday Daily Express*, London, October 24, 2015.

sixteenth century over the Irish hills and are thought to be the location where a doorway leads to the land of spirits.[47]

For generations the Irish people who live in towns closeby have said it is very dangerous to walk through the hills during the late summer and early fall. They believe a person could mistakenly slip into the land of fairies or be abducted by them, never to return home again.

Although atmospheric experts in China, Europe, and the United States cannot fully explain these apparitions, they think it was caused by rare phenomena called Fata Morgana.[48]

Fata Morgana can be seen on land or sea and involves the optical distortion and inversion of distant objects reflecting off the ground. Particles of light called photons[49] can carry information to form an image from any object they reflect. The image can then be focused through a lens and projected on a screen. According to scientists, on a humid day the layers of a temperature inversion act like a lens and the sky, which has considerable water vapor, makes the perfect screen.

Having studied meteorology, it is my opinion the phenomenon mentioned above is possible, but highly unlikely to be the cause of so many manifestations. Most witnesses do not accept this explanation. Many believe it was an alien city appearing through a portal to another dimension. Some thought it was caused by Satan and was a sign of impending doom or a secret government experiment testing out a holographic device. It seems highly unlikely the government is involved, since this type of phenomena has been occurring for thousands of years. Today the reports are more frequent. Is this because there are more people in the world to see them and we have a much greater method of conveying

---

47 *Nature*, May 1882.

48 Fata Morgana is Italian for the sorceress Morgan le Fay in Arthurian legend. It was once believed that these images were created by Witchcraft to lure sailors to their deaths.

49 Photons are the fundamental particles of light. The wavelength of photons that our eyes can see is called the visible light spectrum. This part contains the colors from violet to red.

information? Or is the explanation more exotic? Could it be our reality is aligning with another?

Images of similar manifestations have been posted on YouTube. However, with today's computer technology, you can't really tell if they are authentic or just hoaxes.

There are modern theories in cosmology that state our universe is one of an infinite number of parallel universes. All of these realities are in constant motion in relation to each other. On occasion two or more parallel universes in this complex multiverse cross over and connect by an Einstein-Rosen Bridge.[50] In theory this connection could create a window or portal allowing matter and energy to transverse both realities.

The celestial dome that encompasses our planet seems to be a very strange place. Are these phantom images projections of the past, present, and future? Do they originate from another reality or are they just a type of rare mirage? What ever the true answer is, these sky sightings have generated not only fear, but have played a role in the way mankind views reality. If you would like more information concerning this type of phenomenon, then please read the works of Charles Fort—the first person in modern times credited with documenting this unusual phenomenon.[51]

---

50   In 1938 Albert Einstein and his collaborator Nathan Rosen proposed a theory in which wormholes are formed in our universe and connect with a "mirror universe" on the other side.

51   Charles Fort (August 6, 1874–May 3, 1932) was an American writer and researcher who specialized in documenting paranormal phenomena. His books are still in print today.

5

Gods, Aliens, or Myths

One phenomenon that has frequently been reported in the celestial sphere is the appearance of UFOs. There is considerable evidence that these anomalous objects have been seen in the heavens since recorded history. In Ancient Greece and Rome they were called "flying shields." In the Bible, Qur'an, and Hindu holy books they were thought to be manifestations of God, gods, angels, or other supernatural beings. In the twentieth and twenty-first centuries, a considerable number of ideas have been proposed as to what these mysterious objects are, however, alien visitors from another star system is still the most popular theory.

Mythologists who show an interest in the phenomena say alleged paranormal events like UFOs are nothing more than modern myths in the making. It is important that researchers and scientists consider that reports of close encounters and alien contact could be much more than the imaginations and fantasies of human beings.

In 1968 the paperback book *Chariots of the Gods* by Erich von Däniken[52] was published in the United States. The book centered on his

---

52 Erich von Däniken is a Swiss author of several books who claims that extraterrestrials influenced human culture.

proposal that aliens from other worlds in our galaxy visited Earth in the past and our ancestors looked upon them as being gods or other types of supernatural beings.

The main evidence to support this theory are the many strange and unexplained artifacts that scientists have found during archeological digs in the past 150 years. Structures like the Giza pyramids, the stone works of the Toltec, and many more were conceived as being the work of aliens or humans guided by extraterrestrials.

The book was a big hit, and I too was fascinated by the material Mr. von Däniken presented to support his conclusions. After reading the book it was easy to believe that ancient aliens did in fact visit Earth for many centuries, and their influence resulted in the start of global civilizations and basic technology. Based on Mr. von Däniken's evidence it was conceivable that extraterrestrials might have been viewed as gods or other types of mystical creatures by humans of the Stone and Bronze Ages.

As with all controversial material that becomes highly popular, Mr. von Däniken was verbally attacked by every skeptic seeking publicity for themselves. Many scientists rejected his ideas, claiming the book's conclusions were based on faulty research and weak evidence. Despite the attempts to discredit the book, *Chariots of the Gods* became a bestseller and still in print.

In the present day, being considerably older but perhaps not any wiser, I am no longer a fan of Mr. von Däniken's books, but his work did stimulate a new era of research that showed the connection between ancient cultures and the night sky.

The subject of visitations by ancient aliens became a popular topic, and countless documentaries, books, and movies would follow. The original television series *Battlestar Galactica* in the 1970s was loosely based on the ancient astronaut fad.

Today, decades after the publication of *Chariots of the Gods,* the subject is still significantly in the public interest. The History Channel cable television show *Ancient Aliens* apparently seems to have picked up where Mr. von Däniken left off. The show is well done and has been active for quite a number of years, but on the other hand it is my opinion the writers and producers are stretching their evidence to keep the program alive. One has to remember American television programs that deal with the paranormal and borderline sciences are not science shows. They are intended as entertainment since an opposing argument is usually not presented.

I have been on the show three times, and although much of my interview was edited and taken out of context, *Ancient Aliens* is still an interesting program. However, as of late the producers seem to be crediting almost every mystifying legend and artifact to ancient alien visitations.

It is my opinion that the latest books and television documentaries on the subject do not give credit to mankind's ingenuity. Perhaps much of what the ancient astronaut theorists think are the result of an alien influence might be nothing more than the effort and ingenuity of some very smart men and women and not gods or aliens.

Not all our ancestors were savages, as we learned earlier. Ancient Greek mathematicians like Eratosthenes calculated the circumference of Earth around 200 BC to within an error of 1 percent without any futuristic instruments or help from the "gods."

Many of the anomalies that ancient astronaut enthusiasts claim are the result of extraterrestrial involvement span a considerable length of time, and they would have us believe Earth was once a popular stop for space explorers. Perhaps our tiny backwater planet was once the Disney World for a multitude of spacefaring people who would come to our world and engage in recreational activities by playing gods or watching primitive humans struggling to survive and engaging in warfare. To a highly evolved technological society, human beings might have offered many forms of entertainment, similar to the aliens in the *Predator*[53] movie franchise.

In some cases these magnificent beings that came from the stars were not called angels or gods, but demons. An expert on the origin of languages once told me it is from the word "demon" that we get the modern word "demonstrate," though two different linguistics experts who were also consulted told me the word "demon" in "demonstrate" is just a coincidence and has no bearing on the origin of the word. Christianity of the Middle Ages insisted that all knowledge must come from the Holy Trinity and not from demons. The priests of that time therefore told the people these entities were from Satan and should not be believed. Today we still label something dark, hideous and evil as being demonic in nature even though it may not be the original meaning of the word. Also, the origin of these beings called demons was changed by the church in Rome as not coming from the sky or a designated bright star, which they believed is only God's domain, but from deep in the earth.

Legend also tells us these super beings or demons gave early humans a code of conduct that included moral behavior so the early inhabitants of planet Earth would not destroy themselves. To break the laws of these powerful beings would result in dire circumstances. It was respect, mystery, and fear in the belief of these mighty celestial beings that kept people together and allowed their culture to survive for many centuries. This influence is still with us today, since many faiths teach that if you break God's laws you will be punished, not be allowed in paradise, or be denied eternal life after the physical body dies.

Over the years I have become more skeptical concerning most of the so-called evidence that is used as proof to validate the claim of ancient

---

53   The *Predator* movies are based on the idea that alien hunters have been using Earth as a game reserve to hunt humans. The movies, especially *Alien vs. Predator*, are based on the ancient astronaut theory.

alien visitations; nevertheless, there are historical records that indicate extraterrestrial or interdimensional beings could have interacted in several ways with the human race in the past. These cases are, in reality, few in number when compared to the volumes of "evidence" claimed by UFO investigators and ancient astronaut enthusiasts. We have to stay skeptical concerning the proof presented by the television media, but must keep an open mind to the possibility that people of long ago experienced something extraordinary.

The Garuda

In both Hinduism and Buddhism, the Garuda is a divine creature of the sky. It is associated with the constellation of Aquila, the eagle. Paintings and statues of a Garuda show it as having the golden body of a muscular man with a white face, scarlet wings, and an eagle's mouth with a crown on its head. This ancient deity was believed to have the power to change its size from a small bird to one large enough to block out the sun. The legends state that when the Garuda flew in the sky, it created winds so powerful that it could rip up trees and blow away homes.

According to the Hindu myth, the first Garuda appeared in the sky as a raging fire equal to the inferno that destroys the universe at the end of every age. When the people saw the fire they became terrified and prayed for mercy. Garuda then reduced himself in size and apologized for scaring them. He told the people he was there to protect all life on Earth and rescue them from evil forces that were coming to enslave them.

The Garuda were the sworn enemy of the Naga, a race of lizard-like beings who travel the multiverse with the purpose of enslaving and harming all life. The Garuda legends are told in Japan, Indonesia, the Philippines, China, India, Thailand, Cambodia, and Mongolia. In Thailand the Garuda is a national symbol and statues of the creature can be found in the many temples.

The Naga: Malevolent Aliens or a Myth

Like the Garuda, the Naga are present in Hinduism and Buddhism. Legend describes them as dragon-, lizard-, or snakelike people that have magical powers and can take human form.[54] Their home is on the celestial sphere in the "seventh dimension" and normally their intentions are malevolent to mankind. In Southeast Asia the Naga are often represented by the king cobra. During my time in Thailand, I have seen the king cobra a number of times in the wild and can understand why this animal was thought to be the personification of a powerful, dangerous supernatural being. In Christianity the devil is often identified as a snake or dragon. In the Muslim belief, evil spirits often take the form of a snake while on earth. In the Thai and Chinese zodiac, the constellation of Draco, the dragon, is often depicted as the origin of the Naga.

In Cambodian legend, the Naga were a reptilian race of beings and masters of a large empire until they were driven away by the Garuda. Some of them left our world while others sought refuge in India. It was said the Naga king married an Indian woman and from their unification came the Cambodian nation.

According to UFO enthusiasts, the Naga may still be with us today in the form of the reptilian aliens who abduct human beings and experiment on them like laboratory animals. Whether or not you believe that the twentieth and twenty-first century claims of alien abductions are true, it's apparent that what our ancestors described thousands of years ago is still being reported today. People are just using different language and terminology to describe their encounters.

The conjecture that reptilelike aliens are interacting with humans has been around for a very long time. In many of the mythological stories and modern-day science fiction and fantasy films, the reptilian being is usually the bad guy. Perhaps it's because many mammals, including human beings, have an aversion to snakes and cold-blooded

---

54   The description is very similar to the Persian djinn.

animals. The first mammals that appeared during the Mesozoic era[55] were apparently hunted by reptiles and dinosaurs. Who can really say how much genetic information was carried to all mammals of the modern age.

Legend tells us the Garuda and the Naga were ruled by kings and built magnificent cities. Their mighty machines could burrow through the earth or sail the heavens with magical wings. Frequently, a small Garuda or Naga would emerge from a larger individual in the sky, land on the ground, take human form, and interact with humans.

The Aztecs have a similar myth describing snake or reptilelike beings. The Tzitzimime, a race of powerful beings who once lived in the heavens, were cast out by the gods of the shining star (potentially Sirius) and exiled to Earth to become lords of the dark underworld. Since they could not walk the earth during the day, they came out at night or during a solar eclipse. Each dawn and dusk they would battle the sun for supremacy of the land. It was very dangerous for a person to encounter them, since no matter how great a warrior you were, they would take your life and eat your dead body.

At the end of the Aztec fifty-two-year cycle, if the fire of the sun did not shine on earth, the Tzitzimime star demons would once again rise out of the darkness and control this world. It was prophesied that if this came to pass, the entire race of reptile star demons would descend to earth and devour the humans who survived the destruction of the world.

The Native American Thunderbird

The thunderbird is a legendary creature found in the mythology of many Native North American tribes. It is considered a supernatural

---

55   Began 225 million years ago and ended 65 million years ago with the extinction of the dinosaurs.

being of great power and strength that protects the people of earth and hails from the stars of Aquila.

In Algonquian mythology, the thunderbird controls the upper world while the underworld is controlled by giant serpents. The thunderbird throws lightning at the snakes to keep them from taking control of the ground and air. When the thunderbird flaps its wings, it is said to be so powerful that it blows over trees, and when it moves in the sky, lighting and thunder shoots out of its body.

The Menominee tribes of Wisconsin tell of a vast mountain that floats in the western sky that is the place where the thunderbirds live while on Earth. The thunderbirds are the enemies of the great horned snakes and have prevented them from destroying the earth and slaughtering the human race. Legends also state a long time ago the thunderbirds would take human form and come down from the sky to select new chiefs for many tribes. Early Native American people also believed the thunderbird gave the people a moral code of behavior to live by; breaking this code would result in punishment.

There are a great number of similarities between the Garuda and the thunderbird legends. It's quite clear that if these stories were not of extraterrestrials and their vessels interacting with humans on a global scale, then someone knew how to create powerful myths that kept their people together, controlled behavior, and helped them deal with their fear of the unknown.

In today's technologically advanced world, we as human beings would still like to believe that some powerful benevolent supernatural force is watching over us as we sleep. You see, we are not too far removed from our ancestors.

A Thai Myth

While in Thailand I was stationed near what was then a small town by the name of Korat, which is located about eighty miles northeast of Bangkok. During my time in the country, I made friends with a number of the Thai people who worked for the United States military. On several occasions we would visit the Buddhist temples in Korat or travel north to the religious retreat and temples at Chiang Mai.[56] I was greatly interested in the many myths of the Thai people, which had their origins in antiquity, and the temples seemed like a good place to obtain information.

During my second and final visit to the Wat Chedi Luang temple in Chiang Mai, I was introduced to a monk who was the temple's historian and curator of all ancient sacred documents and books. This person spoke no English and my mastery of the Thai language left a great deal to be desired. Luckily, two of my Thai friends were with me on this trip and acted not only as travel companions but translators.

As we walked to the temple of Guan Yin[57] there was a large stone statue in the hallway that looked very strange. It seemed to be some type of creature which was part bird and part man. Subsequent to taking a number of pictures, my curiosity got the best of me and I asked what it was. The monk then began to tell a story that apparently centered on the Garuda myths and how these creatures saved the human race more than once. There was no note taking and after the translation some of the story may have been missed. The legend below is not a quote or a transcript; it was written to the best of my recollection.

Thousands of years ago, the land was ruled by gods who were selfish and used mankind to benefit their own designs. The gods had possessed a liquid that gave them long life and could cure any disease; this was the source of their power. Then one day a terrible sickness came to the mortals of earth and many died. The people prayed to the gods to give

---

56   Chiang Mai is a city in northern Thailand that was founded in 1296. The city is also
      home to many elaborate Buddhist temples, including fourteenth-century Wat Phra
      Singh and fifteenth-century Wat Chedi Luang. For centuries the city was considered a
      Buddhist religious retreat for all of Southeast Asia.

57   In Buddhism Guan Yin is the goddess of mercy and compassion. Her Roman
      Catholic equivalent would be Mary, the Lady of the Rosary.

them the liquid so they could be healed and stop the deadly plague, but the gods refused. The wise men told the people that out in the stars are more powerful gods that would help, so they began to pray to the stars for deliverance. After many days, one afternoon the sun and the sky went dark and a giant eagle appeared in the sky. The gods, seeing this, became frightened and donned their battle armor and most powerful weapons. The eagle defeated all the gods, sent them scattering to the heavens, and obtained the elixir. The people were saved and the eagle stayed with them for many years and protected the earth from false gods and the snake people.

It wasn't until about ten years later, after looking at the pictures from that day, that I realized the statue was a Garuda and the snake people could have been the Naga. Legends of similar beings are common in most of the Asian countries and some of these myths may have made their way to the people of the Americas.

It was once thought cultures separated by large bodies of water remained isolated from each other, perhaps this is not the case. There is more and more evidence being discovered every year that North America may have been explored by seafaring cultures from Europe and Asia long before Columbus or the Vikings.[58]

Children of the Gods

Legends tell us that, while in human form, Garuda kings had romances with mortal women and produced children. These offspring had superior strength and intelligence, but were aggressive and became very powerful warlords or kings who were very cruel and eventually had to be killed, overthrown, or taken from the earth.

There are quite a number of examples in mythology where the offspring of a supernatural being is born with abilities greater than the ordinary person. The Qur'an warns that having children with

---

58   The Vikings reached northeast America around the tenth century AD.

interdimensional beings called djinn is forbidden; it was believed to be an abomination and against the law of Allah. According to legend such children grew up to be seductive, attractive adults with incredible mind control powers. They exhibited sociopathic behavior, desired supremacy over kingdoms, and created chaos and violence wherever they went.

The Queen of Sheba [59] was said to be the child of a human male and a female djinn (called a jinnini). In the Kabbalah,[60] the Queen of Sheba was considered to be the queen of the demons. An Arabic myth maintains she was actually a djinn in human form and used her mind powers to seduce Solomon and manipulate the pharaoh of Egypt and the kings of Mesopotamia. To assure her rise to power, she murdered everyone in her way without hesitation or remorse.

According to Islamic myth djinn live beyond the celestial sphere in great palaces made of green emeralds. In ancient Persia it was thought if a traveler walked far enough to the end of the sky and chanted an ancient prayer, they would be able to walk through the firmament and into the world of djinn. This legend is very similar to the experience of my Thai friend's grandfather that was presented in chapter 4.

In Greek mythology children born of the celestial gods became great heroes like Hercules, Achilles, and Perseus, but sometimes they became monsters and had to be destroyed. Finally, modern-day Christians firmly believe Mary, the mother of Jesus, had a vision of the archangel Gabriel, who told her she was going to give birth to the son of God. Mary then fell into a deep sleep and was pregnant when she regained consciousness. According to the New Testament, Jesus had great power and could control the weather, raise the dead, walk on water, and manipulate matter and energy.

---

59 There are many legends of the Queen of Sheba. It is believed by historians Sheba is Yemen of today and her name was Bilqis or Billkis.

60 An ancient Jewish tradition of mystical interpretation of the Bible.

Ancient astronaut enthusiasts think perhaps the offspring of gods, angels, or djinn with humans are the result of extraterrestrials performing genetic experiments on Earthlings. This belief is still around today since many UFO true believers think aliens are abducting and artificially inseminating Earth women to create a hybrid race.

It doesn't matter what modern people or our ancestors called these supernatural beings or even if they exist or not, their alleged origin is the same—the heavens! If such creatures and beings are not real then we see the powerful influence the celestial sphere has on the human mind.

Spacecraft or a Vision from God

The Bible, Qur'an, Torah, and the Hindu epic the *Mahabharata*[61] contain many descriptions of strange clouds, flying scrolls, disks, pillars of fire, flying chariots, and globes of light that appear in the sky. We can't discount that perhaps many of these stories are nothing more than misinterpretations of some type of natural meteorological or astronomical phenomena. These experiences were used by people of long ago to confirm the existence of gods and today by modern UFO enthusiasts to support the ancient astronaut theory.

The most frequent manifestation mentioned in the sky, especially in the Bible was called a "cloud."[62] The translation from early versions of both the Old and New Testament show the word cloud was also used to denote an obscure object that is not fixed to the celestial sphere. The reference to "clouds" appearing and associated with some type of supernatural materialization is prominent throughout the Bible, Qur'an, and Torah. In many of these cloud encounters, some type of communication is established as a result of the cloud's appearance. Below is a list of some of the more interesting encounters with clouds from the Bible.

---

61   A Sanskrit epic dating to around the ninth century BC.

62   The word is used in the Qur'an as a symbol of the divine presence.

As he was saying these things, a cloud came and overshadowed them, and they were afraid as they entered the cloud. And a voice came out of the cloud, saying, "This is my Son, my Chosen One; listen to him!" (Luke 9:34)

They will see the Son of Man coming in a cloud with great power and glory. (Mark 13:26)

When he had said these things, as they were looking on, he was lifted up, and a cloud took him out of their sight. And while they were gazing into heaven as he went, behold, two men stood by them in white robes, and said, "Men of Galilee, why do you stand looking into heaven? This Jesus, who was taken up from you into heaven, will come in the same way as you saw him go into heaven." (Acts 1:9:11)

When Moses entered the tent, the pillar of cloud would descend and stand at the entrance of the tent, and God would speak with him. (Exodus 33:9)

God came down in the cloud and spoke to him, and took some of the Spirit that was on him and put it on the seventy elders. And as soon as the Spirit rested on them, they prophesied. But they did not continue doing it. (Numbers 11:25)

When Jesus, Elijah, Enoch, Moses, and Muhammad left the earth, they ascended into the sky in their physical bodies. A cloud or light was mentioned as the method of transportation by historians or painted by artists of a later time to illustrate the event. In Revelation 11:22, two prophets who are killed by the followers of the Antichrist are raised from the dead and ascend to heaven in their physical bodies on a cloud. In the Hindu epic the *Mahabharata*, Yudhishthira is believed to be the only human to ascend to the realm of the gods in his mortal body surrounded by a glowing cloud of light.

Then again not all who try to ascend to heaven make it. In the first century AD, Simon Magus, a Gnostic who claimed to have magic powers, tried to rise up to the heavens from the top of a Roman tower but was severely injured when he hit the ground. In his case there was NO cloud!

A Biblical Close Encounter

The most famous account of a possible close encounter with an alien spacecraft comes from the book of Ezekiel. The account was meticulously analyzed by NASA engineer Josef F. Blumrich who originally was a skeptic of the ancient astronaut theory. After carefully reading the account of Ezekiel he became convinced the prophet had a sighting of what we would today call a UFO and may have been one of the first persons in history to report contact with extraterrestrials.

The late Mr. Blumrich published a book in 1974 on his analysis of the Ezekiel encounter, which is still in print today.[63] His work on the subject was viciously attacked by skeptics who tried to discredit him by stating a scientist should not get involved with nonsense like ancient astronauts.

If you recall from chapter 2, the ideas of Bruno, Kepler, Galileo, and Copernicus were considered "nonsense" for their time, yet today they are considered to be the fathers of modern science. If all the innovative thinkers throughout history listened to the skeptics of their time we would still be in the Dark Ages!

An edited version of the experience of Ezekiel is presented below. It represents the account of a credible person who had an encounter with something incredible, but didn't have the understanding to express his experience with the language available at his time.

> I looked, and beheld a whirlwind coming out of the north and a large cloud with flashing lightning surrounded by radiant light. The center of the fire looked like glowing metal and in the fire

---

63   Josef F. Blumrich, *The Spaceships of Ezekiel* (New York: Bantam Press, June 1974).

were four living creatures. In appearance their form was that of a man but each of them had four faces and four wings. Their legs were straight; their feet were like those of a calf and gleamed like burnished bronze. Under their wings on their four sides they had the hands of a man.

All four of them had faces and wings, and their wings touched one another. Each of the four had the face of a man, and on the right side each had the face of a lion, and on the left the face of an ox; each also had the face of an eagle. Their wings were spread out upward; each had two wings, one touching the wing of another creature on either side, and two wings covering its body. The appearance of the living creatures was like burning coals of fire or like torches.

Fire moved back and forth among the creatures; it was bright, and lightning flashed out of it. As I looked at the living creatures, I saw a wheel on the ground beside each creature with its four faces. This was the appearance and structure of the wheels: They sparkled like chrysolite,[64] and all four looked alike.

Each appeared to be made like a wheel intersecting a wheel. As they moved, they would go in any one of the four directions the creatures faced; the wheels did not turn about as the creatures went. Their rims were high and overwhelming, and all four rims were full of eyes all around. When the living creatures moved, the wheels beside them moved; and when the living creatures rose from the ground, the wheels also rose. When the creatures moved, I heard the sound of their wings, like the roar of rushing waters... Then there came a voice from above the expanse over their heads as they stood with lowered wings. Above the expanse over their heads was what looked like a throne of sapphire, and high above on the throne was a figure like that of a man. I saw

---

64   A greenish mineral similar to olivine.

that from what appeared to be his waist up he looked like glowing metal, as if full of fire, and that from there down he looked
like fire; and brilliant light surrounded him. (Ezekiel 1)

Ever since the nineteenth century, there have been many attempts to
explain Ezekiel's experience. Some say it was a vision from God, while
others believe he encountered angels and given a prophecy, while still
others believe he had contact with extraterrestrials or interdimensional
beings. Many modern-day meteorologists speculate it was nothing
more than a powerful storm with lighting, hail, and a possible tornado.
Finally there are those who think he just made the whole thing up to
validate his position as a prophet.

If we had a vessel that could change our position in time and space,
it would be fascinating to travel backward to Ezekiel's encounter and see
for ourselves what he saw, but until this happens we will never know for
sure what exactly took place that day a long time ago.

A Psychic Connection

Over the years quite a few people have contacted me regarding the psychological effects the spectacle of a clear, dark night sky had on them.
There are psychic effects as well, and although every experience in my
files cannot be presented, one very strange occurrence will be offered.
This case not only involves a connection the witness had with the nighttime celestial sphere but also episodes of psychic (or thought) photography and claims of alleged extraterrestrial contact.

Psychic photography is the so-called capability to produce images
from a person's mind to photographic film. It first emerged in the late
nineteenth century when photography became more widely used. One
of the first books to mention "psychic photography" was entitled *The*

New Photography, written in the late nineteenth century by Arthur Chatwood.[65]

In the twentieth century skeptics and professional photographers considered psychic or thought photography to be faked or the result of flaws in the camera, film, exposures, film processing errors, and light flares produced on the lens.

Ted Serios was perhaps best known for his creation of psychic images on film, which were endorsed by psychiatrist Jule Eisenbud who believed Ted's psychic abilities were authentic. However, professional photographers and skeptics have argued that Ted Serios and his photographs were fraudulent. This was also the opinion of magician and paranormal skeptic James Randi, who actually was able to duplicate Serios's psychic imaging using sleight of hand.

In 1984 the late John G. Fuller[66] and I were working on a special for Fox TV called *Into the Unknown*. Besides UFOs and metal-bending with the mind, there was going to be a segment on psychic imaging, but all the people we interviewed could not produce anything worthwhile so we searched for an alternate topic.

John replaced the segment with a local New England faith healer who at the time was of interest to a number of skeptics including James Randi. This was my one and only contact with Mr. Randi, and although I found him to be a very interesting and intelligent person, he was far too aggressive in trying to discredit the faith healer. In my opinion there really wasn't enough evidence to disprove or validate her claims, but John thought she was the real deal, so she had a part in the show.

---

65 Chief engineer and London manager for Patent Safe and Lock Company.

66 John G. Fuller (November 30, 1913–November 7, 1990) was an American author of several non-fiction books and newspaper articles, mainly focusing on the theme of extraterrestrials and the supernatural. For many years he wrote a regular column for the *Saturday Review* magazine and *Reader's Digest*. His books include *The Ghost of Flight 401*, *Incident at Exeter*, and *The Interrupted Journey*. John was a dear friend of mine for many years.

In the case of most skeptics, there is no open mind; you are guilty even if proved innocent. *Into the Unknown* wasn't a great hit, but on the upside I got to meet film icon Bette Davis, who was staying at John's home during that time.

There are many examples of psychic or paranormal photography in my files and most are undoubtedly fakes, however there are a few cases in my collection that were studied under controlled conditions and defy explanation. Some of these cases can be found in my book *Files from the Edge*. The case presented below has never been published and although it took place over forty years ago, it still is a mystery. There is no satisfactory explanation for what took place.

Aliens from the Great Bear

After leaving the military in July of 1975, my focus became the investigation of UFO sightings with a secondary interest in other types of paranormal phenomena. I was a guest on a number of local radio programs and arranged to have several newspaper articles published. As a result of this publicity, a good number of people contacted me regarding their experiences, especially with what they considered to be a UFO sighting.

Most of the reports were of a type of sighting that UFO investigators classify as a nocturnal light. In a nutshell, a nocturnal light sighting is of an unexplained light that may stand still or make fantastic maneuvers in the sky. The majority of these reports turned out to be nothing more than misinterpretations of conventional and natural objects such as aircraft, satellites, the planets (Venus, Jupiter), and bright meteors called bolides.[67]

In the late summer of 1976, I received a call from a young man who claimed to have had extraterrestrial contact and was able to produce pictures of "alien ships and shadow images" on conventional black-and-white

---

67   A meteor that explodes in the atmosphere.

film using a standard 35mm camera. This was my first contact case and an appointment was quickly made to meet with him the next day at his home in southern New York.

During the interview he told me that his experiences began two months ago, a day after his twenty-first birthday in July of 1976. After a visit from friends he took a walk out to a nearby field, it was about eleven o'clock on a warm, clear summer night. He often did this and would look at the stars, especially the Big Dipper (Ursa Major), which was his favorite constellation. He always felt drawn to this constellation, a feeling that was inexplicable to him.

While looking up at the great celestial bear he noticed a "new" star in the center of the bowl. He thought this was strange since there was never a star in that position before and this one was brighter than the others, with a deep amber color that made him hypnotically gaze at it.

As he stared at the starlike object, it "flared and burst into a beam of light" that knocked him to the ground. When he opened his eyes and looked up, the star was gone and his body felt numb. He then walked back to his home and discovered it was 1:45 in the morning; there was at least ninety minutes of time that he could not account for.

That night he had an agitated sleep and had terrifying dreams of being on an "operating table" with "scary men who looked liked they were partly both human and reptile." They were doing something with the side of his head and placed a device that felt like a vibrator against his skull. He could not move and was afraid they were some type of extraterrestrials who were going to dissect him as a "school laboratory lesson." Then there was a flash of light and he woke up in his bed in a cold sweat yelling something in a language he didn't understand. He got dressed, went to work, and decided the entire thing was just a bad dream and wanted to forget it.

He was concerned about losing his sanity and went to his doctor who performed "all types of tests" and X-rays but could not find a thing wrong with him. His doctor made an appointment with a neurologist for him, and once again a clean bill of health was given. At no time was the encounter with the strange light or dream mentioned to his doctors since he thought they would think him crazy.

Several nights later he felt an urge to go out to the field at night with his camera once again. The feeling was so strong it was as if something was controlling him. While out in the field, he pointed his camera to the Big Dipper and noticed the strange bright star that he saw during the night of his blackout was no longer there. Raising his camera he started taking pictures with no flash.

When the film came back from the developer, there were a multitude of images. When he pulled out the prints from a manila envelope to show me, I found them quite attention-grabbing. There were large bright blobs that looked like giant jellyfish and transparent stingray-like figures slightly out of focus. I have to say this did impress me. He saw nothing with his eye, yet the film picked up something that looked more like amoebas and giant one-celled life-forms rather than spaceships. I then asked to go out to the field with him on his next trip.

We had to wait several days because of bad weather, but when a clear night finally arrived I was excited and brought my camera loaded with Kodak Tri-X film.[68] We both started taking pictures of the night sky; the exposures were 1/125 second. We sent both exposed film canisters to the same lab in Mystic, Connecticut. Ten days later my pictures came back in the mail and they were all blank. I called the experiencer and was told he had eleven unusual images on the twenty-exposure roll.

When I got to see the images, they once again looked like several types of life-forms darting around the sky, but as with the first bunch, they were fuzzy looking, almost out of focus. My first explanation was perhaps there was something wrong with his camera and the images

---

68   Kodak Tri-X 400 is a high-speed black-and-white film for photographing dimly lighted subjects or fast action.

are nothing more than flares on the lens created by the light from street lamps and nearby homes.

A few days later on a clear moonless night after loading my camera with Kodak Tri-X, we both went out to the field, but this time he used my camera and I used his. I also asked if he would shoot different parts of the sky and was told it only works when he is pointing at the Big Dipper. Nevertheless, he did shoot a few frames of the opposite part of the sky.

We completed our experiment in about an hour, but this time I took both canisters of film home to be developed in my darkroom. To my surprise there were images of the same type of amoeba blobs and stingray-like objects, but only in the north near the Big Dipper and the star Polaris and only on the film that he used—my entire roll was blank. Of course using a shutter speed of 1/125 and 1/250 seconds there were no stars visible, just these fuzzy transparent-like things on a black (clear on a negative) background. We were able to repeat the experiment two more times before the anomalous images stopped and the negatives from both our cameras came out blank.

Two days later he called and asked me to come over to his home. Upon arriving he said that ever since the light knocked him out he had been getting "communication" from aliens who told him he was collecting information for them, and every night they would tap into his brain and take the images that he saw.

They told him the creatures on the film were from another dimension and for the most part they are invisible to the human eye. The "aliens" explained that when they took him that night they "rewired" his brain so he would see the creatures on a subconscious level, but they had no idea the images would be transferred to photographic film. He said, "even these aliens from another star system were baffled on how it happened." I asked about the "creatures" on film and he said, "I was told they are from another dimension and they move very fast. The reptile extraterrestrials who took me that night said they are a scientific expedition from a planetary system near the star in the Big Dipper we call Mizar. They have visited Earth on a regular basis for the past ten thousand years; our ancestors thought they were gods. They have been studying these creatures ever since they discovered them by accident during a recent scientific survey of Earth and its life, but they know very little about them. The aliens said the creatures shy away from them, but for some reasons are attracted to earth life-forms."

After our last meeting, he had no further communication from the "reptile people" and produced no more pictures of the sky creatures. This was the first time but not the last in which a contactee or paranormal experiencer would get in touch with me on the topic of strange images on black-and-white and color film of something invisible darting around on the celestial sphere.

In the case of the person above, we have to ask why did the images only happen near the Big Dipper? One possible answer is these so-called sky critters are attracted to the magnetic field of Earth. The images may have looked blurry, because maybe they give off light in the infrared. This would make them invisible to us and, since the lens on a camera is set to focus on visible light objects radiating in the infrared, the camera would produce an image that is blurry and ghostlike on standard emulsions. Yet, this does not explain why on the same night he got images and I did not. This to me is still unexplainable; perhaps the images were placed on the film using some short of psychic photography.

It wasn't until 1986 after reading a book called *The Cosmic Pulse of Life* by Trevor James Constable [69] that a possible partial explanation surfaced for me for the images on the film. Constable's ideas were so revolutionary they must be presented in this book as another mystery of the celestial sphere.

---

69   Trevor James Constable was a writer who believed that the UFO phenomena was explained by the presence of enormous amoeba-like animals inhabiting Earth's atmosphere.

Sky Creatures

About fifty years ago, paranormal researcher Trevor James Constable discovered that when infrared film is used in a camera with a wratten number [70] 25 red filter and a very fast shutter speed at a location high in altitude, you get images that look like a blob or single-cell life-form.

Constable speculated in our atmosphere exists a life-form that is invisible because it moves so fast and radiates a great deal of infrared radiation from its body that cannot be perceived by the human eye. Constable called these beings "sky creatures" and today the idea that they possibly exist is all but forgotten in UFO research circles. As Constable says in his book, "The existence of these organisms seems to be plasmatic having the outline of their form expressed in heat substance. They travel in a pulsating fashion, swelling and shrinking cyclically as they move through the air."

So can we list these creatures as a possibility of being one small part of the UFO puzzle? You bet we can! Perhaps when dimensional windows open, it's like a rush of energy, and living creatures that exist in a parallel reality may be pulled in unintentionally and trapped in our universe where they appear to us like a strange alien life-form.

There could be many forms of these sky creatures who may have mistakenly entered our reality where they stay trapped until they can find their way back home. The late, great biologist and paranormal researcher Ivan T. Sanderson had this to say about the sky creatures, "They are Unidentified Aerial Objects, but they don't look like machines at all. They appear to a biologist like horribly unicellar life-forms, complete in some cases with nuclei, vacuoles, and other organelles. Some are even amoebic in form." [71]

Another type of phenomenon that seems to be related to the sky critters are "spook lights. " Spook or ghost lights are phenomena that

---

70   Wratten numbers are a labeling system for optical filters.

71   Ivan T. Sanderson, *Uninvited Visitors* (Cowles Educational Publishing Group, 1967).

are well documented. There are cases all over the world of mysterious balls of light that seem to follow people and then move away when you try to approach them. These phantom lights behave more like playful animals rather than highly intelligent beings. They are known in many Native American legends and were thought to be nature spirits of some sort. The settlers in the Old West also reported the lights and thought they were Indian spirits or the damned souls of people who died.

I have witnessed spook lights in action and can tell you that they act more like a thinking life-form than some electrical phenomena of nature like piezoelectric sparks.[72]

As for the sky critters, Mr. Constable's photographs do make a strong case for the existence of these creatures. If you have a 35mm camera, then get a roll of infrared film and take a few pictures of the sky, you might catch one of these critters swooping about in the atmosphere looking for a way home.

As for the experiencer mentioned above, he passed away in 1998 from a cerebral hemorrhage. From the last of his brief experiences in the mid-seventies to the date of his death, there were no more paranormal pictures taken and no further claims of alien contact.

---

72   When certain solids such as quartz-bearing rocks are subjected to pressure, they emit a burst of electricity. This can happen in nature near fault zones.

6

Sirius: Star of Mystery and Wonder

While watching television during a hot week in August, a commercial for air conditioners came on and the announcer began talking about the hot days of August, calling them "dog days." It was apparent the advertiser had no idea what the "dog days" of summer meant, and most people in North America and Europe don't have a clue to the origin of this saying.

It is true that the dog days of summer are the hottest days of the year, but they have very little to do with terrestrial canines. The *Farmers' Almanac* lists the dog days of summer from July 20–August 25. These dates have varied depending on the time in human history and location in the Northern Hemisphere.

The hot August days have been recognized and celebrated by many cultures throughout recorded human history. The Druids and most of the Celtic tribes in northern Europe and the British Isles called this time of the year "Lughasad" after the god of the harvest, Lugh. It was a time when the crops were ready to be picked. Lugh was also a sun god. The Celtic people believed he brought the hot, muggy weather and drought if not appeased.

The early Christians celebrated this event as Lammas, a time when all nature reached its growth peak and slowly would decay in preparation for winter. In this they were reminded that all life is limited in time and subjected to the cycles of nature and the will of God.

Today, Lammas and Lugh are still celebrated, but most people know this time of the year as midsummer. Midsummer according to legend is supposed to be a very magical time, when fairies and other playful creatures of mythology come out to celebrate the central point of summer. Shakespeare made this time of the year popular with the play *A Midsummer Night's Dream*.

The hot, muggy days of midsummer get their name from Sirius, the Dog Star, which is the brightest star in the constellation of Canis Major, the Big Dog. Sirius is the most luminous star in the sky as seen from Earth. During August, Sirius can be seen in the east rising just before the sun. The Dog Star was thought to bring hot, muggy weather during midsummer and because of this belief hot August days became known as "dog days."

It was also a time that marked the mid-point of summer, when the sun would rise halfway between the summer solstice and autumn equinox. The ancient Greeks also thought the star brought the hot weather and named it "Seirios," meaning "scorcher." In the *Iliad*, Homer mentions Sirius as bringing heat and sorrow during the Greek war with Troy. "Sirius rises late in the dark morning sky, On summer nights, brightest of stars, Orion's Dog they call it, Of all, an evil omen, bringing heat and fevers to suffering humanity." [73]

Sirius has long been associated with a great celestial dog. The Greeks, Romans, Chinese, Persians, and even the Native American tribes saw

---

73   Homer, *Iliad*, translated by Stanley Lombardo (Indianapolis: Hackett Pub. Co., 1997), 22.33–37.

the star as representing a dog or large wolf. The people of Alaska knew the star as "Moon Dog." Sirius is mentioned in the Qur'an, where it is given the name "The Dog Leader Who Helps Protect the Crops."

In ancient Egypt, Canis Major was seen as the dog of the God Osiris, who assisted with the passage of souls to the underworld. In Mesopotamia, the star was known as "The Dog Star." The Assyrians knew Sirius as "The Dog of the Sun." In Thailand it was called the "Dog Star that Leads the Sun." The Persians of the first millennium called the star "The Director of the Sun."

Ancient Egyptian stargazers watched intensely for the first yearly rising of Sirius. If the star appeared red on the horizon, the harvest would be poor, because the month would bring little or no water. However, if the star appeared bluish-white, then a plentiful harvest would be expected due to increased rain.

This was not all just superstition; there is some science behind it. Sirius will flicker red low on the horizon if there is a great deal of haze in the sky. Atmospheric haze is a sign of air stagnation, no wind, no cloud formation, and most important of all, no rain. Bluish-white is the normal color of the star that meant the atmosphere is clear and the wind would be pushing moisture off the water to the land.

Sirius was also seen as the star that gave life or death, since it always appeared in the sky just before sunrise at about the same time as the annual flooding of the Nile River. Sirius was the foundation of Egypt's sacred structure, since pharaohs were buried with the star rising and setting. Some archeologists and historians believe the construction of the Great Pyramid of Giza was aligned at one time with the rising of Sirius.[74]

---

74 Due to the proper motion of stars as they orbit the galaxy, over a long period of time the stars would shift position on the celestial sphere. If this were true concerning the alignment of Sirius and the Great Pyramid, then this structure might be a great deal older than archeologists thought.

Since Sirius is a bright star, it was noticed to flicker a great deal in the sky, especially during times of atmospheric turbulence. The ancient Greeks believed if you stared at the star too long at this time it could cause ill health, make a person make rash decisions, or drive you insane. Anyone suffering from this effect was said to be "starstruck." The inhabitants of coastal cities of the Aegean Sea would offer dog sacrifices to Sirius in the hope of bringing good sailing weather and a cool breeze during the hot summer days.

The ancient priests of most cultures in Europe would wait to observe the first rising of Sirius. If the star appeared sharp and clear on the horizon, it would mean good fortune. If it was misty or faint, then it foretold pestilence and drought. Coins retrieved from Greece in the third century BC show dogs looking at a large star (Sirius) that is emanating rays, indicating the significance of Sirius and its effects on the earth. The Romans celebrated the setting of Sirius sometime around the beginning of April, sacrificing a dog so that the star's twinkling emanations would not cause drought, pestilence and fungus to grow on the crops.

Sirius in Mythology

In Greek mythology Sirius is the alpha star in the constellation Canis Major. Together with Canis Minor, whose alpha star is Procyon, they were known as the Big and Little Dogs of Orion, the hunter. As Orion rises in the east his two faithful dogs are never far behind.

A Greek tale tells us the Big Dog was a canine known as Laelaps and was noted for his great speed. The myth goes on to say Laelaps ran so fast that no animal could escape him. For an entire month an extraordinarily fast fox was plaguing the Greek city of Thebes. Laelaps was sent by his master to chase the fox and kill it. It was an even match; the chase lasted for weeks. Zeus, who was watching the drama, finally got bored and placed the dog in the stars without the fox. The dog then became the constellation of Canis Major, the great hunting dog of Orion, the hunter.

Another similar story from a later Greek myth also involves the celestial dog and a fox. The gods gambled on a race between Canis Major and a fox. Zeus was the only one to bet on the dog. Seeing he was about to lose, Zeus called the contest a draw and froze both animals in their tracks by turning them into stone statues. He then placed the dog in the sky with Orion and left the fox on the earth where, in time, it disintegrated into dust.

In still another Greek legend, Sirius (Canis Major) was celebrated as being the watchdog of the gods. His job was to guard the cattle of the sun god Apollo and to safeguard the entrance to Olympus. Legend says his warning bark was louder than thunder and would shake the earth and destroy buildings.

The Pawnee of Nebraska saw Sirius as a wolf that protected the evening star from the amorous intentions of the morning star. In a great battle, the morning star defeated the celestial wolf and won the hand of the evening star, and their union created the world. The Wappinger of New York believed Sirius was a great wolf spirit who protected the earthly wolves and made them powerful. During clear winter nights when Sirius was at its peak in the sky, they would hear the howl of the wolf; this was a time to stay indoors, since the animals spirit was at its greatest power.

Wishing upon Sirius

Star light, star bright,
First star I see tonight.
I wish I may, I wish I might,
Have the wish I wish tonight.[75]

---

75 An English language poem first recorded in the nineteenth century. The author is unknown.

Most of us have heard the poem above and at some time in your life you most likely went outside as the sun was setting in the west and looked for the first star to appear in the sky and made a wish. Since the Middle Ages people of Europe believed if you were sincere and made a wish when Sirius was visible in the night sky your request would be granted.

For countless centuries Sirius has played an important role in the superstitious beliefs of human beings. The belief that Sirius possesses magical powers and is the home of supernatural beings dates back to cave paintings found in France known to be at least 70,000 years old. The images show tribes of humans sitting on the ground around a campfire and pointing up to a bright star in the sky with magical beings flying around it. Although some would speculate that the ancient art might show UFOs and ancient astronauts, to me it represents primitive people trying to connect with the magic and power of the star to help with hunting, protection, and basic survival.

During the early Renaissance, theologians thought Sirius was the dwelling place of angels looking down upon the earth to make sure the will of God was done. Today there are those who firmly believe Sirius is the home of aliens who periodically visit Earth and interact with human beings. Although Sirius had a great influence on the beliefs of ancient cultures, the star's impact was based mostly on superstition. However, there are four mysteries of the Dog Star that have been carried into the twenty-first century—mysteries that have not been satisfactorily explained.

The First Mystery: Bloody Sirius

When we look at Sirius in the sky, it blazes with a brilliant, beautiful, white light, however in ancient times the color of Sirius was recorded as being red. In many accounts dating back to 2000 BC, the star was often called "Bloody Sirius." Was Sirius red in ancient times? Did it change color over the past twenty centuries?

In the *Iliad*, Homer refers to Sirius as gleaming in the sky like the copper shield of Achilles. The earliest observations from Babylon referred to Sirius as "shining like copper." The Greek writer Aratus and the Roman poet Cicero referred to Sirius as being "redder than Mars." The Persians astrologers as far back as 450 BC refer to Sirius as being red like blood. Ptolemy, who in AD 170 was one of the greatest astrologers of his time, compared the color of Sirius with the star Antares, which is an indisputable red-colored star.

Today we know that Sirius is a star that is mostly white and about 25 times brighter than our sun. It is close by, only 8.6 light-years away (about 58 trillion miles). That may sound very far, but when you consider the size of our galaxy and the number of stars it contains, Sirius can be compared to the distance of a neighbor's home less than 150 feet away.

According to our current knowledge of stellar evolution, Sirius could not have undergone such a drastic change in 4000 years. This would mean that Sirius went from a cool red star to a very hot blue-white star in a very short time. If you want to put this time frame into human perspective it would be like a one-year-old child growing to a fifty-year-old man in ten seconds. It is very possible that there are forces at work taking place in the core of Sirius that astronomers are unfamiliar with.

If the star is collapsing and getting hotter it is possible that Sirius may become a flare star. This means that in a very short time it would expel millions of years of energy that would be built up in its core. If this happens, then for a period of 100 years we could have two suns in the sky. The bad news is the radiation from the star would have a devastating effect on the ecosystem of our planet.

Astronomers and meteorologists feel that Sirius has not really changed in the past 20–40 centuries and the color difference may have been caused by a great deal of dust in the atmosphere of Earth due to volcanic activity during that time. This could have made the star appear red, especially when it was low in the sky.

A few historians have even speculated that the eyesight of people thousands of years ago was slightly different when compared to people of more modern times. It was suggested that perhaps human beings had vision that was more sensitive to the red end of the visible light spectrum. This makes some sense since our ancestors primarily used fire for light, and ever since the twentieth century, we have been dependent on electric lights. The human eye will slowly adapt to the frequency of light. While the light from a fire or heat source is red, fluorescent and incandescent lights are shifted more to the blue end of the spectrum. No one really knows for sure, and the mystery of "Bloody Sirius" is still unexplained today.

Mystery Two: Sirius and the Dogon Tribe of West Africa

In 1862 astronomers discovered that Sirius was actually a double star. The larger star is referred to as Sirius A and the smaller companion, a white dwarf star, was named Sirius B. A white dwarf star is a very old star at the end of its life. At one time Sirius B was about the size of our sun, but as stars age they use up their energy reserves and collapse inward due to the overwhelming force of gravity.

Although Sirius B is now smaller than Earth, it still has the mass of a star the size of our sun. Matter in the star has been crushed down so densely by gravity that one cubic centimeter (less than a thimble) of Sirius B would weigh over 10,000 tons on Earth! The orbital period of Sirius B around Sirius A is about fifty years and it can only be seen from Earth for a short time, when it is at the farthest point of its orbit from Sirius A.

Although Sirius B was only discovered 156 years ago, it seems that a primitive tribe in Africa knew of its existence for thousands of years. The Dogon (it's interesting to note the tribe's name since Sirius is called the Dog Star) are located in Mali, West Africa, and are believed to be of Egyptian descent. The tribal priests have star tales that date back to 1100 BC, and in 1943 the tribal elders told an amazing story to two French anthropologists of a secret Dogon legend regarding Sirius and a companion that is invisible to the eye.

The Dogon priests said the companion of Sirius moved in an elliptical orbit around the star and, although it was very small, it was incredibly heavy and it was spinning rapidly. All of these detailed points the tribal priests said about Sirius B are scientifically accurate, but what is so amazing is that, although Sirius B was first seen in 1862, most of the information mentioned above by the priests was not verified by astronomers until 1970.

The Dogon name for Sirius B is Po Tolo, which roughly translates into English as "little seed." The Dogon could not have known about Sirius B since they have no optical instruments. The priests and tribal elders claim the knowledge was given to them by beings from the stars. The Dogon have a legend of star creatures called the Nommo who came to earth a very long time ago in a vessel of fire and thunder. The Nommo were described as being half fish and half man and could live on the land, but dwelled mostly in the sea. This depiction is very interesting, since the Dogon are describing intelligent spacefaring beings that are amphibians. In most cases "star beings" were described by ancient cultures as being something more common, like lizards, birds, or other land animals. It was from the Nommo that the Dogon claim their awareness of the heavens originated, and every fifty years they hold a great festival that is enigmatically timed with the orbit of Sirius B around Sirius A.

In 1977 American astronomer Dr. Carl Sagan announced that he had a simple explanation for this Sirius mystery. He claimed the Dogon could have gotten their knowledge of the Sirius system from modern informants. Dr. Sagan asserted that westerners had probably visited the Dogon many times and discussed astronomy with them, which they quickly added to their legends. Shortly after Dr. Sagan's comment French anthropologist Germaine Dieterlen called Sagan's theory "absurd" in an interview on BBC television. She then displayed a Dogon carving crafted 400 years ago that clearly showed Sirius and its white dwarf companion. Dr. Sagan refused to make a comment regarding this new information.

The unexplained connection with Sirius and the Dogon continues to be just that, a mystery. It's clear in the case of the Dogon; the myth of the Nommo and the rituals they perform has kept the tribe intact despite frequent contemporary visits and cultural contamination from Eastern and Western civilization. It is the mystery and wonder of the Nommo and the promise that one day these beings from the stars will return that keeps the Dogon culture alive. Albert Einstein once said, "The most beautiful thing we can experience is the mysterious. It is the source of all true art and science."

Mystery Three: Sirius and the Paranormal

Sirius is a dazzling luminous object on the celestial sphere, and when you looks up during a clear winter night, it immediately captures your attention. The star has always been popular as being the origin of super-natural beings and modern-day claims of alien encounters. Recently, a number of websites have appeared on the internet claiming that aliens, demons, devils, the Antichrist, and super beings from Atlantis are all from the Sirius star system.

For ages those who have studied the mystic arts claimed Sirius is "the sun behind the sun" and from its energy one can tap into the power of the multiverse. The Freemasons call Sirius "The Blazing Star" and gave it a place of importance in all Masonic lodges. Freemasonry also taught that the Blazing Star is a symbol of the power of God who knows all and sees all. They believe Sirius is the sacred place where all must ascend to achieve divine power. In the tarot the seventeenth numbered major trump card, the Star, shows Sirius surrounded by seven other smaller stars emanating energy from the multiverse.

In 1980 a person who belongs to a small metaphysical group contacted me and claimed psychic contact with an extraterrestrial by the name of Baltomu. It seems this Baltomu is one of many highly evolved beings who are stationed around the galaxy keeping an eye on things.

Baltomu's interest is the planet Earth. His followers claim the being is stationed close by on a small astronomical body orbiting the star Sirius. Despite my depredations, an appointment was scheduled to meet this group of people the next time Mr. or Ms. Baltomu decided to contact them.

Shortly after the first call, I was invited to a private home in Connecticut and was introduced to a small gathering who claimed to be psychics and had the "power" to channel extraterrestrials. In a case like this, my approach is just to sit back and not ask any questions, but since the alleged information was coming from Sirius, a great number of inquiries were planned.

To make a very long story short, as Baltomu began channeling information through a process called automatic writing, the hand of the medium, a young woman, began shaking violently and her eyes were closed, displaying what look like REM.[76] In the course of ninety minutes, she produced a number of drawings of what other aliens stationed in our section of the galaxy looked like. This assembly of aliens is supposedly part of some type of council or federation that governs backward planets like ours whose inhabitants are bent on self-destruction.

One of the beings in the drawings was of an extraterrestrial by the name of Monka, stationed under one of the Martian pyramids. Monka is a popular entity channeled by psychic contactees, and during my research the name Monka has popped up many times.

Although I could not explain how the writings and diagrams were produced while her eyes were closed, most of the things channeled were of a spiritual nature. The few bits of scientific information that

---

76   REM stands for rapid eye movement. It is displayed in humans and some animals
     when experiencing a dream during sleep.

came through did not make sense or were inaccurate. The answers to my astronomy questions were also incorrect and evident of someone with a limited scientific background. As a matter of fact, most of the astronomy questions could have been answered by a school senior in my astronomy class.[77] Also, if Baltomu was on a body orbiting Sirius then it would have to be a considerable distance from the star, because it is very hot. If Baltomu did exist, it's doubtful he (or she) was really from Sirius. That evening it almost seemed as if some force was playing a cosmic joke on the people in this group and was getting very entertained by the entire session.

It is amazing how the star Sirius has been the center of focus for dozens of small groups who want to believe they are in contact with extraterrestrials. Some of these groups have merged together to create what can be considered a cult. Their claims center around not only on Sirius A and B but, also on an alleged Sirius C[78] and D.

The contactees believe that on Sirius C there is an advanced alien civilization that colonized Earth thousands of years ago and founded Atlantis. They also claim the aliens from Sirius C live on a world with no night as the result of a complex orbit around Sirius A. This gathering of "psychics" supposedly channels teachings from these aliens with the majority of the information consisting of warnings of the upcoming destruction of our civilization and the beginning of a new age.

---

77   From 1986 to 1995 I taught a high school astronomy course at the Windward School and a continuing education adult course on astronomy at Greenwich High School.

78   It seems there is some indication that Sirius C might exist, but nothing is confirmed as of the publication of this book. The following paper addresses the Sirius C question: Drs. Benest and Duvent, "Is Sirius a triple star?" *Astronomy and Astrophysics Journal* 299, (1994): 621.

Mystery Four: Sirius and the Hopi

In 1984 at the request of Dr. J. Allen Hynek,[79] I flew to Scottsdale, Arizona to discuss a number of UFO sightings we were investigating. After our work it was my intention to do research on the so-called extraterrestrial connection of the Hopi. Dr. Hynek felt it was all just superstition and nonsense and would have no part in it, calling my venture a "waste of time." Luckily, there was someone who was also staying with Dr. Hynek who knew the area and was kind enough to take me to the right people. At the time I knew very little about the Hopi beliefs and what the Kachina dolls represented. We spent the day talking to people and exploring a number of locations that are rich in legend and modern-day paranormal events.

In the twenty-first century, there has been a great deal published about the Hopi prophecies, so only the highlights from what was learned that day are presented. An ancient Hopi prophecy states, "When the Blue Star Kachina makes its appearance in the heavens, the Fifth World will emerge." The Hopi name for the star Sirius is "Blue Star Kachina." It will come to earth dancing in the plaza and will remove its mask. According to ancient alien astronaut theorists, they believe the Blue Star Kachinas are aliens from a planet revolving around the star Sirius. It is also believed by some that the Nommo of the Dogon and the Blue Star Kachina are the same aliens. After examining the evidence, there is a noticeable similarity between the Kachina mask of the Hopi and the Nommo mask of the Dogon.

---

79   Dr. J. Allen Hynek was the foremost authority on the UFO phenomena. He was the Air Force consultant to UFOs for twenty years and founder of the Center for UFO Studies. Dr. Hynek also was a member of the Apollo team and helped in selecting a landing site for Apollo 11. He was one of the scientists who contributed to the Manhattan Project. Dr. Hynek was professor of astronomy at Northwestern University.

Sirius Magic

Stars have always been artistically expressed in the shape of a pentagram with the two points facing downward. It was thought for countless centuries that stars used their power to contain evil under the earth and keep it from emerging to the surface and the heavens. Even today there are Christian groups who associate the brightest stars in the sky with angels. In many Hollywood movie productions from 1930 to 1960, angels were shown as stars with five points having conversations with each other concerning the activity of humans on Earth below.

The earliest known use of the pentagram can be found around 3500 BC in ancient Mesopotamia, where the star symbol was used as a sign of power over evil. In ancient Greece, the geometry of the pentagram and its metaphysical associations were explored by the Pythagoreans who believed it was the shape of the universe and a symbol of perfection and power. The early Buddhists and Hindus also viewed the pentagram as a symbol of power from the stars. The Buddhist and Hindu priests may have got this belief from the Pythagoreans since there is some historical evidence the followers of Pythagoras traveled east.

In a great number of ancient cultures, including the doctrines of pre-Christian pagans, the pentagram represented the "Blazing Star" (Sirius) and could be used to harness the power radiating from that celestial body.

Helena Blavatsky[80] and Alice Bailey[81] both considered Sirius to be a source of supernatural power. Blavatsky declared that Sirius exerts a direct influence over all of humanity and can be linked with the foundation of every religion. Bailey believed there was a force emanating from

---

80   Helena Blavatsky was a Russian occultist and spirit medium who co-founded the Theosophical Society in 1875.

81   Alice Ann Bailey was an English writer of more than twenty-four books on theosophical subjects and was one of the first to use the term "New Age."

Sirius whose origin is in the distant center of the galaxy.[82] She was sure the star Sirius acted as a focusing element directing this power to earth, where it could be used to perform amazing feats of magic.

The American flag actually contains pentagrams, not stars with the points pointed downward, indicating a country that stands for good and works to abolish evil in the world. The star Sirius was considered the "Blazing Star" by the founding fathers of the United States, many of whom were Masons. The Pentagram is also used on the flags of Ethiopia and Morocco just to name a few. The star Sirius was always seen as the center or progenitor of this pentagram.

A reversed pentagram, with two points projecting upwards, was considered a symbol of evil and was thought to attract sinister forces. It is very easy to see why occultists assumed this, since the stars image was inverted; they believed the power would be reversed and would be a magnet for evil and not repel it. The overturned pentagram is still used today by covens that practice the dark arts and is a symbol of the Church of Satan.

However, when the average person sees a pentagram, most do not know the difference between the upright and reverse symbol so they assume it is a sign of evil and the devil. In modern times there are many people who practice Wicca[83] that wear the pentagram as jewelry. A few days ago, after checking in with the secretary at a professional office, I noticed she was wearing a pentagram necklace. There was also a sign on the wall that read "Yes, I'm a witch so deal with it!"

---

82 During her time astronomers had no idea a supermassive black hole was at the center of our galaxy emitting enormous amounts of energy.

83 Wicca is a form of modern Paganism that was founded in England and spread to North America in the mid-twentieth century. Wicca followers claim its origins in pre-Christian religions. In modern times there are a considerable number of people who have left twenty-first century traditional beliefs and have embraced the old Pagan way of life.

It's amazing how things have changed in New England, if this was in the 1950s she probably would not be allowed to display the sign. Worse still if it was the seventeenth century, this woman would have been arrested, tortured until she confessed to consorting with the devil, jailed, and then hung in a public assembly.

Since there is a perceived association of the pentagram with Satanism, many schools in the late twentieth century sought to prevent students and teachers from displaying the symbol on clothing or jewelry. Even today in several schools in the northeastern United States children have been suspended for simply wearing the pentagram as a pendant given to them by their parents. Teachers who are Pagan are afraid to wear their spiritual jewelry to work, for fear of reprisals by other teachers, school administrators, and parents.

In New England there are a considerable number of people who have gone back to the old Pagan religions. The fear of Satan and image of the stereotypical witch are still with many people in a number of states; this is especially true in New York and Connecticut. As a result those who openly practice Wicca have been mistakenly looked upon as some type of weird freaks who worship the devil. In Westchester County, New York, a local town government and the board of education fired two teachers and several town workers who discussed their Pagan beliefs with coworkers or students.

In the late eighties I was writing an astronomy column for the local paper in the Westchester County town mentioned above. After doing a story about the Druids and how they used Stonehenge as an astronomical calendar, my column was canceled. I was told the article "supports the witches in town." The persecution of those who practice nontraditional religions and beliefs did not disappear with the New England witch trials, it is still going on today.

During my forty-plus years of researching the paranormal, many groups, cults, and individuals have and continue to get in touch with me, claiming to be in contact with extraterrestrials from Sirius or have mystical powers from the star. It is my opinion that since the star Sirius is so vivid in the night sky, people are drawn to it. It is also feasible to presume the visual appearance of the star acts as a catalyst in building a foundation for the creation of a fantasy, but then again I have been wrong before—the multiverse may be full of cosmic jokers.

It doesn't matter if you are an astrologer, a mystic, a contactee, one who channels supernatural aliens, an astronomer, or just a casual stargazer; everyone still gazes in wonder at the phenomenal Dog Star.

7

The Pleiades: Sisters of the Night

The Pleiades is a very beautiful open star cluster that is visible to the naked eye and a spectacular sight in binoculars. Depending upon where you live, six or seven stars can be counted on a clear moonless night by someone who has good vision, but there are actually fivehundred members and all are about the same age. The Seven Sisters are located 443 light-years from Earth, and from our viewpoint in the galaxy, it is part of the constellation Taurus, the bull.

The brightest star in the celestial bull was named Aldebaran, which is an Arabic word meaning "follower." The star was apparently given this name because it seems to follow the Pleiades across the sky from east to west. In Japan, the Pleiades is known as "Subaru," which means "come together or gathering," and has given its name to the car manufacturer whose logo incorporates six stars on their automobiles to represent the company.

The Pleiades is a very young cluster, only 20 million years old. Although this may seem like the stars of the Pleiades have been around for a long time, they are newly born infants in the galaxy. If you were to compare them to the life span of a human, the Pleiades would be several weeks old. The Seven Sisters shine like tiny, beautiful, perfect gems in the sky and was the main inspiration for the rhyme "Twinkle, Twinkle, Little Star," especially the line "Like a diamond in the sky." [84]

The Pleiades was always believed to be connected to natural disasters. Legend has it they were directly overhead at midnight the night before the great biblical flood took place. They were also used as an indicator for fair weather by seafaring cultures. Centuries ago, when Greek sailors saw the Pleiades low on the eastern horizon just before sunrise,[85] it was a sign that you could begin safe long journeys by sea. It was believed that ocean voyages planned before the Pleiades were visible would end in disaster. There is some scientific credence in this belief since the Pleiades begins to rise in mid-spring, which for the most part was suitable for sailing. The season for safe sailing came to an end during the first week of November, when the Pleiades was directly overhead at midnight.

In early Greece it was believed if structures were aligned to the Pleiades and Hyades,[86] the buildings would be protected from natural disasters. At least six Grecian temples were built this way, including the Hekatompedos[87] of 550 BC and the Parthenon of 432 BC.

The number seven has always been significant in the mystical arts. It is very possible the importance of seven was based on the Pleiades. For example, the following passage from Revelation in the King James Bible states, "The mystery of the seven stars that you saw in my right hand, and the seven golden lamp stands, the seven stars are the angels of the

---

84   "Twinkle, Twinkle, Little Star" is a popular English lullaby from an early nineteenth-century English poem by Jane Taylor.

85   This takes place on May 1.

86   A much older loose open cluster not far from the Pleiades in Taurus.

87   The Hekatompedos was an ancient Greek temple built in Athens from limestone and once stood in the position of the present Parthenon.

seven churches, and the seven lamps stands are the seven churches"
(Revelation 1:20).

During my research at the New York City Public Library, I discovered a bizarre reference to the Pleiades in *Astronomica*, a first-century
AD book by Manilius.[88] Although the alleged influence of the Pleiades
on human behavior goes on for several pages, only the significant part is
presented here, paraphrased. It has to do with the Pleiades influencing
men to dress, act, and look like women.[89]

The Pleiades are seven sisters who shine with each other's radi-
ance. Under their influence are the devotees of Bacchus[90] and
Venus,[91] men born into the light. These are men whose lack of
concern runs free at feasts and banquets and who strive to rouse
sweet mirth with stinging wit. They will always take pains over
personal embellishment and an elegant appearance they will set
their hair in waves of curls or confine their tresses with bands,
building them into a thick topknot, and they will transform the
appearance of the head by adding hair to it; they will smooth
their hairy limbs with the porous pumice, hating their manhood
and longing for sleekness of arm. They take on feminine dress,
footwear and paint their face not for wear but for show, and display an affected effeminate way of walking. They are ashamed of
their sex; in their hearts dwells a meaningless passion for display,
and they boast of their woe, which they call a virtue. To give their
love is never enough; they will also want their love to be seen.

---

88 *Astronomica* was written by the Roman poet Marcus Manilius during the reign of
    Augustus or Tiberius. The five-book work describes celestial phenomena, the zodiac,
    and astrology.

89 Explained to me by a curator in the rare book section at NYC Public Library main
    branch.

90 God of wine and lust.

91 Roman goddess of love and beauty.

The Celts of northern Europe marked the day of the festival of Beltane when the Pleiades were first seen in the east rising before the sun; this took place on May 1. The festival of Beltane was named after the Celtic sun god Belenus, who was one of the most ancient and widely worshiped Celtic deities. Beltane[92] (today known as May Day) heralds the return of the light half of the year, the start of warm weather, and the sun god ruling over the moon. However, when the Pleiades were directly overhead at midnight, it was the beginning of the supremacy of night over day. This was Samhain, the commencement of the dark half of the Celtic year, which was ruled by the moon. To the Celtic people this represented the ageless battle between light and dark, growth and decay, life and death.

The Druids warned the people of the clans that when the Pleiades reached their highest position in the sky at midnight, it marked a time when our reality crossed with another. It was at this point in time that spirits who lived in this parallel reality could cross over to our world. They also believed it was possible to talk with relatives who lived in the past and those who have yet to be born. It was considered to be a dangerous time for those who were alone, so people of the clan grouped together and stayed awake all night eating fruit and sweets and playing games, hoping the creatures of the night would pass them by. In Ireland the Celtic people would light great bonfires below the Pleiades, which could be seen throughout the land, and watched the embers rise up to the sky in a gesture to hopefully please the celestial sisters of the night.

The Celtic people called this festival "Samhain" and saw it as the night that did not exist in time; today we know it as Halloween. In the present day Samhain is still celebrated by the many Wiccan groups in England and the United States as a time when the sun god gives up supremacy to the moon goddess. It is also acknowledged by those who practice the

---

92   The Pagans of the northeastern United States still celebrate this day with a three-day festival in northwest Connecticut at a secluded field and forest. I was a guest speaker two years in a row and have to say it was a time to remember.

black arts since they believe that at this time they can channel power from the universe through the Pleiades. Also, groups of contactees who claim to be able to communicate with extraterrestrials from the Pleiades say the "messages" are much clearer during Halloween night.

From 45 to 5 BC the Pleiades reached its highest point on the celestial sphere during midnight of October 31–November 1; this is still held as the traditional date for Halloween and Samhain. In the twenty-first century, due to the wobbling of our planet as it rotates on its axis, called precession of the equinoxes, the Pleiades now reaches its highest point at midnight on November 20–21.

I know of at least one large group of people who practice Wicca that still perform their Samhain rituals on midnight October 31–November 1 claiming their ability to do "magic" is at its greatest. Since Samhain was timed by an astronomical event and the Druids believed the Pleiades triggered some sort of dimensional cosmic happening, today my Wiccan friends might be celebrating the holiday at the wrong time. It seems human imagination and determination is the greatest power of all.

In Mesoamerica the Pleiades was used to calculate the seasons of the year. It was considered the great divider between summer and winter. When the Pleiades began to ascend in the east just before sunrise it was a sign to plant the crops. When the cluster reached its highest point on the celestial sphere at midnight, it was time to complete the harvest since colder weather would soon follow.

To the Aztecs, the Pleiades were the most important group of stars in the sky. They believed when they reach their highest point in the heavens at midnight, horrific natural disasters would begin the next day and the sun would not return unless some sort of sacrifice was made. Perhaps in their history a powerful storm, earthquake, or some other natural catastrophe occurred the day after the culmination of the Pleiades, and the priests blamed the group of stars for the event, so they decided something must be done to appease the heavens so that it doesn't happen again.

Mythology of the Pleiades

The ancient Greeks saw the seven stars as being the daughters of Atlas; they were named Electra, Maia, Taygete, Alcyone, Celaeno, Sterope, and Merope. There are quite a number of stories on how the seven sisters got in the sky. One version is that they committed suicide from the grief of their father, who was forced to hold up the entire world as a punishment by Zeus.

In still another legend the seven sisters were the attendants of Artemis, the goddess of the hunt, who turned the young maidens into doves after Orion cornered them and threatened to take away their virginity. As the doves flew up to the sky, they changed into seven tiny stars. The legend goes on to say that when Orion died he was placed in the sky close to the Pleiades and is still pursuing them for all eternity in the heavens above. As a last resort Artemis placed the powerful Cretan bull Taurus in the sky between the mighty hunter and the seven sisters, keeping them apart for all time.

In Greek literature seven stars are mentioned, but the native tribes of North and South America mention six stars in their legends. In modern times only six stars are distinctly visible to the naked eye. In a later myth the ancient Greeks identified the vanishing Pleiadian sister as Merope and created a story to explain her disappearance.

It was declared by Zeus that all the sisters of the Pleiades were to be consorts to gods. But Merope fell in love with a mortal man and became his wife. When her sisters found out, they looked away from her in shame and her divine powers faded. The Greek legend of the disappearing star is similar in Jewish, Hindu, Muslim, Persian, and Buddhist mythology.

Today astronomers think the star actually faded some time around 200 BC. The Chinese, who were meticulous observers, noted seven stars in the cluster as far back as 1200 BC. They were called the "Glowing Hair of the Tiger" in the northern providence and "Seven Concubines" in the south. Additionally, in the eastern providence, they were known as the "Seven Sisters of Industry." From this information we can assume the fading of the seventh sister took place sometime between a time span of one thousand years.

The Pleiades is still shrouded by the nebulous clouds of hydrogen gas that created them. Modern telescopic observations of Merope show it densely engulfed in this gaseous cloud. Of course one of the reasons we can only see six stars with the naked eye today is because of light pollution caused by the multitude of electric lights used by our cities at night.

In Thailand the Pleiades are known as the "Little Chicken Stars" and get their name from a very ancient legend. The myth goes on to say; a poor elderly couple who lived in the forest owned a hen and six baby chicks. One summer afternoon a monk arrived at the home of the couple on a pilgrimage to a nearby holy place. Afraid they had no decent food to offer him, the elderly couple decided on cooking the mother hen. The hen overheard the conversation, and rushed to say goodbye to her offspring. As the mother hen was being cooked over a fire, the chicks threw themselves into the flames so they could die with their mother. The goddess of compassion was so impressed by their devotion to their mother she immortalized the six chicks and the mother hen by placing them in the stars together forever as the Pleiades.

The Blackfoot Tribe of North Dakota consider the Pleiades not seven sisters but six brothers that lived in poverty and would beg for food and clothing from the more well-off tribe members. The people were heartless to the boys because of their tattered clothes and uncombed hair. The brothers were teased by the children who wore fine buffalo skins and had parents who cared for them. The boys no longer wanted to be people, so they decided to become stars. They reasoned that stars are always beautiful and high in the sky—safe from all cruel people and dangerous animals. One night the boys ran up a mountain trail and leaped off a cliff. Instead of falling they floated up to the sky to become the Pleiades. The people who treated them so cruelly looked in amazement as they were transformed into beautiful stars. The sun welcomed them and the moon called the boys her long-lost children. From that day on whenever the Pleiades reached its highest point in the sky at midnight all the populace including the high chiefs honor them with song and dance. Its clear that the story was intended as a lesson to the children of the tribe to respect and help all people.

From the Inuit Tribe of Alaska, who believed the earth was flat, comes a legend saying the Pleiades were once a great bear being chased by a pack of wild, ferocious wolves. The bear tried to escape by running away over the ice but the wolf pack followed close behind. For many hours the chase went on. Finally the bear began to tire. The only escape the bear saw was to run to the edge of the world, which the horde of wolves didn't seem to notice, and jump off. They all fell off the earth and floated into the sky. The moon saw what was taking place and saved them all by transforming the bear and wolf pack into stars, they then became the Pleiades.

A Pawnee myth says the Pleiades were six brothers who were killed while protecting children from a great bear. At their funeral the Great Spirit changed them into stars and the brothers flew up into the sky to become the Pleiades.

The Shasta tribes of the Northwest tell a story of a raccoon that was killed by a coyote. The children of the raccoon then killed the coyote, avenging their mother's death. As a reward for their brave deed, the universe turned them into beautiful stars and placed them high in the sky where they became the Pleiades

The Kiowa tribe of North America has a legend about the Pleiades saying they were once seven maidens who were being chased by a giant bear. To save the young girls, the Great Spirit created the Devil's Tower [93]

---

93   A national monument in Wyoming made famous in the movie *Close Encounters of the Third Kind.*

and placed them on top and out of the reach of the bear. With its great claws, the bear began climbing the sheer cliff. When the bear was ready to pounce on the maidens, the Great Spirit turned them into stars and placed them in the sky away from harm.

Over the years I have seen a number of great nighttime photographs of the Pleiades right over Devil's Tower taken by amateur and professional photographers. When you see these spectacular photographs it's easy to understand how the myth was inspired.

In the late 1980s, during my research on the many mysterious megaliths and stone chambers found in the Northeast United States,[94] I found a conical shaped carved rock composed of limestone inside one of the stone chambers. Etched in the rock was a pattern that looked exactly like the Pleiades, showing all seven members, which tells me the stone may have been carved before 200 BC. The stone chambers are theorized to have been built by European explorers several thousand years ago. There is no doubt in my mind that whoever built these structures held the Pleiades in high regard.

The Pleiades look very strange in the sky, so it's easy to see why they were held in such esteem. Novice stargazers who first see them remark how the stars look like the Little Dipper. On a crisp, clear, dark winter night they appear like shimmering ghostly spirits. This explains why the cluster of stars was observed all over the world throughout human history and inspired songs, myths, legends, folklore, the Holy Bible, the Noble Qur'an, and many works of classic literature.

In today's fast-paced world, despite all our technological wonders, the sisters of the night continue to get attention; however, the manner in which some view the Pleiades in the present day is a great deal stranger than our ancestors could have ever imagined.

---

94   Further information about the stone chambers can be found in my book *Celtic Mysteries: Windows to Another Dimension in America's Northeast.*

Who Are the Pleiadians?

It has been seven decades since the start of what has been called the "modern age of UFO sightings" and although the phenomenon seems to come and go in cycles, there is no indication that sightings and close encounters with strange objects and aliens have vanished—to become part of our mythology.

It all began on June 25, 1947, when Kenneth Arnold, a private pilot, witnessed a number of unknown objects flying over the Cascade Mountains in Washington State at great speed. When he was asked by the media to describe the strange objects, he replied "they looked like saucers skipping across water," thus the term "flying saucer" was born. Arnold never said what he observed were saucer or disk shape, he was relating to the press how the objects flew across the sky. In a report to the Federal Aviation Agency, Arnold described the strange objects as looking chevron in shape, but definitely not like saucers. Nevertheless, the mystifying objects were still called flying saucers by the media, and from that time on people from all over the world reported seeing thousands of saucer-shaped objects each year.

Since the majority of these reports came from the United States, the task in dealing with them was turned over to the Air Force. In a time period from 1947 to 1969, under several different project names, the reports of "flying saucers" were investigated to determine if the unexplained objects were a threat to national security or held some type of scientific value.

In the 1950s the Air Force was barraged with calls and written reports from people who saw something strange in the sky. Most of these sightings were from individuals who had never looked up at the night sky, and now, because of the flying saucer craze, almost everyone was watching for the mysterious disk-shaped ships.

Cashing in on the craze, Hollywood began making pictures like *Earth vs. the Flying Saucers, It Came from Outer Space, The Day the*

Earth Stood Still, *Invasion of the Saucer People*, and *The Thing From Another World*, just to name a few. These now-classic science fiction movies resulted in a tenfold increase in the number of reports of spaceships and alien encounters made by Americans.

In the 1950s and early '60s it was common for people from New York to Los Angeles to host "flying saucer parties" where groups of people would watch the sky while having hamburgers, hot dogs, and many alcoholic drinks with the hope of seeing one of these mysterious objects. The celestial sphere hadn't received this much attention since the golden age of Greece. The people at these parties would report bright stars, Venus, Jupiter, meteors, and even conventional aircraft as UFOs. Those who attended these gatherings wanted to be thrilled, so they watched the skies until their imaginations, perhaps stimulated by alcohol, transformed conventional or natural objects into spaceships full of little green men.

The reports made to government officials at this time were easily dismissed. However, it wouldn't be long before a number of individuals came forward with claims of contact with the alien occupants of the flying saucers. For government and private UFO researchers, this was an entirely new situation, but not unexpected.

On November 20, 1952, George Adamski and a number of his friends were in the Colorado Desert when they allegedly saw a large cigar-shaped object moving slowly in the sky. As the UFO moved about a mile from their location, he told his friends to stay and wait since he believed the occupants in the ship were looking for him. Later, Adamski reported, a "scout ship" made of semi-transparent metal landed close to him and an alien from the planet Venus named Orthon came out of the ship and greeted him. Adamski claimed the people he was with stated on record that they could see him in the distance near the ship talking to someone. However, neither these sworn statements nor the individuals materialized during Mr. Adamski's lectures and numerous television and radio interviews.

Adamski described Orthon as appearing human, of average height with long sandy-blond hair and light skin that seemed slightly tanned only on the face. During their conversation, which was all done by telepathy, Orthon told Adamski he feared the human race would destroy themselves by nuclear war. Adamski later wrote, "The charisma of this man was like the warm embrace of great love and understanding."

Adamski claimed Nordic[95] looking aliens are present in Earth's solar system and regularly visit our planet. In his 1955 book *Inside the Spaceships*, Adamski said that Orthon arranged for him to be taken on a trip to see the solar system, which included the planets Venus, Mars, and Jupiter. Also on this voyage he was taken to the moon, where the aliens have a base on the dark side.[96]

Adamski believed he had been specially selected by the aliens to bring their message of peace and salvation to Earth people. He further claimed aliens were peacefully living on Earth in every country and that he had met with them on a regular basis in bars and restaurants in Southern California. He mentioned once in a radio interview that they are vegetarians and their favorite Earth drink is a vodka martini.

George Adamski began speaking at flying saucer conventions in the early 1950s, was paid well for his time, and definitely seemed to enjoy the newfound attention he was getting. There was a great interest in UFOs and aliens at the time. It was all new to American culture and people flocked to these conventions by the hundreds. Soon Adamski's stories became old, so he added more dramatic alien contact tales to his show. Many of the true believers began to consider him an ambassador and a

---

95   Physical characteristics of people from Scandinavia, Finland, or Iceland.

96   The so-called dark side of the moon is the surface that is never seen from Earth because the moon is gravitationally locked with one side facing us. When we experience a "new moon," the dark side is fully illuminated, though we can't see it.

wise teacher, while others who were more skeptical considered Adamski to be nothing more than a crafty con man. As a result of his newfound popularity, he had several books published and was a much sought after guest on many television talk shows and radio programs.

Seeing Adamski's success, dozens of other people came forward with their own claims of alien contact and interplanetary travels with whom were called the friendly "space brothers"[97] from Venus. These other people included Howard Menger, Daniel Fry, George Van Tassel, Truman Bethurum, Ruth Norman (also-called Spaceship Ruthie), Andy the Mystic Barber, Martin the Martian, and Saucer Sam. Some of these people would appear on television with tinfoil or a wire mesh on their head and glued-on antennas and give the audience "live" messages from the space brothers.

The majority of the public laughed at them and it made the entire UFO experience look ridiculous. People who had legitimate encounters were now afraid to report them for fear of being put in the same category as some of the more extreme contactees.

In the late twentieth century UFO investigators who were heavily into government conspiracy claimed many of the ludicrous contactees like Andy the Mystic Barber were actually recruited by the secret government or the CIA to spread disinformation and to help cover up their covert contact and agreements with the aliens. I remember seeing these people on TV and in my opinion some of them were just publicity seekers and several were, without a doubt, out of touch with reality.

When astronomers in the early sixties discovered that Venus is inhospitable to human life, the origin of the Nordic aliens changed from Venus to the Pleiades. Contact with the so-called Nordic aliens from

---

97   Space brothers? Are there no space sisters? Is outer space male dominated? Space brothers is a term invented in the late fifties by Adamski and his followers. It's a term one might expect at that time from a male-dominated society, proving the saying *space brothers* came from people of twentieth-century Earth and not enlightened aliens.

the Pleiades escaladed throughout the sixties to the present day, where literally hundreds are claiming some type of contact with these beings. As a result, dozens of groups have formed in the United States alone and meet on a regular basis to channel messages from one or more of the Pleiadians. Adamski and the rest of the early contactees have all passed on, but their legacy continues to this day.

Billy Meier, a Swiss author, has been claiming contact with the Nordic aliens from the Pleiades since the 1970s. Mr. Meier has produced crystal clear photographs of the alien ships, which the majority of skeptics and true believers alike have labeled fake. However, Mr. Meier still has been able to attain a very large following, a publishing deal, a bestselling book, and a number of television contracts over the years. Despite being verbally attacked by the paranormal community, Mr. Meier continues to report contact with the Pleiadians and sticks resolutely to his claims.

In 1988 I spoke at a UFO convention in Long Island. My presentation was a detailed study of the sightings in the Hudson River Valley of New York that were still going on at the time. One of the presenters, a contactee, spoke for a solid hour on her communications with aliens from the Pleiades. The audience had mixed feelings about her presentation, with some closing their eyes and looking up to the ceiling saying, "Yes! Space angels talk to us!" While others would interrupt the speaker's presentation to voice their objection to having to pay and sit through what they considered a "ridiculous claim."

During a break one of the skeptics asked me why I didn't object to her presentation. My reply was that I respect the beliefs of all people, and besides, arguing with this person is not going to convince her to see things a different way. It was clear to me that day the people who came to hear this speaker viewed her presentation as more of a religious experience based on faith rather than extraterrestrial contact.

During the last week of December 1988, shortly after the Long Island convention, I wrote a story in my Connecticut newspaper astronomy column addressing the Pleiadian contact claim. I simply stated the Pleiades are a very young star cluster, so young they haven't been around long enough for planetary formation to begin, so how can a civilization that some contactees claim is millions of years old originate from one or more of the stellar members in this group?

It was clear the contactees who made up the Pleiadian story had little or no knowledge of basic astronomy. As time went on the people who claimed contact with the Nordic aliens from the Pleiades would change their story by saying this group of extraterrestrials are spiritual beings from a higher dimension whose portal to our reality is located in the Pleiades.

Several people who have claimed contact with the Nordic aliens from the Pleiades have reached out and contacted me over the years. It is my opinion that some of these individuals had a very troubled life and were trying to escape it with a fantasy, while others just wanted a sympathetic ear and attention. In one such case the individual channeled a number of technical diagrams, writings in some sort of language, and music. Despite years of considerable research and investigation, this case remains a mystery and unexplainable.

In the twenty-first century, the Pleiadian connection developed into something incredibly complex. Imaginative contactees and true believers over the years have added multiple layers to the story with new people joining in all the time and building on where their predecessors left off. It seems they are trying to make us believe the Pleiadians are part of a federation of civilizations in the multiverse. It's amazing what these people have created; it's a tale any fantasy or science fiction writer would have been proud to have written. Are these people bonding together to share a fantasy or are they really in contact with something other than their own make-believe world?

It is my belief we are seeing a modern myth in the making. Many of us who are familiar with the Greek legends of the stars find it humorous that people of those ancient days could have really believed in the stories of gods, monsters, and demigod heroes. Perhaps in 2,000 years, human beings of our distant future will look at the stories that we have of the stars, especially claims of alien contact from the Pleiades, laugh, and say, "Did they really believe in that stuff?"

8

Orion: Giant of the Heavens

To many ancient stargazers, Orion was known as a hunter who possessed great strength and enormous stature. They also saw the constellation as the father of giants and the behemoth god who dwells in the great mountain. The ancient Egyptians were the first to mention Orion in their mythology, around 3000 BC. They associated the stars of Orion with Osiris, the god of life and rebirth. According to the myth, Osiris was killed by his jealous brother Seth and his body was dismembered. Despite his brother's attempt to finish him once and far all, Osiris was resurrected, and left Earth to make his home in the belt of Orion. Escaping the wrath of Seth and to await the resurrection of Osiris, his queen Isis went to live on Sirius.

The myth goes on to say Osiris will return to earth someday from his home in Orion and once again rule the world as a benevolent god. To the ancient Greeks, Orion was not only the greatest hunter who ever lived but a giant demigod so powerful that even the Olympian deities respected and feared him.

The Sumerians believed a race of giants who once enslaved mankind came from one of the stars in Orion's Belt and one day would return to destroy our planet. This myth may be the source for those who believe today that hostile giant aliens from the belt of Orion are planning to invade our planet in the near future.[98]

Chinese astronomers also knew Orion as Shen, a mighty giant who was a great hunter; this is one of many cases in which a constellation was visualized almost exactly the same way by people thousands of miles apart. Shen was always looking down at Earth, watching and waiting to pounce down on unsuspecting prey; this included animals and humans. According to a Chinese legend, the children who emerged "out of Shen's mouth" became the giants of their legendary stories; in the Bible, Orion was associated with the giants called "Nephilim." [99]

The Nephilim

In the Aramaic language, the term Nephilim refers to the constellation of Orion and to the offspring giants of biblical mythology. Our legends are full of stories of powerful colossal humanoids that controlled and terrified the land. In many of these legends, giants were feared by man since the myths tell us most of them were evil, aggressive, power-hungry, and some even cannibalistic. Genesis 6:4 describes the violent nature of the Nephilim: "They lie with the warriors, the Nephilim of old, who descended to Earth with their weapons of war. They placed their swords beneath their heads and their shields upon their bones, for the terror of the warriors were upon the land of the living."

In an account that has its origin in Judaism and Christianity, angels from heaven descended to earth and had children with mortal women. Their offspring were called Nephilim and, like the children of

---

98   There are a few websites but I do not suggest that you visit them. On the other hand, if you don't believe in some of the crazy ideas, you might be amused.

99   This word is translated to "giants" in the King James Bible.

djinn mentioned in the Qur'an, they had great power and ambition. They were considered an abomination in the eyes of God and had to be destroyed. "When man began to multiply on the face of the land and daughters were born to them, the sons of God saw that the daughters of man were attractive and they took them for their wives as they chose. The Nephilim were on the earth in those days, and also afterward, when the sons of God came to the daughters of man and they bore children to them" (Genesis 6:1).

The New American Bible [100] identifies the paternity of Nephilim as heavenly beings that came to earth, had sexual intercourse with women, and produced a race of super beings that ruled over mighty kingdoms and waged war with each other. They corrupted the human race to a point that God had to wipe the earth clean with a great flood, sparing only a handful of those who were not degraded by the influence of the Nephilim.

There are some researchers who believe the epic of the hero king Gilgamesh [101] is about a Nephilim who survived the flood, since Gilgamesh is described as being larger and stronger than any man on Earth and originally a harsh, cruel, powerful ruler. In the epic, there is clear reference to the flood and the near extinction of the human race.

Alien contactee groups have stated the Nephilim were the result of genetic manipulation of human beings by extraterrestrials from the constellation of Orion. They also claim the Nephilim were genetic hybrids with great power and ruled Earth in preparation for an invasion by their masters from the third star in Orion's belt. These modern-day contactees also believe the Nephilim married and had children with

---

100   *The New American Bible* (Oxford University Press: 2004).

101   The epic of Gilgamesh is probably the oldest series of stories known that came from Babylonia. It describes the change of heart and great adventures of a powerful, cruel king with great strength who was one-third human and two-thirds god. The story takes place sometime in 3000 BC. Gilgamesh is sometimes compared to the Greek legends of Hercules.

human women. This statement is supported by the book of Enoch, which has been translated as saying that the children of the Nephilim were called the "Elioud." The Elioud were not violent like the Nephilim, but had greater physical and mental abilities when compared to mortal men. However, they shared the same fate as their parents and were also destroyed in the great flood. It seems that someone, rival aliens, God(s), angels, or simply mother nature tried to rid the world of the Nephilim and their offspring by wiping the earth clean of their genes, but who? The answer to this question will depend on who is giving the narrative.

Jews, Christians, and Muslims believe it was God who destroyed the Nephilim and their offspring with a great flood. The Greeks of 500 BC believed Zeus commanded the constellation of Aquarius to empty his colossal vase of water down on the earth, drowning all the people who had become corrupt. This genetic cleansing also included giants and other creatures of Greek mythology. Contactees and ancient alien buffs will tell you it was another group of aliens from a planet in the constellation of Aquarius who were at war with the giants from Orion. In order to stop the evil Orion aliens and save the human race, the Aquarian extraterrestrials caused a magnetic cataclysm that reversed the poles of Earth and created the flood.

Fossils of Giants

If there were giants on the earth in those ancient days, one would think after centuries of excavating someone would have discovered the remains of a colossal human. As with most topics in the paranormal, there are several unconfirmed reports of such finds. In 1705 the fossilized remnants of giant leg bones and teeth were discovered near Albany, New York. It was believed by many Bible scholars of the eighteenth century to be the remains of a Nephilim giant who perished in the great flood.

This was a time before the discovery of dinosaurs and the bones caused quite a sensation. They were placed in the basement of the Museum of Natural History in New York City, where they remained a mystery for over 200 years. During the early twentieth century, paleon-tologists were able to identify the fossils as mastodon remains.[102]

A complete giant humanoid skeleton that was said to be 12 feet in length was discovered in France around 1890 by anthropologist Georges Vacher de Lapouge in a Bronze Age burial ground.[103] A French news-paper story from 1894 mentioned the discovery of bones of human giants, unearthed at a prehistoric cemetery at Montpellier, France, that belonged to a race of humanoids "between 10 and 15 feet in height." [104]

In the last two cases, the bones mysteriously vanished and were not available for inspection by scientists and medical doctors. It was thought they were stolen by a radical religious group who wanted to conceal the truth of the origin of the Nephilim. The second possibility is that they are in a secret government warehouse similar to the one shown in two Indiana Jones movies along with the Ark of the Covenant and remains of the aliens of Roswell, New Mexico. The third possibility is perhaps the bones of the giants never existed in the first place.

The Cherokee, Hopi, and Toltec tell of a great flood long ago that wiped out a race of giant men. The Cherokee claimed that on some hillsides the bones of these giants can be seen after a heavy rain. In the early twentieth-century scientists intrigued with the story asked to see the bones of the giants. To make a long, complex story short, the bones turned out to be fossils of dinosaurs that existed in the Mesozoic era.

It is possible the Nephilim were not giants at all. During the time when the stories of the Nephilim were written, the word giant was also used to describe a great warrior or king. In the twentieth century the saying "he was a giant of a man" didn't necessarily imply the person was physically large; it usually meant the individual did great things in his

---

102   Mark Rose, "When Giants Roamed the Earth," *Archaeology Magazine,* December 2005.

103   *The Popular Science News,* August 1890.

104   *The McCook Tribune,* 1895.

life. For example, to describe successful businessmen like Rockefeller, Getty, or Carnegie, we say "they were giants of industry."

Perhaps the great flood mentioned in the historical records of many cultures was just a natural event and had nothing to do with gods or aliens. After such a devastating occurrence, prescientific societies always believed it was the judgment of an angry god or other type of supernatural force. In the case of the great flood, it seems some cultures indirectly held Orion responsible for the disaster, probably because the pattern of stars looks so incredible and ominous in the sky. On the other hand, we cannot discount the stories of giants or dragons for that matter, since accounts of these creatures can be found it the ancient literature of most civilizations.

Theory of Alignments

In 1989, engineer and amateur archeologist Robert Bauval first published a theory proposing that the Giza pyramids were a physical representation of the three stars that make up Orion's belt.[105] Although his idea did not receive much support in the scientific community, it fueled the imaginations of dozens of amateur archeologists and followers of the ancient astronaut theory in looking for similar alignments around the world. Ten years later these groups of enthusiastic researchers claim to have found hundreds of such alignments centering on not only Orion but also the star Sirius. In some cases UFOs, extraterrestrials, and supernatural beings of all kinds were included in these far-out ideas as being responsible for the alignments.

The three stars in Orion's belt look quite extraordinary as seen from Earth. They appear equal in brightness and form almost a straight diagonal line in the sky. The ancient Egyptians as well as many other civilizations of that time must have noticed this unique configuration in the heavens and attributed significant meaning to it. It's not astonishing to

---

105   *Discussions in Egyptology*, Vol. 13 (Oxford: 1989).

believe that many of these people would mention these three stars with great importance in their mythology and align their temples and other important structures to the stars in Orion's Belt.

The Orion Effect

Just below the third star in Orion's belt is the hunter's sword. Here you will find the Great Orion Nebula, a secret place in the universe where new stars are being born. This amazing object can be seen with the naked eye on a clear moonless night as a fuzzy patch. Using a small telescope it reveals itself as consisting of multiple embryonic stars, luminous gas, and hydrogen and helium dust clouds. The Great Nebula in Orion is at an approximate distance of 1,500 light-years from Earth and is frequently photographed by amateur astronomers since a moderate-sized telescope will result in a fantastic picture that appears like a colorful colossal cumulus cloud.

Lately, there has been a great deal of chatter in the paranormal-contactee circles describing a wormhole in the Orion Nebula that is being used by hostile aliens as a rapid transit system to Earth. There have been unconfirmed claims that a huge ship, which was supposedly photographed by the Hubble Space Telescope, has been seen emerging from the nebula and is now heading for our planet.

It seems the government conspiracy theorists joined in on the action, claiming the secret government and NASA are covering it up. Ten years ago, while I was still actively researching the contactee phenomena, an anonymous letter was sent to me claiming that an Orion warship is coming to Earth from the nebula, bringing a powerful being named Sladden who will destroy all life on our planet.

This claim is remarkable, but unbelievable. The nebula is 1500 light-years away from us; in order to be seen by the space telescope, the ship would have to be the size of our solar system. It's clear once again that the people who are making these fantastic statements have little or no knowledge of basic astronomy.

As the saying goes, "Extraordinary claims require extraordinary evidence." When dealing with mainstream science, this statement is true, but evidence may be difficult to present if it exists outside our reality and our instruments of technology and science are blind to it.

I think the late Dr. Sagan would have agreed that when it comes to the paranormal, most skeptics believe in the Newtonian view of the multiverse, which is cause and effect. In this view of the multiverse we can determine the results from A to B with considerable accuracy. However, we exist in a quantum universe full of variables we don't understand, so the results of A to B cannot be determined with any certainty. The scientific method is based on the idea of the Newtonian view of the multiverse. Therefore a study of the paranormal cannot be done using the scientific method.

Many of the contactees making these fantastic claims about Orion seem to be looking for attention with the hope of a publishing deal, a television reality show, or just a following of people who will give them the attention they long for. I have talked with perhaps 80 or more of this type of contactee and 75 percent or more show the same psychological pattern. It seems they tend to have a great desire to feel important since deep inside some feel they failed in life. Perhaps this type of individual never got any social attention or was not popular in school. This individual could then use the paranormal or alien contactee scenario and sometimes even religion to fill that gap in their life to fulfill the need for respect. Then again, there are some contactees who say they are experiencing alien contact that keep to themselves and don't care if you believe their extraordinary claims or not. This type of person may visualize themselves as being specially selected by angels or aliens. And oftentimes, the more verbal abuse they get from skeptics the more they seem to like it. They view themselves as being a martyred prophet and suffering for a greater cause.

Throughout recorded history the constellation of Orion has had and continues to have a great effect on the minds of some people by being the stimulus to induce not only myths and legends but also flights of the imagination. In the modern world the human race has created an entirely new set of stories about the mighty hunter of the heavens that someday may be called the myths of the twenty-first century.

9

Moon Madness

Since the dawn of recorded history, the moon has fascinated human beings. Because of this a great deal of mythology and religion was based on it—not only the full moon but also its phases. Everyone, at one time or another, has taken a walk at night during a full moon; its silver luminescence brings light and comfort to the darkness no matter the time of year. The sight of a full moon against a dark velvet sky and a starry background is a beautiful spectacle that leaves us Earthlings staring in awe and wonder.

The connection we have with the moon is an important one. The earliest calendars found in the Middle East and Europe were based on the lunar cycle and date back to 6000 BC, with twelve months, each identified by one full moon. The modern Islamic calendar is also lunar with twelve months and twelve full moons in a year. For the most part, this calendar is used by many Muslim countries mainly for religious purposes, but in Saudi Arabia it is the official calendar.[106]

Today, religious holidays such as Easter, Passover, and Ramadan are timed with the full moon or a crescent phase. The Hindu festival of lights

---

106   A lunar calendar has 364 days while the modern Gregorian solar calendar we use has 365 days.

takes place at the new moon, and the Chinese New Year occurs on the second new moon after the winter solstice. In Buddhism, the full moon pays an important role in many aspects of the faith. It is believed that several important events took place in the life of Buddha on days when the moon was full, including his birth, abandonment, enlightenment, the day of his first teachings, and the day of his ascension. The May full moon festival is still an important day at many Buddhist temples. I have been to several of them at the Chuang Yen Monastery in New York and for me they were always days to look forward to and remember.

The phases of the moon were also used to determine the passage of time by Native Americans. The time from full moon to full moon is 29.5 days. We have all heard the saying from old westerns of "many moons ago," which is still used by some northeastern tribes of the United States when telling stories.

A Native American lunar calendar located in Bighorn, Wyoming, is called the "Medicine Wheel." This ancient artifact is a mysterious arrangement of stones on the ground that is thought to be pre-Columbian[107] in origin and constructed by an unknown ancient people. The Medicine Wheel has a diameter of 80 feet with 28 spokes marked by stones radiating out from a central point and 7 carved cairns[108] arranged around the circle. It is theorized the 28 spokes plus a standing stone represent the number of days in a month using a lunar cycle from full moon to full moon. The Medicine Wheel also marks the rising of the sun during the summer solstice and evidence has been found that some of the stones line up with the bright stars Rigel, Sirius, Aldebaran, and Arcturus.

---

107   Pre-Columbian refers to the time before Columbus came to the North America. The Medicine Wheel could be a great deal older since no indigenous people in the area have claimed its construction. Rick Laurent, *The Big Horn Medicine Wheel, Crossroad of Cultural Conflict,* University of Wyoming, Laramie, 1996.

108   A cairn is a human-made stack of stones or a carved single stone used for a variety of purposes from prehistoric times to the present.

Ancient supernatural beings called "Little People" are believed to appear to those who fast and pray during the night at the Medicine Wheel. The Little People are said to have come from the sky and now live underground in caves below the Medicine Wheel. In modern times UFO contactees have claimed to have meditated at the Medicine Wheel and actually met the Little People, who they say are gray aliens from the Reticulum system in our galaxy. Since the "aliens" would not offer proof of the encounter, the stories are dismissed by most paranormal researchers.

During the Middle Ages the moon inspired tales of the supernatural, and in modern times, romance. In the twentieth and twenty-first centuries, no less than forty songs have been written about our love for the moon, including "Harvest Moon," "Shine On, Harvest Moon," "Moon River," "Fly Me to the Moon," "Moon Dance," "Bad Moon Rising," "Walking on the Moon," "Man on the Moon," "Dancing in the Moonlight," "Bark at the Moon," and my favorite from the early days of rock and roll, "Blue Moon."

For centuries the moon was considered to be a perfectly smooth sphere, a ball of light made by a supernatural being to illuminate the night. It wasn't until the year 1612 when Galileo, using a relatively new instrument at the time called the telescope, discovered the true nature of the moon. Using his crude, small, home-built telescope, Galileo discovered the moon was covered with mountains, craters, and large dark areas that he mistook for seas. Today we still call these large ancient basins "the seas of the moon." Because of his discoveries the moon was no longer a glowing object in the sky; it was now a real place. And this established a stronger connection between us and our nearest neighbor in space. From that day on space became the new frontier and human beings set a goal to one day explore the moon and claim it for the entire human race.

Just like other celestial bodies in the solar system, our moon has a name. Using words like "moon" and "natural satellite" to classify our companion is like calling your child "boy" or "girl" and not by their name, which identifies them as individuals. The official name of our moon is Selene, who according to Greek mythology, was the Titan goddess of the moon. She is the daughter of the pre-Olympian gods Hyperion and Theia, her brother Helios is the original sun god, and her younger sister is Eos, goddess of the dawn.

Selene's responsibility as a powerful deity was to bring light to the world after sunset. She was depicted as a woman either riding side-saddle on a horse or in a chariot drawn by a pair of winged black and white stallions. Her lunar sphere and crescent was represented as either a crown set upon her head or as a shining semicircular emblem on her gown. The ancient Greek poets and storytellers of long ago identified Selene as the principal lunar deity.

The Romans also adopted Selene as their primary moon goddess and called her "Luna." [109] In modern times we use this word to describe a physical feature of the moon, such as the lunar mountains, craters, and so on. In the twenty-first century, an astronomer who studies the moon as their specialty is known as a selenologist. If some sort of intelligent life existed on the moon they might be called Selenites. In preparation for the first manned lunar landing, the astronomers involved, including Dr. J. Allen Hynek, were called the selenology group. When I mentioned this to people, including teachers and other well-educated individuals, they had no idea what a selenologist was.

Although a number of Greek goddesses were also associated with our moon, Hecate seems to be the most ancient, and once had a very large cult following in not only ancient Greece but also the Roman Empire. There are, however, sculpted statues that date before the fifth century BC that show three goddess representing the moon as a trinity. Artemis is shown as the waxing crescent, Selene as the full moon, and Hecate as the waning crescent.

---

109   Sometime after 35 BC, the Romans identified the moon with the goddess Diana, who is the equivalent to the Greek goddess Artemis.

Physical Features and Formation

From the time astronomy was first considered a science to the conclud-
ing part of the twentieth century, no one knew for sure how our moon
was formed or how it ended up in its current unique orbit. One of the
contemporary theories from 1930 to 1980 was that the moon formed
independently as a rogue planet in our solar system and was captured
by the gravity of Earth. This idea didn't work since the angular momen-
tum of the Earth–moon orbit is considerably different then what would
be expected if this was the case. Another theory was a piece of Earth
broke off during formation and formed our moon. This explanation
was also rejected when the Apollo astronauts brought back samples of
moon rocks and found their chemical composition different than those
found on Earth. The third and most accepted theory at the time was
that our Earth and moon were created together from the aggregation of
dust, gas, and debris during the formation of the early solar system. This
theory was considered until the 1970s, but later rejected and once again
the formation of our companion Selene remained a mystery.

In 1984 after an exhaustive study from the scientific data from the
Apollo moon missions, scientists at NASA proposed the accepted current theory that the Earth–moon system formed as a result of a rogue
planet the size of Mars colliding with Earth in the early stage of its
formation. The impact of the two planetary bodies nearly destroyed
them both and blasted out material in orbit around Earth, which then
accreted by gravity to form the present day Earth–moon system. The
name for this hypothetical planet was appropriately named Theia, after
the Titan mother of the Greek moon goddess Selene.

The Earth–moon system is unique in the solar system. Our companion Selene has a diameter of 2,159 miles, which makes her over one-
quarter the size of Earth. When you compare the size ratio of Earth
and our moon with the other planets that have natural satellites, the

Earth–moon system is closer to being a double planet, and this makes it one of a kind in our solar system.[110]

As with most planetary bodies, the moon's orbit is elliptical not circular. During one part of its orbit, the moon is closer to Earth (called perigee) and at another point it is farther away (called apogee). This elliptical course results in the distance between the moon and Earth varying from around 221,500 to 252,700 miles.

On November 14, 2016, the moon was closer to Earth during its full phase than it had been since 1948. This lunar apparition was called the "super moon" by the media and was 30 percent more luminous and 14 percent larger than it normally appeared in the sky. On the night of the so-called super moon, people in my neighborhood braved the chilly evening air and came out to look at Selene as she was rising in the east. There were quite a few oohs and ahs, then after five minutes most went back into their homes to watch television. One hundred million years ago, the moon was much closer to Earth; it must have been a fantastic sight, since every night was a super moon during the age of dinosaurs. I wonder if the super moon of the Mesozoic era got more attention from a Tyrannosaurus Rex than humans give it in the twenty-first century— of course it did; they didn't have cable!

The gravitational influence of the moon on Earth helps stabilize our planet as we orbit the sun. If there was no moon, Earth would wobble significantly as it rotates on its axis and revolves around our star. This would result in a world that would be plagued with continuous natural disasters. If Theia missed our planet and Selene was never born, then life as we know it would have never emerged on this planet. It is hard to believe that the formation of the Earth–moon system was nothing more than a cosmic accident. It is my belief that some universal intelligence had a hand in the event.

---

110   If Pluto was still considered a planet, it would also be unique since its largest moon, Charon, is half Pluto's size.

According to recent studies, the moon seems to be pulling slowly away at a rate of about 1.5 inches per year and eventually may establish its own orbit around the sun and become a new planet. When this happens, Earth will not only become moonless, but also perhaps lifeless, and our planet will have lost two of the things that made it exclusive in the solar system.

Moon Folklore

Having taught astronomy and operated a school observatory for many years, the question that was asked recurrently from students and their parents was about the man in (or on) the moon. The man in the moon is usually seen during the full moon as an old man carrying a bundle of sticks upon his back. If you have a good imagination, the man in the moon can be seen outlined by the dark lunar basins.

I would often use the lowest magnification on the telescope with a special filter to reduce the glaring lunar light and begin telling the tale. There are many European legends explaining how the old man got there. My favorite story to tell during my classes at the observatory came from a German myth during the Middle Ages and my take on it is presented here.

A very long time ago during a beautiful Sunday morning an old man walked into the forest to find wood for his fire. He spent all morning picking up sticks and put them in a bag and when it was full he threw the sack over his shoulder. On his way home he met a tall man in a bright-colored spring Sunday outfit with long flowing blond hair slowly walking toward the church. The man said, "Why are you dressed in your working clothes, don't you know today is Sunday and all good Christians should be in church?"

The old man laughed and said, "Sunday on Earth or Monday on the moon; it's all the same to me!"

The well-dressed man then turned into an angel and said, "Then bear your collection of sticks forever. Since you do not value Sunday on Earth, yours shall be an everlasting moon day and you shall stand forever on the moon, a warning for all to see who do not recognize the Sabbath." Then the angel waived his hand and the old man was banished to the moon to carry his bag of sticks forever.

The ancient Greeks saw a rabbit on the moon rather than an old man, and believed this is where the winter constellation of Lepus, the rabbit, spends his summer. Lepus is a very ancient constellation; it is so lost in antiquity that no one can agree upon what people first named this group of stars. We do know that the Greeks as far back as 600 BC saw Lepus as an object of Orion's hunt.

The Hindus called the dark areas of the moon "marks of the hare." Ancient Sanskrit tales mention the palace of the king of hares on the moon. The people of Mexico and Central America saw the constellation of Lepus as a hare whose home was on the moon.

According to an Aztec legend, a long time ago the god Quetzalcoatl was living on Earth in human form. There had been a great drought; food was scarce and many living creatures were dying. After expelling a great deal of energy to remedy the situation, he became very weak and hungry and tried to turn back into a god but could not. With no food or water around, he thought he would die. A nearby rabbit saw the starving god in human form and offered himself as food to save his life. Quetzalcoatl, moved by the rabbit's gracious offer, transported him to the moon, then brought the rabbit back to Earth and said, "You may be just a rabbit, but everyone will remember you; look, your image is now on the moon for all people to see for all times."

In another Aztec legend, the lunar deity Tecciztecatl was once the old man that lived on the moon whose greatest desire was to be the god of the sun. One day he came to Earth to look up at the sun and tell him of his longing. Seeing the threat, Nanahuatzin, the sun god, changed Tecciztecatl into a rabbit and hurled him up in the heavens and back on the moon. In some depictions he carries a large white seashell on his back, which is supposed to represent the full moon.

In a Buddhist story that dates to the fourth century BC, a monkey, an otter, and a rabbit were determined to practice charity on the day of the full moon. They noticed an old woman lying on the road starving and pleading for food. The monkey gathered fruits and nuts from the trees and the otter collected fish. The rabbit could only get grass so he offered himself as food instead. The old woman built a fire and the rabbit jumped in; however, he did not burn. The old woman revealed herself as Sakra, the mother of the gods, and was so touched by the rabbit's sacrifice she drew the likeness of him on the moon for all to see. A version of this story can be found in the folklore of China, Japan, Korea, Thailand, Vietnam, and Cambodia.[111] In another version of this myth the old woman is presented as an old man.

Another myth of the lunar rabbit that can be found in the Asian countries of China, Korea, Thailand, and Japan says the rabbit on the moon was placed there as a pet for the lunar goddess. The Chinese saw him using a mortar and pestle to make the elixir of life for her, while the Japanese saw the rabbit making rice cakes for the gods.

A very old German myth says that the hare (Lepus) was at one time a bird that was changed into a hare by the goddess of the spring as punishment for flying into the moon. The goddess imprisoned the hare on the moon, only allowing her to return to Earth once a year (on Easter) to lay eggs. This is why the Easter rabbit is associated with bringing brightly colored eggs on its back during spring.

Prior to the first moon landing in 1969, the lunar rabbit was mentioned in a radio conversation between Houston and astronaut Michael Collins of the Apollo 11 crew.

---

111   As told to me at the Chuang Yen Monastery a Buddhist temple in Putnam County, New York. The temple is home to the largest indoor statue of a Buddha in the Western Hemisphere.

Houston: Among the large headlines concerning Apollo this morning is one asking that you watch for a lovely girl with a big rabbit. An ancient legend says a beautiful Chinese girl has been living there for 4,000 years. It seems she was banished to the moon because she stole the elixir of immortality from her husband. You might also look for her companion, a large rabbit, who is easy to spot since he is always standing on his hind feet in the shade of a cinnamon tree. The name of the rabbit is not reported. Michael Collins: Okay. We'll keep a close eye out for the bunny girl.[112]

There are some people in the UFO–government conspiracy community who believe the rabbit and bunny girl was really a code name for aliens. It is my belief the controllers at Houston were just taking a pause in the dry technical conversations with a little humor, which the press always loved. The only thing about the statement that bothers me is I had never heard this version of the myth before, but there are so many variations I'm sure it does exist.

The image of the rabbit on the moon was noted by many different cultures separated by great distances and long periods of time. There is no acceptable answer why this is so, but it most likely has something to do with the moon being meticulously observed by people all over the world at all points in time. And with a little imagination and excellent eyesight, the dark basins do resemble a rabbit or hare with its ears pointing upward.

Special Moon Names

The moon was always considered important to the Native Americans of the United States. It is mostly from them we get the names given to the full moon of each month. The tribes used the names of the moon to keep track of each month and the seasons.

---

112   *The Apollo 11 Flight Journal*: National Aeronautics and Space Administration.

January: The Wolf Moon

In the cold and snow of winter, the wolf packs howled close to Native American villages since game was scarce at this time. It was considered to be very dangerous to go out at night during this month. There is a superstition dating back to colonial times in the United States that says werewolves run wild during the wolf moon. This belief has survived to the present day since there is actually an organization in the United States that claims to hunt werewolves. They warn that during the wolf moon a lycan's power to transform is enhanced and their appetite for human flesh is uncontrollable. They recommend that during the Wolf Moon you stay indoors at night, barricade your door, and place silver and wolf bane on your windows. They warn that even the nicest, gentlest person you ever met could be a werewolf, and if you let this person into your life they will hunt you down the next wolf moon and tear you apart and eat your flesh. It seems this warning is related to the poem below.

> Even a man who is pure in heart
> and says his prayers by night
> may become a wolf when the wolf bane blooms
> and the moon is full and bright.[113]

I hope these guys, whoever they are, don't have pistol permits!

February: The Snow Moon

Since the heaviest snow falls during this month, Native tribes of the north and east named this month the snow moon.

March: The Worm Moon

As the ground starts to thaw, earthworms come up to the surface and many types of birds appear to feed on them, especially the robin and crow.

---

113   Curt Siodmak, *The Wolf Man*, film, directed by George Waggner (1941).

April: The Pink Moon
This name came from the blooming of the earliest wildflowers of spring.

May: The Flower Moon
A month when flowers are abundant everywhere.

June: The Strawberry Moon
Named for the short time in which trawberries can be harvested.

July: The Buck Moon
July is the month when the new antlers of bucks push out of their foreheads.

August: The Red Moon
As the moon rises, it appears reddish through the summer haze. Some tribes knew it as the blood moon.

September: The Harvest Moon
The September full moon is actually the month of the harvest moon, which is the full moon that occurs closest to the first day of fall. However, once in every three to four years the harvest moon occurs in October. The harvest moon will rise when the sun sets and is visible all night, allowing colonial farmers to work late into the hours of darkness by the light of the moon. During most of the year the full moon is visible above the horizon an average of 52 minutes later each night, but for two to three nights around the harvest moon, it will rise at nearly the same time.

October: The Hunters Moon
The leaves are falling from trees, vegetation is thinning out, and deer can easily be seen by the hunters. This was a time to begin storing up meat for the long winter ahead.

November: The Beaver Moon

This was the time to set beaver traps before the swamps froze to guarantee a supply of warm winter furs.

December: The Cold Moon

During this month winter begins. Days are shortest and nights are longest.

Unique Lunar Names

Blue Moon

The blue moon is when two full moons are observed within the same month. This takes place at the beginning and end of a month once every two to three years. The saying "once in a blue moon" is still used to designate some unusual, rare event. Although the actual color of the moon has nothing to do with the term, there is one documented report that the moon did indeed appear blue for two years after the eruption of Krakatoa in 1883. This blue moon effect was caused by micrometer-sized dust particles in the atmosphere that scattered the red and yellow light from the moon and allowed the blue light to pass through the atmosphere. The visible blue moon is a rare event since the particles of dust have to be exactly the right size to make the moon appear that color. A red or an orange moon is more common since most atmospheric haze, volcanic dust, and large forest fires produce particles that scatter blue light and allow red light to pass through.

The Green Cheese Moon

That the moon is made of green cheese is one of the most popular children's proverbs from late sixteenth-century English literature and is still around today. As far as my research shows, the moon never appeared green in the sky, although it is possible the moon might flicker with green flashes when very low on the horizon during times of extreme haze. This rare phenomenon was noted in the summer of 1910 as the planet Venus set in the west after a very hot, muggy day. However, atmospheric refraction of the lunar light does not seem to be the source of this proverb.

In the mid-1950s there was an old black-and-white cartoon from the 1930s on television showing a number of mice looking at a picture of the moon with the caption: "The moon is made of green cheese." The mice then get all excited, build a spaceship, and land on the moon. When they leave their ship the mice begin scooping up the surface of the moon and start eating until they are all fat. Back on Earth an astronomer is looking at the full moon through his telescope, and very quickly the moon shrinks to a thin crescent as the result of the hungry rodents. The Apollo lunar landing missions proved once and for all that our moon is not made of green cheese but various types of volcanic basalts.

Honey Moon

In ancient times the honey moon was that month when the honey from beehives was at its sweetest. In the sixteenth century, the honey moon was used to describe the first month of marriage, which was said to be the sweetest. Today, "honeymoon" is used to denote a short time in which a newly married couple get away to be alone together, supposedly for the first time.

Ashen Moon

This haunting, beautiful display called the ashen moon can be seen just before sunrise in the east or after sunset in the west when the moon is a thin crescent. The darker section of the lunar surface appears a light red or gray and you can actually make out detail. This phenomenon is known as earthshine and was first recorded nearly 500 years ago by Leonardo da Vinci, who correctly explained it as sunlight reflected off our planet, striking the moon, and reflecting back to Earth. His conclusions were pretty amazing since he lived before the invention of the telescope.

He called it "the moon's ashen glow"; today we know it as the "old moon in the new moon's arms" or "new moon in the old moon's arms."

Moon Magic

I grew up in an Italian family with strong superstitious beliefs. My great-grandparents and great-uncles and aunts all came from southern Italy, and although they were devoted Roman Catholics, they still followed some of the old Pagan ways of life.

My aunt, who was trained in the "old ways," would often get calls from people in the neighborhood to remove things like the "evil eye" or say a prayer to help an illness or get rid of an evil spirit from a home or person. I would often ask her about the things her mother and grand-mother taught her and would always get the same answer: "You don't want to know. It is dangerous and only women are allowed to know." My aunt believed the full moon gave her power, so when faced with a difficult task, she would always wait for the time of that particular lunar phase.

Sometime around 1965 she saw me reading a magazine on UFOs and laughed and said, "You really believe in that nonsense, don't you?"

I replied, "But you believe in curses and the evil eye and think you can cure a disease and a headache with a prayer." My aunt replied "Yes, but that is real. What you are reading is stupid and make-believe." She had two sons and didn't pass her knowledge down to anyone after her passing. She was adamant in her belief that it takes a woman to use the power of the moon to help people and free them from the influence of evil spirits.

Drawing power from the moon to cast powerful spells is a common belief found in many ancient cultures. Such practices are also wide-spread amongst modern followers of Neopagan beliefs and forms of Witchcraft which include Wicca. In almost all of these rituals, a deity is attributed to the moon's influence and the conjurer or worshipper invokes the name of the god or goddess to obtain power or some favor.

The majority of lunar deities are female, but male lunar gods are also present in the mythology of the north Native American tribes and the legends of the people in the Near East. If a culture considered the sun as a male deity, the moon was almost always female. Modern science has adopted the female representation of the moon from the ancient Greeks and Romans with the goddesses Selene and Luna.

Traditionally in Wicca, the moon is seen as a Triple Goddess and is symbolized by the waxing crescent moon, full moon, and waning gibbous or crescent moon, signifying the maiden, the mother, and the crone. The Wicca community of the twenty-first century identifies the waning gibbous moon with the ancient goddess Hecate and, because of this, there is a strong belief in many Wicca circles that only women can draw upon the lunar power.

Hecate is recognized as the crone goddess of Wicca. She is also a goddess of protection, but only to those few mortals she favors. Since she sees through illusion and deception, her followers must be completely honest when invoking her. Hecate enforces the laws of the universe and will not allow any living being to upset the balance of creation. Hecate is the queen of magic, Witches, the wilderness, and the spirit realm. She is also the protective mother of life and will use her power to heal. Hecate believes in freedom of choice, but will also answer your questions and provide guidance; however, since she believes in free will, Hecate cannot be called upon to correct the mistakes you make in life. She is the ancient representation of the Hag Witch that the early church used to scare children so they would not follow the old Pagan ways. Hecate does not desire youth, beauty, love, or admiration; these things are meaningless to her. Hecate has the power to transform into any form and can give back lost youth and health.

Hecate: Alien, Ascended Being, or Myth

The Byzantines[114] were especially devoted to Hecate, believing the goddess saved them from an invasion by Philip of Macedon's army.[115] According to legend, one moonless night the army of Philip of Macedon attempted a surprise attack on the city, but was hindered by a bright light that appeared suddenly in the heavens, temporarily blinding them. The light also startled all the dogs in the town and roused the garrison, who were able to prepare a defense in time. This strange phenomenon that saved the city was attributed to Hecate. In her honor they erected a public statue to the goddess.

To this day the glaring light in the sky that blinded the entire invading army has never been explained. There are ancient astronaut enthusiasts who believe it was caused by a UFO and aliens who have been manipulating the destiny of the human race by interfering with major historical events.

In AD 330 the Romans placed Hecate's symbol, the crescent moon with a star, on the walls of Constantinople to show invaders the city was under her protection. Hecate was considered the patron goddess in Constantinople and great temples were built in her honor. Also, strange stories about Hecate appearing in a bright cloud spread throughout eastern Europe, and many cults were formed in her name.

Hecate in the Twenty-First Century

My experience with Hecate, or should I say her followers, began about seventeen years ago. A friend of mine invited me to a local coffee shop, which at the beginning of the twenty-first century was a popular spot for Neopagans to meet. This was my first time at this establishment and

114   Byzantium was an ancient Greek colony in early antiquity that eventually became Constantinople and later Istanbul. Byzantium was first colonized by the Greeks in 657 BC.

115   Philip of Macedon was the king of the ancient Greek kingdom of Macedon from 359 BC until his assassination in 336 BC.

I was curious about the type of people that frequented it. The atmosphere was very relaxed and the coffee was very good.

My friend finally explained the nature of our get-together; he was interested in getting an update concerning my investigations into the unseen reality. He also mentioned that we were going to meet with a person who requested an introduction, an individual that he was sure I would find quite interesting.

Our discussion quickly geared to UFOs and things that go bump in the night. After fifteen or twenty minutes, a tall woman with long jet-black hair and dressed in the same color came in to the shop and sat with us. After the usual introductions, the woman said she was excited to finally meet me, since she had read many of the things I had written over the years and was an avid reader of my newspaper column and books.

She began telling us about being the organizer and high priestess of a group of people who were followers of the goddess Hecate. We spent the next several hours talking, but before we said our goodbyes, she invited us to a moon ceremony for Hecate that was to take place in a few days after midnight. Although my friend could not attend, I quickly and graciously accepted and took down the details.

As the night of the ceremony arrived, the meteorological conditions were ideal, with clear summer skies and a comfortable temperature. If Hecate was real, then she did an outstanding job with the weather, since you could not have asked for a more perfect midsummer night. I arrived on time at a private home, which was located on a large estate deep in the hills of northwestern Connecticut, and was introduced to a coven of thirteen women of varying ages. I was allowed to interview most of them and got some fascinating information on not only their background in Wicca but their experiences with the paranormal.

As midnight approached they all put on robes, which were white on the left side and black on the right, indicating the waning moon that

Hecate is identified with. The ritual area was in a beautiful section of the backyard with multiple sculptures of Greek and Celtic gods surrounded by breathtaking flower beds. There was a circle, perhaps twenty feet in diameter, with a large bowl in the center that was full of hot, glowing coals. They first spent considerable time making offerings to Hecate, individually praying, and making requests to their goddess. Well after midnight, each member went up to the hot coals, ignited a torch, then took their position around the center and faced the moon.

As soon as the waning moon was high enough in the sky, the high priestess stood at a point directly south and began the invocation, which was repeated by each member. It was quite a sight; the moon and the glowing torches illuminated the lighter parts of their robes, making the fabric glow. In contrast to the darker fabric, it gave the impression of an eerie half-moon effect. The ritual was amazing and the women moved in a graceful manner. It was apparent this was something they had done many times and were very good at.

The fire of the torches added a supernatural aura to each woman and this combined with the chanting made me feel as if I were transported three thousand years in the past to the temple of the moon goddess.

I could not identify the language they used during the ceremony; the only word that was understood was the name Hecate. I knew it wasn't Latin since this is a language that has been familiar to me from my early days, learning Latin in my Roman Catholic Sunday school.

I sat about ten feet or so south of the circle with my back to the moon, and every once in a while one of the younger members of the group would look in my direction to see my reaction at what they were doing. I have done many investigations into the world of the unseen and have witnessed a great number of events that defy conventional explanation, and what I witnessed that night was delightfully wonderful.

My past experiences exploring the paranormal convinced me there were a great number of dimensional beings in the multiverse that were incorporeal in nature, and some of them may have posed as gods, goddesses, or some other supernatural beings to prescientific cultures. According to the Greek myths and legends of many countries, these entities were powerful, but for some reason needed to be worshipped or acknowledged by intelligent physical beings. If they were not worshipped, they would eventually lose their power and fall into some type of coma until they were once again awakened by worshippers. Because of this need, some of these entities may have used their power to terrorize or cause seemingly natural disasters to create fear so people would continue to pray to them. It is possible these beings fed on energy given off by humans during prayers, rituals, and even fearful situations. In Christianity, Islam, and Judaism, the Holy Scriptures insist one day a week is reserved for praying to God. Also, we cannot forget the part of the Bible that states, "Thou shall have no other gods before me." [116]

The early Christians of Ireland believed the old powerful Celtic gods of the Tuatha Dé Danann [117] lost their power and were reduced to fairies when the people adopted Christianity and stopped praying to them. According to one of many legends, the main gods and other lesser deities were stripped of their power by Saint Patrick and exiled into the hills where they became the leprechauns and other fairy spirits. Here they wait until the people of the world lose their faith in Christianity and once again worship them so they can regain the supremacy they lost. Perhaps it's the same with the gods of the Greeks and other cultures of the world. The bottom line is in all religious beliefs, gods need to be worshipped or they fade in oblivion.

In modern times, with each generation there are an increasing number of people who once again are worshipping the ancient gods, and as a result these weakened, forgotten deities may be getting their power back.

---

116   Exodus 20:3.

117   A supernatural race of beings in Irish mythology believed to be the main gods and goddesses of pre-Christian Ireland.

Perhaps this is one of the reasons why we are seeing an increase in paranormal phenomena on a global scale.

In Islam, the Noble Qur'an teaches us that God made the angels from light, humans from the mud and clay (matter), and djinn from fire. It very well could be that many of these ancient gods are what the Qur'an identifies as djinn.

In my long history of investigating the paranormal, my curiosity may have angered several of these primordial creatures by uncovering things about them that they preferred to keep secret. Knowing the reputation of Hecate from legend, my plan that night was to observe and be respectful of this group and their beliefs just in case she did exist. It seemed like an excellent idea to stay on the good side of the goddess.

After an hour the ritual was over and we all retired to the patio where we had unbelievably good tea and snacks. I had a great number of questions and everyone was eager to give me a detailed answer. It was explained to me the language they were using during the ritual was ancient Greek. It must have required a considerable amount of dedication to learn the words of the invocation in a language that is more ancient than Latin. This impressed me greatly.

I was told the ritual they performed that night was one of many and is used to give health, long life, healing, and protection for their loved ones. Whether or not they had success is hard to say, but they believe their efforts always yield results, and there is no greater power in the multiverse than faith.

As we sat on the deck enjoying our refreshments, the air seemed charged with a great deal of psychic energy emitting from each person; this is something that cannot yet be proven, only felt. However, there is one thing that even the most skeptical person would have noticed if he or she was present that night. The facial features of all the women in the ceremony seemed noticeably younger. I don't know if it was the light of the moon, the glow of the coals and torches in the distance, or being enchanted by the presence of such amazing people, but all of the ladies looked different. Was the answer to this mystery simply a physiological or psychological effect, or was it a gift from Hecate?

A week later with permission, I wrote an article on the followers of Hecate for my column on the paranormal, and my editor refused to publish it. He felt it supported and glorified Witchcraft and was sure the story would generate scores of angry letters from Connecticut residents.

Over the next several years, I kept in contact with the followers of Hecate and attended several more of their moonlight rituals in honor of the goddess. Each ceremony was quite different and they were all beautifully and carefully prepared with a great deal of time and effort.

As life would have it, eventually most of the members moved away and the property was sold. I wonder if the new owners would have purchased the property if they knew it was once the home and ritual site for a coven of Witches.

One last item; if you think Hecate has not been influential in the United States, take a good look at the Statue of Liberty at Ellis Island in New York. Also, the next time you watch a movie, take notice of the toga-dressed lady holding a torch at the beginning of Columbia films. I will leave this part of the mystery for you to solve.

Shape-Shifting and the Moon

Sorcerers of ancient times believed performing rituals during certain phases of the moon could bring about the physical transformation of the conjurer into an animal, especially a wolf, or increase the power of the sorcerer. These rituals have traditionally occurred on or around the full moon and, to a lesser extent, the new moon.

My great-grandmother, who was born in Calabria, Italy, to my mother's side of the family, also believed the full moon had an effect on people. She thought an evil man could turn into a werewolf when the moon was full.

When I was about six or seven years old, my great-grandmother and I were in a small neighborhood Italian grocery store picking up a few things for dinner.[118] There was a tall, slim man in front of us, and as he turned his head to look at us, my great-grandmother gasped and made the sign of the cross. She then grabbed my arm and we quickly walked to the back of the store until the man left. After asking her what was wrong, she said one word in Italian, "Lupo."[119] When we arrived home she acted upset and was raving on and on in Italian about something that upset her.

Finally, seeing my confusion, my grandfather (her son), told me the man we saw was evil and every full moon would turn into a wolf and go after people, especially babies, and eat them. He said, "You can tell if a man is a werewolf and has a deal with the devil because they always have thick, hairy eyebrows that come together over the nose and their eyes are very dark."

In Italy, they believed that a man could turn into a werewolf if he prayed to the devil and slept outside on a summer night with the full moon shining directly on his face. The werewolves of Italy were said to kill and eat sheep and would attack people if other food could not be found.

From that day on I would often dream about wolves—and movies like *The Wolf Man* and *Werewolf of London* didn't help. As a matter of fact, even today I still have dreams about changing into a wolf or being chased by a werewolf.

The concepts of the werewolf, vampire, and zombie and their relationship to the cycles of the moon is an interesting one. There are however very few cases and myths in recorded history that show a connection between the werewolf and the full moon. There is also no documented evidence of multiple witnesses seeing a werewolf or being present when

---

118   Nona was a fantastic cook and to this day her lasagna has never been matched.

119   A male wolf.

a human transforms into one. Most of the stories of werewolf sightings are hearsay or have one witness who saw something in the dark. Sounds a great deal to me like modern-day paranormal accounts or alien encounters. One witness is still no witness no matter what the century. The most documented arrest and trial of an alleged werewolf took place in Germany in the late sixteenth century.

In 1589 a German farmer named Peter Stump was accused of being a werewolf and a cannibal; he had one of the most shocking werewolf trials on record. Following his arrest Stump was tortured for hours until he confessed to having practiced the black arts. He claimed the devil offered him a belt made of wolf hide that gave him the power to change into a powerful, large, hungry wolf with sharp fangs and claws. According to the historical account of Stump's case, it was the wolf belt that caused his transformation and not the moon. During the investigation no such belt was ever found.

For twenty-five years, Stump had supposedly been an insatiable killer who ate the flesh of sheep, men, women, and children. He confessed to killing and eating fourteen children over a period of twenty years while in the form of a wolf. Stump was executed on Halloween Eve in 1589 in the most horrible fashion one could imagine. The flesh was torn from his body and the bones in his legs and arms were crushed with sledge hammers. He was then beheaded and his body burnt so he could not rise from the grave. His skull and bones were then buried in two separate places miles apart so they could never unite. When word got out of the alleged hideous crimes of Peter Stump, it created a werewolf scare in Europe resulting in many people, who were most likely innocent, being hunted and killed.

Algonquin and Wappinger tribes of the northeast United States have legends about powerful medicine men that could shape-shift into a bear or wolf by using the full moon as a catalyst. The tribal elders of today accept the simple fact that it is impossible for a human being to physically change into an animal and then back again. They explained to me that a medicine man must first leave his body and "spirit walk." [120] As a spirit, he can then shape-shift into a wolf or any animal.[121]

As a spirit animal, the medicine man (shaman) can come back into the material world and perform physical tasks and cannot be harmed by any weapon. As a wolf, the shaman can disappear and reappear at will and possesses great strength and ability. His only weakness is that his physical body, which remains unprotected at this time, can be killed. If this happens the wolf vanishes. For this reason they pick a secret, isolated place to perform the ceremony.

When I asked if any of the tribal shamans have this ability and, if so, if it would be possible to talk with them, the answer to my questions was yes then a stern no. Although the ancient ways of shaman magic are still passed down to each generation, much has been forgotten, and what is retained is kept secret.

One thing is clear; the full moon or energy radiated to Earth during certain lunar alignments was believed to be a catalyst in the shape-shifting ritual of these people.[122] The next time you are taking a walk during the full moon on a clear night and hear a howling in the distance, pay attention—it may not be the neighbor's dog.

The Lunar Effect

Although most scientists and medical doctors keep insisting the full moon has no effect on a human being, there are many people on a global scale and from all walks of life who still believe the lunar effect is real, and in some cases, that it can be extreme.

---

120   Astral projection.

121   This is much different than a skinwalker. A skinwalker is a powerful witch who has the ability to physically change into an animal.

122   During my research into mysterious stones, artifacts, and paranormal in the New England area, I spent a great deal of time with many members of the Wappinger and Algonquin tribes to obtain information on their history and myths.

Professionals who work in emergency rooms, law enforcement, and even teaching often will blame the full moon for a busy night or disciplinary problems in class with students. Throughout my teaching career, I often heard teachers talking in the staff room about a day of energetic students, asking if it was a full moon since they had trouble with classroom management as well as a number of other disciplinary problems.

While still in the military, there was one incident involving a female patient who was suffering from the disease Lupus.[123] The young Thai woman would go into episodes of psychotic-paranoid behavior at night that was apparently timed with the appearance of a full or nearly full moon. The doctor ordered that the shades in the room be closed at night so that the patient could not see the moon. I was assigned to keep an eye on her and there was a definite change in the behavior of this person at night, especially during times of significant lunar illumination.

For centuries people of the Near and Far East knew the moon was responsible for high and low tides and believed it also had a great effect on animals and humans. The Buddhist priests held true that the moon and all other celestial bodies in the multiverse have an influence on the health and behavior of human beings. Since the days of ancient Rome, it was observed that people suffering from various types of mental illnesses were at their worst during times of the full moon. The word "lunatic," denoting such behavior, comes from the Latin word "luna," which refers to madness caused by the moon.

Throughout the recorded history of the human race, the full moon was blamed on everything from an increase in violent crimes and psychotic behavior to physical illness and the frequency of UFO sightings.

---

123   Lupus is a chronic inflammatory disease that occurs when your body's immune system attacks your own tissues and organs. The disease was called Lupus as far back as the Middle Ages, since doctors during that time thought the red marks and sores that appear on the face and body looked like the bite of a wolf. "Lupus" is Latin for "wolf."

Nineteenth-century lawyers in England used the defense "guilty by cause of the full moon" to declare that their clients could not be held responsible for committing a violent crime because they were acting under the moon's influence.

In his book *How the Moon Affects You*, psychiatrist Dr. Arnold Lieber proposes the theory of "biological tides." Dr. Lieber states the human body contains anywhere between 65 and 75 percent liquid, which theoretically should flow more freely at times of the full moon. This increase of fluid pressure in the human body could trigger many types of behavior. It is also possible the electrical and cell activity of the brain and body could be affected by the moon's tidal forces.

As for other physiological effects in humans, many researchers have pointed out that the menstrual cycle of women is timed close to the lunar month of 29 days. Physicians who have studied this similarity believe the moon has no effect at all on women and the alleged correlation between the lunar cycle and the human menstrual cycle is nothing more than a coincidence. However, a Buddhist priest at the Chuang Yen Monastery told me a very long time ago, "In the multiverse, there is no such thing as a coincidence."

Paranormal researchers claim that there are more incidents of UFO sightings and strange happenings during the new and full moon. Over the years I have collected hundreds of reports, and one day, with the help of two enthusiastic assistants, we compared the date and time of 615 well-documented cases with the lunar phase for that particular day. The results obtained were totally unexpected and were double-checked for accuracy.

The study showed there was not an increase of paranormal activity on the new and full moon but one to two days after. The chart below is the result of several weeks of work. It plots occurrences of paranormal phenomena from 1975 to 2008. Of course one has to remember if we had access to more data over a longer period of time our findings could have been somewhat different.

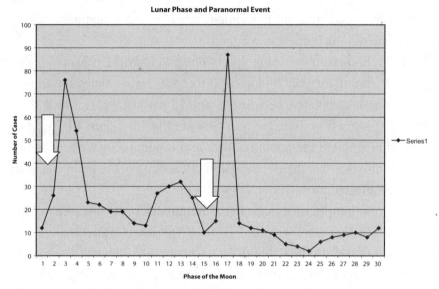

Figure 1: Paranormal activity and lunar phase: 1= New Moon: 15=Full moon

Does the lunar phase really affect human behavior? The answer to that question is no one really knows for sure. There is one thing that is certain; there is a connection between the orbital positions of the Earth–moon system and the occurrence of all types of paranormal phenomena. The question as to why strange phenomena, especially UFO reports, are more frequent shortly after the new and full moon can't be answered. This is a study that needs to be done in greater detail by some young, enthusiastic researcher. Always remember—we find the answers to nature's mysteries by building on the work of those who came before us.

The next time you are taking a walk at night and you look up and see the full moon rising, if you have the uncontrollable urge to howl like a wolf[124] or give in to irrational urges, it just might be the lunar effect!

---

124   I have seen people do this and with some it seems to be an uncontrollable urge.

Transient Lunar Phenomena

The moon is our closest neighbor and the most frequently observed and imaged celestial body by amateur and professional astronomers. There have been reports of anomalous lights and unexplainable formations on the lunar surface for several centuries. An observation of this type of lunar event is called transient lunar phenomena or TLP. The types of TLP that have been reported over the past 250 years include red glows and flashes in craters, abnormal reflections, large bridge-like formations stretching across craters that disappear and reappear, and balls of light floating across the lunar surface seemingly under intelligent control.

The official explanation by astronomers for such lunar phenomena is the lights and other TLP manifestations suggest nothing more than static electricity on the moon, ionized gases emitting from ancient lunar volcanic activity, or an optical illusion caused by the abnormal reflection of sunlight or earthlight.[125]

Observations of TLP date back to the time of Sir William Herschel who, in 1781, discovered the planet Uranus. On April 19, 1787, Herschel reported in his journal that on a number of occasions while observing with his telescope he witnessed odd globes of lights jump from crater to crater. To Herschel this was proof that there was life on the moon, but the astronomers of his day did not accept his theories and soon his observations of TLP were forgotten.

TLP was even reported by Apollo 11 astronauts as they orbited the moon. Although, besides a short statement from NASA stating that they did see some type of phenomena, a detailed report by the Apollo astronauts has never been published. This led many conspiracy theorists to suspect a cover-up, claiming what they really saw were alien spacecraft on the moon.

---

125 Earthlight is sunlight reflected off Earth to the moon. Our planet is quite bright as seen from the lunar surface. It is in fact bright enough to cast shadows in the lunar mountains and high crater walls.

The best example of TLP that I have ever seen was taken in Connecticut by an amateur astronomer who photographed a series of images showing a strange, brilliant light moving across the lunar surface. The light then hovered above a crater, illuminating the crater floor, then increased in altitude, and with a burst of energy shot off into space.

The image was analyzed by a number of experts in the fields of photography and astronomy, who found it to be an intense light source moving across the lunar surface and not the result of any type of optical illusion or photographic trickery. However, no professional astronomer or photographic expert would support the conclusions that the light represented a form of TLP that seemed to be under intelligent control and therefore unexplainable.

Every professional consulted in the fields of astronomy, physics, and photographic imaging would not go on record to say the light had no conventional explanation; they all gave me the same answer, "I have to think about my job and career."

Aliens on the Moon

In 1977 author George Leonard published a book entitled *Somebody Else Is On the Moon* [126] that claims aliens who have been exploring Earth for a very long time have portable bases on the side of the moon we observe from Earth and a large permanent base on the so-called dark side of the moon. Mr. Leonard's book contains a number of "official" photographs from NASA pointing out "unusual formations," which he believes were artificially constructed by aliens.

After carefully reading this book and taking a good look at the pictures, the so-called alien bridges, large machines, domes, and other structures that he claims are in the images all elude me. Although the photographs in the book are very low resolution, in my opinion most of the so-called alien artifacts can be explained by reflected sunlight and shadows.

---

126   George H. Leonard, *Somebody Else Is On the Moon* (New York: McKay, 1976).

In 1982 after contacting NASA, I was able to obtain many of the same photographs published in Mr. Leonard's book with much better resolution. The alleged "alien artifacts" were in the photographs and scrutinized carefully under a high-quality stereomicroscope in my science lab, but they still looked like natural reflections and shadows. If one is going to try to prove that there are alien bases on the moon, then they are going to have to come up with a great deal more evidence than the material presented in Mr. Leonard's book.

When my findings were made public, a number of die-hard UFO true believers contacted me claiming NASA probably took the originals and doctored them to make the alien machinery and construction look like natural phenomena. Some even accused me of being a government agent spreading disinformation. A number of the angry responses to my opinion were very similar to that of a religious fanatic responding to someone who said something negative or contradictory about their faith.

This incident showed me how much paranoia exists in the UFO community, since two "UFO investigators" who contacted me as a result of my story were quite angry and would not give their name because they thought the phone was tapped.

The majority of people who see and report UFOs and other forms of paranormal phenomena are not crazy; it's many of the people investigating UFOs and the paranormal that are the crazy ones. A late, great paranormal investigator and bestselling author once told me that the people who investigate UFOs are the lepers of paranormal research.

According to alien moon base believers, Neil Armstrong, the first man to walk on the moon, observed two massive alien spacecraft as the Apollo 11 Lunar Module touched down on the moon's surface in July 1969. This was never confirmed by Armstrong or anyone in NASA, and today it's still a hot topic of discussion in the UFO community.

During the Apollo 11 mission, the public was allowed to hear the radio transmissions from mission control to the astronauts. Armstrong was heard to say he could see a light on the edge of a nearby crater. Mission Control asked for more information and then there was silence for several minutes. This is actually true.

The conspiracy theorists claim NASA cut communications on the public frequency and switched to a private one where they thought no one could listen in. The following transmission has floated through the internet in different forms and was supposedly received by an amateur radio operator during the several minutes of radio silence.

Neil Armstrong: What was it? What the hell was it?

Mission Control: What's there?

Neil Armstrong: These babies are huge, enormous. Oh, God you wouldn't believe it! I'm telling you there are spacecraft out there, lined up on the far side of the crater edge. They're on the moon watching us!

To my knowledge the conversation above was not recorded and NASA denied the authenticity of the transmission. The original source of the "secret transmission" is even more questionable, but it is possible to decode and receive government transmissions of frequencies they believe are secure.

For example, in the early 1990s while working on a research project sponsored from a private grant, I was able to decode satellite transmissions from American, Soviet, and Chinese satellites. My work in this area was published in the scientific journal *Earth*.[127] That story resulted in a visit from an investigator from the United Nations, a government agent, and several Soviet scientists, but that's another story.

---

127   "Imaging satellite transmissions on your home computer," *Earth,* May 1992. This science periodical was the sister publication of *Astronomy Magazine.*

In 1995 a wealthy Connecticut resident[128] who had a great interest in UFOs contacted me and asked about the alien bases on the moon. After a short conversation, he invited me to his home to discuss it further. After a three hour conversation about UFOs and lunar phenomena, he told me the reason for the visit. He knew I had access to an observatory and wanted to know if it was possible for him to come and look at the moon. My reply was of course, so we set a date when the moon was half full and the night was clear.

During our observing session the gentleman was so impressed with the clarity of the lunar features that he was willing to finance the observatory for a year and supply the funds to purchase new equipment on our wish list. The only condition was that we spend a number of nights within that year to photograph the lunar surface with high-resolution film looking for TLP and the alleged alien bases and structures. I agreed to the project but made it very clear the chances of success were very low. He replied, "Yes, this is understood. But if we don't try, our chances of success are zero."

Over the next year or so, we took hundreds of frames of the moon at various magnifications at varying times, under all conditions, and during all phases. We even used special equipment like filters and high-resolution color and black-and-white film.[129] During the project we also used a variety of different special scientific films that are sensitive to a wide span of wavelengths. Despite being able to obtain amazing pictures of the moon, there was not one incident of TLP captured, no evidence of anything artificial, and no alien bases or equipment.

Who can say for sure? There just might be alien bases on the moon and a NASA conspiracy, however the evidence available to support this theory is very weak. Today, there are still quite a few people who believe

---

128   This person passed away in 2016 and left a considerable amount of his estate to charity and UFO research.

129   This was a time before digital cameras were popular.

that aliens are on the moon and have published images on the internet showing structures of "alien origin." To me and many others they appear to be faked using computer graphics. If there is a cover-up by the government, then those photographs would have never made it to the public. There are UFO-paranormal "researchers" who are going to extremes to attract sponsors for their websites and internet radio shows and many of these people will do whatever it takes to land a show on cable television.

The moon continues to inspire the imagination of the human race and despite all our technological wonders and understanding of the cosmos, it is still a main source on the celestial sphere in which legends originate.

Someday in the near future when Earthlings colonize the moon, the "alien bases" of the twentieth and early twenty-first centuries may be looked upon as nothing more than a myth from a culture who desperately wanted to believe they were not alone in the universe.

10

The Sun King

The sun is the center of the solar system and without a doubt the most important celestial object to all life on planet Earth. No other heavenly object has influenced the human race more than the sun. The sun was and still is the cornerstone of every myth and religious belief. All living things on Earth depend on the sun for survival; it is the progenitor of all energy used by plant and animals. The sun's gravity also keeps the entire solar system in a steady orbit. Without the influence of the sun, our planet and the entire solar system would fling outwards into the cold, dark depths of the galaxy.

Ancient cultures throughout time knew the importance of the sun and always held it in high regard, identifying our star with the most powerful gods. The early Greeks identified the sun with the god Helios, one of the last Titans spared by Zeus, since his job was too important. Later Helios was replaced by Apollo, a favorite son of Zeus, who became the new sun god. What became of Helios? After Apollo mastered the sun chariot, the legend says that Zeus, fearing the Titan Helios would get too powerful, stripped Helios of his power and imprisoned the ancient god with the rest of the Titans for all eternity.

The people of ancient Greece took their belief in the sun god very seriously. In the fifth century BC, when the Greek-Persian philosopher

Anaxagoras said the sun was not a god but a large ball of fire that moves around the Earth, he was imprisoned and sentenced to death for heresy.

Fortunately for him the death sentence was not carried out, but it made him and everyone else think twice before questioning the power and importance of the gods.

Cultists of Mirtha in ancient Persia honored the rising sun each day and saw it as a renewal of life. In Christianity, Jesus rises from the dead on the third day in the morning with the rising sun. There are historians who speculate the story of the resurrection of Jesus was based on legends from the sect of Mirtha.

The Egyptians acknowledged the sun as the main source of life, warmth, and power. They identified the sun with the god Ra who was considered the ruler of the universe. The priests of Ra had great influence and power in their society, since the people of ancient Egypt believed their priests spoke for the sun god himself. It's interesting to note the symbol representing the eye of Ra is similar to other sun gods such as Bel, Belenus, and the Hittite Arinna.

In Norse mythology the sun was called the eye of Odin, since the Vikings believed its power came from the king of the gods. According to legend, Odin lost one eye in battle, which explained to the Norse why there was only one sun in the sky.

In ancient Roman culture, Sunday was the day of the sun. It was later adopted by Christians as the Sabbath day that identified the sun with the light of God. The belief that a powerful God of the universe who was indentified by the light of the sun was handed down to Christianity from pre-Christian pagan beliefs.

The Roman ritual of Sol Invictus was performed on the winter solstice giving hope to the people—even though it is the shortest day of the year, the days following will be longer and longer, indicating the invincibility of the sun god. This ritual is one of several that influenced the date of our modern celebration of Christmas.

The Arabians thought the sun was inhabited by fiery beings they called djinn. These creatures were responsible for powering the sun. They would often visit Earth by floating on the solar wind to the North Pole where they had a great palace. It was said that when these fire spirits reached the earth, their blazing bodies would react with the air and the sky would glow green, yellow, and red.[130] They would then transform into a race of giants with physical form.

The ancient Greeks had a similar legend of a race of giants called the Hyperboreans who lived in the far north in a land where the sun never set in the summer time (the Arctic Circle). They lived in a great palace and their fires were responsible for the colors seen in the sky.

Today people are still affected by the sun. There are many who feel depressed or unproductive during the winter when the sun is low in the sky. Some also feel down in the dumps when it is cloudy or rainy. Let's face it; many prefer a sunny warm day over a cold, cloudy one. Children will draw happy times showing people with smiles on their faces and a bright yellow sun above in a clear sky. The sun not only plays an important part in keeping the solar system in order, but it is also important for the physical and mental well-being of human beings and most animals.

The Sun as a Star

Our sun is one of several hundred billion stars in our galaxy. If you travel ten light-years from Earth, our star will just blend in with thousands of other stars and be so faint it would be difficult to see. The sun is considered to be a main sequence type II population star. This means it is average in size with a somewhat stable energy output and low in heavy elements. The solar chemical composition is 74 percent hydrogen

---

130   Atmospheric scientists today accept that the people of Arabia may have seen a glowing sky, most likely an occasional rare manifestation of the Aurora Borealis.

and 23 percent helium [131] with the remaining 3 percent consisting of a variety of elements like carbon, oxygen, sodium, calcium, and iron.

Stars are classified not only by size, energy output, and composition, but also by the temperature of their "surface," which is called the photosphere. The temperature of a star is directly related to its color; blue stars are the hottest while red stars are cooler. Astronomers use a letter scale to identify the spectral- or color-type of a star.

O: Blue
B: Blue-white
A: White
F: Yellow-white
G: Yellow
K: Orange
M: Red

Using this scale our sun would be classified as a G-type star with a surface temperature of about 10,000 degrees Fahrenheit (5,500 degrees Celsius).

Life on Earth has adapted to the color of the sun. For example plants are green with some yellow in them. They reflect this color of light to protect themselves from too much solar radiation. If our sun was red the grass would be red instead of green. The human eye and most animals are sensitive to yellow and green light. This is one of the reasons why the old-style chalkboards were changed from black to green. The old saying "Don't wear a yellow shirt around bees because they are attracted to yellow" is true.[132]

---

131   The element helium was first discovered on the sun. It was thought to be found only in stars and was named helium after the sun god Helios. In 1868 the gas was discovered in underground pockets in Texas.

132   Bees are attracted to all bright colors that they identify as flowers. A recent study has shown that honeybees see the color yellow as being blue.

The sun is almost a perfect sphere with a diameter of about 850,000 miles and it makes up 99.8 percent of all the mass in the solar system. Its average distance from Earth is 93 million miles. In 200 BC the Greek scientist Eratosthenes, using geometry and trigonometry, calculated the distance from the sun to Earth with less than a 2 percent error—an astonishing feat for his time.

The source of the sun's energy was a mystery until the late nineteenth century. No one could explain how it could continue to expel vast amounts of energy over millions of years without a drop in temperature. Some believed it was beyond the understanding of science; many believed the sun was actually a powerful angel instructed by God to warm the earth until judgment day. Ancient cultures thought it was actually a living being. In the twentieth century the mystery was solved with the discovery of nuclear energy.

There are two basic types of nuclear reactions, fission and fusion. In nuclear fission heavy unstable elements are split into lighter ones releasing a great amount of energy and deadly radiation. This is the method that powers our nuclear reactors and is responsible for the explosive power of the atomic bomb.

In nuclear fusion lighter elements such as hydrogen are combined or fused into heavier atoms such as helium. The result is a great amount of energy with much less radiation. This type of nuclear reaction powers the sun and all stars.

In the core of the sun, fusion reactions take place, creating large amounts of energy. Scientists have not yet figured out how to do this, but someday if the mystery is solved, our energy problem will be solved. On the negative side an atomic weapon could be constructed that would be 1000 times more powerful than our hydrogen bomb. Could the human race be responsible enough to handle such power?

Our sun is about 4.6 billion years old and has enough energy to last for another 2 or 3 billion years. As it uses up its fuel, the sun will change in color to orange and then red. Its outer atmosphere will expand and engulf all the inner planets including Earth and Mars.

Sunspots are dark depressions on the photosphere and the aftermath of gigantic explosions called solar flares. Sunspots appear dark because they are cooler than the surrounding solar surface. The typical temperature of a sunspot complex is still 7000 degrees Fahrenheit. The average number of visual sunspots varies over time, increasing and decreasing on a regular cycle of about eleven years. In 1843 an amateur astronomer by the name of Heinrich Schwabe was the first to note this cycle. The part of the cycle that contains a low sunspot number is called the "solar minimum," or quiet sun, while the portion of the cycle with the greatest number of sunspots is called the "solar maximum," or active sun. It was also noted that the sun would actually expand during an active sun and contract during its quiet phase.

Today astronomers have discovered that a complete sunspot cycle from maximum to maximum is 22 years. According to recent observations we are now in a period of solar maximum when there should be a large number of sunspots visible on the photosphere of the sun.

From 1645 to 1715 there was a drastically reduced number of sunspots during the cycle of active solar activity. This period of time is now called the "Maunder minimum," after the nineteenth-century scientist E. W. Maunder, who discovered it using old records. During the Maunder minimum, temperatures dropped drastically all over our planet. Reports from that time indicate that in snowed in July over much of Europe and New England. This period has also been referred to as the "Little Ice Age," since lakes in the upper northern latitudes stayed frozen all year long. The discovery of the Maunder minimum has led many scientists to believe that sunspot activity may affect the climate of Earth and our sun may vary in its energy output from time to time.

Sunspots have been blamed for a variety of issues like a poor stock market, baby booms, UFO sightings, and other manifestations of paranormal phenomena. Decades ago I did a study with the hope of discovering a correlation between the sunspot cycle and the reports of all types of paranormal phenomena. Despite a great deal of work, there seemed to be no connection.

During times of an active sun, more radiation reaches Earth and most is stopped by the upper atmosphere. This creates magnetic storms and is responsible for the appearance of the northern and southern lights. There have been incidents in which considerable electromagnetic radiation from solar flares has reached the surface and caused overloads at power stations resulting in a massive blackout.

These magnetic storms are also responsible for radio and satellite blackouts and could be the catalyst in the reception of very strange signals that may not originate in our reality. Receiving and documenting these mysterious radio transmissions is part of a personal future project.

The Aztecs and the Sun

The Native American tribes of the Great Plains and Northeast saw the sun as the primary life-giving force. Sun dance rituals were performed every year at the summer solstice to honor and thank the sun for making the crops grow and taking care of the people. In some North American and Mesoamerican tribes, the sun was seen as the king of the universe and many chiefs and other important rulers claimed their heritage from the sun god.

The Huron and Algonquin warriors and hunters believed that if they stripped off their clothes and basked in the sun for several hours, they would absorb its power and be better at the hunt and fiercer and indestructible in battle.[133] However, of all the cultures in the Western Hemisphere, the Aztecs were the most avid sun worshippers and had the most complex beliefs.

---

133   It's possible that the creators of Superman used this old Indian belief to explain how the superhero gets his powers from absorbing photons from our yellow sun.

The names of the Aztec gods are very difficult to pronounce in English and unless someone who has an understanding of their ancient language says their name, you may never get it correct. During a lecture on the Aztecs in San Antonio, Texas, the presenter said the name of several Aztec gods. Many in attendance including myself looked at him puzzled. He noticed this and wrote the names of these gods on the blackboard and then said them once again. Everyone in the audience smiled and gestured that they now understood.

The Aztecs honored the sun god by building great temples. They believed there were five ages, each ruled by a different sun god. The sun gods of the past ages were Tezcatlipoca, Quetzalcoatl, Tlaloc, and Chalchiuhtlicue, and the god of the final sun, which is the age we live in, is Nanauatl.[134]

At the conclusion of each age, the world would experience a great cataclysmic event and the sun god would have to use his or her energy to rebuild the world and the human race. This expenditure of energy would leave the god or goddess drained of power and they would have to sleep and rest for a thousand years. To rule the next age, a new deity would be chosen by a cosmic council and given the power of the sun.

According to Aztec legend, at the end of the fifth age the current sun god would have to sacrifice his life in order for the human race to survive. In appreciation and honor of this great act the Aztec priests began offering human sacrifices to the sun god. A great deal of thought went into each ritual sacrifice, and in most cases the heart was extracted because it was believed to be not only the seat of the human soul but also contain a fragment of the sun that gave the people physical life.

---

134   Four of these gods were male, while Chalchiuhtlicue was female. Her name translates to English meaning "Lady of Jewels (or Jade)."

Shortly after the Spanish conquest of Mexico, the Franciscans[135] persuaded the government to pass a law forbidding the Aztec priests to continue human sacrifice under penalty of death. This led to the formation of secret sun god cults that still exist today in Mexico and the southwestern United States.

Sun Worship in the Twenty-First Century

People who like to travel to Florida in the winter or go to the pool or beach during the summer are sometimes called "sun worshippers." This has nothing to do with their religious beliefs since these people just enjoy the sun.

In the twenty-first century, legitimate sun worship is thought of as being an ancient primitive religion, but in reality it is a complicated system of worship that captivates the mind with its beautiful and complex ceremonies and is still around today in many different forms.

Sun worship has been present throughout thousands of years of human history and formed the basic foundations for Buddhism, Hinduism, Catholicism, and many Pagan groups. The names of the gods have changed, but the method of worship is very similar to the original Babylonian. For example, when Shamash, the Babylonian sun god, plunged into the waters of the Euphrates River, this act of sacrifice allowed his son to enter into the waters of the womb of a chosen woman to be born in physical form as the savior of mankind.

In Hinduism the rising of the sun in the east represents Brahma, at its highest point in the sky it is identified with Shiva, then finally Vishnu when setting in the west. At night, the sun rests in the darkness of the underworld, representing the death and suffering of the sun god, who once again rises from the dead in the morning.

---

135   The Franciscans are a religious order within the Catholic Church, founded in 1209 by Saint Francis of Assisi.

There are Pagan groups today that honor the sun during the equinoxes, solstices, midsummer, and the festival of Beltane. During Beltane (May 1) small groups will travel to the highest hills or mountains in their area that have a clear view of the eastern sky. Dressed in colors of red, yellow, and green, they await the rising sun and honor its return in the sky by lighting a fire, singing songs, dancing, saying prayers, and eating assorted berries for breakfast. The fall equinox and winter solstice ceremonies are performed indoors by lighting dozens of yellow candles and reciting ancient Celtic prayers thanking the sun for all it does to benefit humanity.[136]

There is a small Christian group in New York that identifies the sun as a manifestation of God. They teach their parish that the universe is a giant living being and we are part of it. During mass the priests say our sun is the consciousness of God in our solar system. They also teach there is no coincidence that our sun has a stable energy output and our planet is at a perfect distance from it.

Out of curiosity I attended one of their Sunday sessions. The ministry is very well funded, since the church and grounds were magnificent. Inside the cathedral, the ceiling has many glass panes that have diffraction gratings, making the white light of the sun split up into many colors.

As the priest came out and began mass, he wore white robes with a bright yellow rayed sun on the front and a rayed red sun on the back, which represented the sun during the day and the setting sun in the evening.

The mass itself seemed typical, but there was more in the way of personal teachings and philosophies presented by the priest. After mass I was lucky enough to have a short conversation with the priest and mentioned the sun–God connection his church had that originated

---

136   I have actually been at a number of these ceremonies as an observer and sometimes as a participant. They are interesting and seem to generate a great deal of good feelings and positive energy among the followers.

from pre-Christian religions. He simply replied that the sun is a manifestation of God and one would have to be dull-minded to believe such an amazing object created itself. He also mentioned that in the Christian belief Sunday was to be the Sabbath and the day of the Lord God. He then looked at me directly in the eyes and put his hand on my shoulder then smiled and said, "SUN-DAY! The day of God!"

11

Eclipses of the Sun and Moon

Throughout history, eclipses of the sun and moon were perceived as signs of destruction, terror, an angry god, a bad omen, or the assault of a supernatural monster. Although today we understand what causes an eclipse and the dynamics behind this phenomenon, the sight of the sun or the moon slowly disappearing in the sky still generates a deep feeling of apprehension. Eclipses are not only amazing spectacles of nature, but they also give us insight to the cultural beliefs of many people at all points of history.

The word eclipse comes from the Greek, meaning "abandon" since the ancient Greeks thought the sun or moon was leaving the sky above. Witnessing a solar eclipse was quite disconcerting to all ancient civilizations since they knew the sun was the primary source of energy on earth, and without its light all plants, animals, and even people would eventually perish.

Chinese astrologers as far back as 2500 BC were able to predict solar eclipses with considerable accuracy. They believed an evil flying dragon was coming to slowly devour the sun and unless something was done all life on Earth would perish.

In response to this threat, the king or governor of a province would warn the people in advance and get them ready to frighten the monster away. This was usually done by making a great deal of noise such as yelling and banging pots and drums. In some cases black powder was ignited and fireworks were shot up into the air.

The Chinese believed the same dragon was also responsible for trying to eat the moon during a lunar eclipse. At night they would beat gongs, burn fires, and try throwing torches up in the air to drive the deadly creature away.

The sun was considered to be a symbol of the Chinese emperor. When a solar eclipse was predicted, the emperor would normally eat vegetarian meals, avoid the main palace, and perform rituals to rescue the sun.

According to a Chinese legend from sometime around 2000 BC, Emperor Zhong Kang beheaded two of his court astrologer-astronomers because they failed to predict an eclipse of the sun. As late as 1890 the Chinese navy fired cannons from a ship during a lunar eclipse to scare away what they believed was a dragon eating the moon.

The Mayans and the Incans believed that lunar eclipses occurred when a colossal celestial jaguar would attack the moon and try to eat it. The red moon they witnessed during totality was believed to be the blood of the moon caused by the teeth of the giant predatory cat. They also believed that when the jaguar finished with the moon, the colossal cat would come down to earth and eat their ruler. To protect their king the priests would select a volunteer to masquerade as the king as a diversion while the warriors threw spears and torches at the moon, hoping to drive the monster away and make it spit out the moon. Also, the volunteer who posed as the king was usually killed during mid-eclipse to show the jaguar there is no reason to come down to earth.

In ancient Mesopotamia they also believed that during an eclipse a giant monster was coming down to Earth to kill the king, and like the Incas they had a servant, slave, or prisoner dress up and act like the king while the monarch himself blended in with the crowd dressed in rags. During totality the royal imposter was killed under the eclipsed moon to satisfy the monster's lust for royal blood.

Lunar and especially solar eclipses had a great effect on history. There are several accounts during the many Greek wars that both sides dropped their weapons and called a truce because they believed the sun vanishing was a sign the god Apollo was not pleased with the war. A solar eclipse that took place in 478 BC was seen as a favorable omen by Persian king Xerxes to invade Greece.

Herodotus[137] recorded a solar eclipse that put an end to the conflict between the Lydians and the Medes.[138] Herodotus writes that the day turned into night and both sides were so fearful that they threw down their weapons and the leaders of both armies began peaceful negations.

The Prophet Muhammad stated with authority that eclipses of the sun and moon are not bad omens or evil creatures trying to destroy mankind or the sun and moon, but are natural cosmic demonstrations showing the power of Allah. This one statement convinced the people of the Muslim world to no longer fear eclipses and allowed them to watch these amazing spectacles of God in wonder and not terror. There is a Muslim prayer called the eclipse prayer. Its purpose is to remember the power and love of Allah the Creator during a total eclipse.

A Native American belief from the Hupa tribe in Northern California has a myth about lunar eclipses that says the moon is a great celestial

---

137   Herodotus, fifth century BC, was a Greek historian known as the Father of History. He was the first historian to collect his materials systematically and arrange them in a well-constructed and vivid narrative.

138   Lydia—a name derived from its first king, Lydus, according to Herodotus—also known as Maeonia, occupied the western region of Asia Minor. The Medes were an ancient Iranian people.

being that is very wealthy, having many wives and hundreds of animal servants. One of the pets was a giant ferocious mountain lion and when the moon didn't bring him enough food to eat, the lion attacked the moon and made him bleed. This is how the Hupa explained the red of the moon during totality. When the moon would once again move out of the shadow of Earth and turn white, they believed it was caused by his wives who healed him and restored his health.

To most of the tribes of Southern California, an eclipse signaled that the moon was ill. The tribal members led by the medicine man would gather around a large fire to sing and beat drums loudly until the moon turned white, a sign that its health was restored.

There is a Hindu belief that during an eclipse the "influence" of the moon or sun can cause ill health and other physical or mental maladies. To remedy this many people in India will fast during an eclipse and bathe in a public area to wash the lunar effects off their body. There is also another Hindu belief that warns that if you were born at a time when an eclipse was taking place, the negative effect it will have on you will be much greater than a person not born during one. For this "unfortunate individual" it was considered safe to view the eclipse indirectly.

To Westerners this may sound somewhat superstitious, but scientists and medical doctors really don't know how the full or new moon affects living things. The moon, like any other celestial body, has a gravitational influence on the surface of Earth. However, according to the late great astronomer and skeptic Dr. George Abell,[139] a mosquito landing on your shoulder exerts more gravitational pull on you than the moon.

Gravitons, the elusive theoretical particles responsible for gravity are thought to have the ability to transverse the entire multiverse. This

---

139   George Abell taught astronomy at UCLA. He worked as a research astronomer and was an outspoken skeptic of the paranormal.

means they can pass through all the multiple dimensions and parallel universes. Physicists have to consider that we know very little about the graviton so how can we know in what way this particle interacts with the complex molecules of matter in a human body?

My great-grandmother believed that if you planted flowers or tomato plants during an eclipse they would grow larger and produce larger tomatoes and more beautiful flowers. You might ask if it worked or not—the answer is unknown, but the practice was carried through several generations of my family and other people of similar ethnic background.

Columbus and the Lunar Eclipse

In 1503 during his fourth voyage, Columbus's damaged ships made landfall somewhere on what is known today as Jamaica. His expedition was out of food and fresh water, his ships were not sea worthy, and his crew was on the brink of mutiny. The natives of the island greeted them, but were very curious about these strange visitors who looked very mysterious in their large wooden ships. Columbus and his crew were the guests of the native Jamaicans for one year, hoping the governor of Hispaniola would eventually send a rescue mission, a rescue that, according to history, never came.

Columbus and his crew lived with the indigenous people of the island and eventually learned some of their language. From his diary it seems most of his crew were not ideal houseguests and did things that violated the Jamaicans' social order. As a result of these violations, the elders of the island became angry with Columbus and refused to give him and his crew any more food and water.

Columbus was a terrible sailor, but he was a good astronomer and knew of an upcoming total lunar eclipse on February 29–March 1, 1504. Just before the eclipse, he told the native leaders that he had a strong connection with his god, and if he asked it of him, God would make the moon disappear.

Columbus actually had an almanac and timed his threat with the upcoming eclipse that very night. As the full moon appeared in the sky Columbus kneeled and probably said a few prayers in Latin to convince the elders he was talking to God. At first they all laughed, but when the moon started to vanish, they took Columbus seriously. During mid-eclipse the moon turned a bright red and the native people fell to their knees and begged Columbus to bring back the moon and in return they would give him anything he wanted. I'm sure old Chris made a long list of demands and the moon came back. He then told the elders that if their word was not kept, he would make the sun vanish next. It's a good thing no one called his bluff since there was no solar eclipse scheduled from that location for a very long time.

Columbus and his crew got all the food and water they needed and a great deal more from the people of the island. For the next several months he used the men and women of Jamaica as a workforce to repair his ships and fulfill the needs of himself and his crew. There is no doubt that if it wasn't for this lunar eclipse, Columbus would have never been able to complete this journey and, perhaps, would have been lost in history and not remembered as he is today. It was this one event on the celestial sphere that changed our history and saved Columbus and his crew from an unknown fate.[140]

Every year I would tell the story of Columbus and the eclipse to my sixth-grade science students just before Columbus Day weekend and mention that if it wasn't for this lunar eclipse, perhaps Columbus and his men would have been killed or lost forever.[141] One year, after finishing the story, a student raised her hand and said, "The worst thing would be no three day-weekend for Columbus Day!"

---

140   Samuel Eliot Morison, *Christopher Columbus, Mariner* (Boston: Little, Brown and Company, 1955).

141   This story and follow-up lesson on lunar eclipses was also in a sixth/seventh grade *Earth Science* workbook. Every Columbus Day weekend the section would be assigned as homework.

A Scientific View

The earth casts a shadow in space. Like all shadows it has two parts—a lighter shadow called the penumbra surrounds a much darker shadow called the umbra. A total lunar eclipse takes place when the moon moves into the umbra shadow of Earth. Since the moon shines from reflected sunlight, it appears to slowly vanish in the sky as it enters umbra. This can take place only at full moon since the sun, moon, and Earth have to be lined up.

The reason we don't have a lunar eclipse every full moon is because the moon is mostly above or below the shadow of Earth during the full moon phase. Sometimes only a section of the moon enters the umbra and the result is a partial lunar eclipse.

Lunar eclipses take place within two months of the spring or autumn equinox because the Earth–moon system is lined up perfectly at this time. From any given location the frequency of a total lunar eclipse is once every three years. The frequency of a total solar eclipse from any given location is approximately once in every 360 years.

When the moon is in the shadow of Earth, "totality" occurs; however, it does not vanish completely but turns a shade of red. This phenomenon is caused by sunlight bending (refracting) through the atmosphere of Earth. The blue light from the sun is scattered in our atmosphere, giving us the blue sky effect; the red light is refracted and enters the Earth's shadow and strikes the lunar surface. This red light is then reflected back to Earth, and the result is we see a red moon in the sky during totality. The shade or brightness of the moon in totality will depend on how much dust is in our atmosphere at the time. If there is very little dust, the moon will be very bright red.

In November of 1975 I observed a magnificent lunar eclipse that was a bright copper color during totality. This was the most beautiful lunar eclipse I have ever witnessed in my life. Total lunar eclipses, especially bright red ones during mid-eclipse, have always been important in the magic rituals of many Pagan and Neopagan beliefs. Some paranormal investigators claim a great deal of phenomena, including UFO sightings, take place during a total eclipse of the moon, however this researcher has never been able to verify this claim.

It could be that the eerie atmosphere created during this time triggers a feeling of uneasiness in people, resulting in an induced paranormal experience. It may also be possible, but highly unlikely, the paranormal occurrences witnessed at this time are generated by the multitude of human minds as it shifts into unused parts of the brain, which even physicians claim is still a mystery.

A total solar eclipse occurs when the moon completely obscures our sun. During totality the moon almost fits perfectly in front of the solar disk, allowing the light of the sun to be blocked. What is visible at this time is the outer layer of the sun, called the corona,[142] which appears like a glowing crown circling our star. A solar eclipse can take place only during the new moon phase when the moon is between our Earth and sun and perfectly aligned. A solar eclipse does not take place every new moon, since as seen from the surface of the earth, our moon is mostly above or below the sun.

Since the distance of the moon changes as it orbits Earth, its apparent angular size in the sky varies. A rare type of solar eclipse occurs when the moon is at its farthest point from Earth. This results in the apparent angular size of the moon being smaller, hence the sun being not completely eclipsed, and a bright ring, or annulus, surrounding the dark disk is visible. This is called an annular eclipse and is quite beautiful to witness.

Unlike a lunar eclipse, which can be seen by almost an entire hemisphere, a total eclipse of the sun can only be seen in a much smaller area

---

142   The word "corona" means "crown." The "atmosphere" of the sun appears like a glowing crown surrounding the solar disk. It is composed of intense magnetic fields and high-energy plasma.

no larger than a band of about 435 miles. This is because the umbra shadow of the moon cast on the surface of the earth is quite small. I have seen quite a few partial solar eclipses in my life but only three total solar eclipses and they were all a sight to remember.

On May 30, 1984, an annular eclipse took place that was visible from New York. It was a school day, so with the help of a number of students, we set up our four-inch refracting telescope on the schools outdoor basketball court. It was a cloudy day, and although our chance of seeing the eclipse was getting slimmer as the day went on, our telescope was nevertheless ready with a projection screen so a large number of students could safely view the eclipse. The telescope was covered just in case it rained and we all went back inside to resume class. Several minutes before eclipse time, the sky was completely overcast and it looked like rain so no one went outside.

During the time of totality, there was a notable drop in temperature and it became considerably darker outside. In the science lab, we had a motorized drum that would chart the outside temperature on graph paper with a stylus filled with red ink. During the eclipse the temperature took a plunge downward, then all of a sudden, without warning, heavy rain fell from the sky like a cloudburst was taking place.[143]

The students were all looking out the window and some feared the eclipse did something to cause some terrible flooding disaster. To alleviate their fear, I explained that when the air cools down, the molecules come closer together, turning water vapor into liquid water, which falls as rain. The deluge lasted for about four minutes and stopped shortly after the predicted end time of totality.

Later that day, the biology teacher mentioned that the school's hamsters and guinea pigs all ran into their little shelters during mid-eclipse. This was interesting since they were indoors with bright artificial lights.

---

143   A cloudburst is an extreme amount of rain in a short period of time, sometimes capable of creating flood conditions.

Was it possible the animals were sensing the drop in temperature and light outside or responding to some other influence?

Eclipses and Life on Earth

Tibetan Buddhists priests teach that during a lunar and solar eclipse, the good and bad actions of humans and animals are magnified considerably. Astrologers believe a lunar eclipse can influence erratic behavior in some people and cause wars and cataclysmic events such as earthquakes, volcanoes, bad weather, and magnetic storms in the upper atmosphere.

If the lunar effect does exist, then it would be at its greatest during the time of an eclipse, since the sun, Earth, and moon are in a perfect alignment. During the January 21, 2000, total eclipse of the moon, at the moment of totality it turned a deep red and was quite eerie in the clear sky. About a minute into totality, all the dogs in the neighborhood began barking and howling. Since they were quiet before the event it was apparent they were reacting to the eclipse and somehow it was affecting their behavior. It's hard to tell if they were actually seeing the moon go dark and responding to it or if there were other forces emitting from the lunar alignment that were having an effect on their behavior. I was taking a walk at the time and felt strange and very uneasy. It was if something invisible was following and watching me. Perhaps it was just my imagination compounded by the howling canines, perhaps not.

In 2012 the Department of Anthropology at the University of Pennsylvania conducted an investigation of the reactions from different species of monkeys during a total lunar eclipse. The results showed a marked change in the activity of the animals during totality. It seems they reacted to the decrease in light by becoming quiet. This is not surprising since a recent study has shown that lions and most likely other predatory cats are more dangerous as hunters when the moon is low on the horizon or the night is dark. Animals, including early humans, learned to stay quiet or go into hiding on dark moonless nights.[144] Perhaps this study is the answer to why people, especially children, have a subconscious fear of the dark.

Throughout history, during the darkest hours of the night, human beings have always found the light of a bright full moon comforting. This is one of the reasons why Selene was identified as a powerful goddess. She gave light and hope through the darkest nights.

The Prophecy of the Blood Moon

In the Christian Bible, solar and lunar eclipses were seen as signs of the end of the world and thought to herald the return of Jesus Christ. Also, during the crucifixion of Jesus, it is reported that the day sky turned into night at the moment of his death. Astronomers and historians have tried to find a solar eclipse that could account for this phenomenon, but there was none. Whatever darkened the sky during that time remains a mystery. Agnostics and atheists question if the unexplainable event ever took place and say the supernatural occurrence may have been added by the apostles or the first council of Nicaea in AD 325 to give Jesus a more divine image.[145]

The three biblical passages below are thought to represent a solar and lunar eclipse. They have been used for centuries by alleged prophets and ministers, mystics, and cult leaders of long ago and today to predict the date of doomsday.

---

144   C. Packer, A. Swanson, D. Ikanda & H. Kushnir, "Fear of Darkness, The Full Moon and the Nocturnal Ecology of African Lions" (*PLOS*, July 20, 2011), http://journals. plos.org/plosone/article?id=10.1371/journal.pone.0022285

145   The First Council of Nicaea was a council of Christian bishops convened by order of the Roman Emperor Constantine in AD 325 in the Bithynian city of Nicaea, which is now located in modern Turkey.

And I behold when he had opened the sixth seal, and lo, there was a great earthquake; and the sun became black as sackcloth of hair, and the moon became as blood. (Revelation 6:12)

Immediately after the tribulation of those days, the sun will be darkened and the moon will not give its light; the stars will fall from heaven and the powers of the heavens will be shaken. (Matthew 24:29)

The sun shall be turned into darkness and the moon into blood, before the coming of the great and grand day of the lord. (Acts 2:20)

Eclipses were not only thought to be a sign of doomsday and the second coming of Jesus Christ by Christians of the first century, there are many today who believe that a rare series of lunar and solar eclipses that have taken place this decade is once again a sign the end is near (here we go again). Just when I thought people were getting over the dire prophecies of the years 2000 and 2012, there are those who are again predicting the end of the world before 2021.

The blood moon prophecy is a doomsday predication by a number of Christian evangelists who are telling their followers that four consecutive eclipses that have taken place between 2014 and 2015 are a sign that the end of times is near. However, what they didn't tell their television congregation is that this event is one of eight tetrad eclipses that are to take place during the twenty-first century. The suggestion of the red or blood moon as an omen for the end of times actually has its origin in the three passages from the Bible above.

At the beginning of 2008, two popular television preachers started putting the fear of God into their followers by telling them that the end of the world will happen sometime after 2008, and only the faithful will survive to see Jesus appear in the sky and establish his kingdom on earth. During two of the lunar eclipses, the moon did turn red (as it usually does during totality), and it frightened many parishioners who witnessed it since a great number of them had never seen an eclipse or had the patience to follow it to totality. When the moon turned "blood red," they firmly believed without question their beloved pastor did indeed have the inside track to God and was correct in his assumption that the end was near.

From 2008 to 2010 the income of these ministers increased considerably as devotees gave their church a great deal of money with the hope of buying their way into the new world and heaven. One of the ministers actually wrote a book about the blood moon prophecy and it became a bestseller on Amazon and was on the *New York Times* bestseller list in 2014 for several weeks. One would think he would have published it sooner, since if he really believed 2015 was the end of the world, it didn't leave much time for syndicated and mass market sales, not to mention that greatly sought-after movie deal.

The predicted time of doomsday was to be the fall of 2015 and when it failed to take place, most of the TV evangelists who supported it quickly talked their way out of it by mentioning that God had changed the date and the new time would be secret, so people could honestly repent. It would be a date and a time that not even the angels in heaven would know.

As of the writing of this book, these TV evangelists are not talking about their doomsday predication anymore, but have hinted the new date is 2021. Despite their "mistake" and claim they never predicted doomsday in the first place, the attendance of their congregation has not been affected.

In biblical times the apostles and the prophets used eclipses of the sun and moon to get the attention of people in the hope of converting them. Today, nothing has changed; ministers and self-appointed prophets are still using eclipses to fulfill their own agendas. It's clear in America the God business is big business and the celestial sphere is often used to teach (as the Southern Baptists ministers would say) "the fear of Jesus." The sad part is people are still falling for it. As the old saying goes, "There's a sucker born every minute."

Eclipse Magic

Not all spiritual beliefs look upon eclipses as a prelude to disaster. There are some who view them as a positive event. The Wicca community views the moon as a goddess and the sun as a god, and during a solar eclipse they see it as the two coming together to generate positive energy directed at all life on Earth. It is a time when the two deities commune and reestablish their connection so they can continue to coexist in harmony. Although most Wicca and other Neopagan groups do not acknowledge an eclipse with a special community ritual, many will recognize the event privately.

The total lunar eclipse of August 1989 was a spectacular event and, for me, one to remember. I wanted to photograph this eclipse and carefully prepared for it several weeks in advance. My plan was to go to a field located in an isolated section of town and set up my telescopes and camera early while there was still light.

At the site there was a fifty-foot area of concrete painted white and, on its surface a number of very strange images. There were two circles and each had six human figures (a total of twelve) with their arms in the air as if flying or falling. The human figures on the right side (north) were red, while the left side (south) were white. Each image was about six inches long. Between the two human-shaped images, exactly in the center was a dotted black circle large enough for a person to stand. The paintwork appeared as if it was done a short time ago and seemed to be the work of one of the many occult groups in the area. This was not a Wicca ritual design, but whoever they were, the number six seemed to play an important role in their faith.

As the time of first contact of the eclipse began, several cars and a van pulled into the parking area and out walked a group of people carrying a number of items. They went over to the ritual area and began setting up a number of effigies. At first they didn't notice me, but when they did I decided to go over and introduce myself and ask them if they would like to see the eclipse through one of my telescopes. At first the leader, a middle-aged woman, was a little defensive.

As we talked they all donned robes—six red, six white—matching the images on the ground. The woman who was in charge slipped on a robe that was black with a red and white reversed pentagram on the back surround by a white circle with symbols on each point of the star. She told me they were a coven that worships angels who were cast out of heaven and were trying to make their way back to a dimension where matter and energy are one. She explained although the chief deity in their religion is a fallen angel known to Christianity as Satan, that is not this angel's real name, nor is it Lucifer. The word Satan [146] actually means "deceiver" or "accuser" and was used to identify a given group of angels, humans, or djinn who defied the word of God.

She then told me the powerful angel they worship is called Samael,[147] who was once a freedom fighter and was cast out of heaven for breaking the rules and fighting for the right of free thinking and independence of the angelic heavenly host.

I asked if they were afraid of getting repercussions from the established religious community who would label her group as Satan worshippers. She calmly responded, "The constitution of the United States guarantees free religion, and as long as no laws are violated, there's really not much anybody can do to stop us legally. The law is on our side."

She then explained many organizations like the Church of Satan use the name Satan since it is something easily recognized by the general

---

146   In Islam, Satan is called "Shaitan," which means "those who oppose Allah."

147   In Judaism, Samael is said to be the angel of death and is sometimes associated with Satan. Samael refers to a poison angel who tempts people to sin. Samael is considered to be good and evil and, in Christianity, a fallen angel. Samael is also listed in *A Dictionary of Angels, Including the Fallen Angels* by Gustav Davidson (New York: Simon & Schuster).

public. She also believes all the so-called Satanic churches are just mixed up people simply looking for publicity, attention, and to get a rise from others or feel different and important. She continued to explain that their group is no way connected to these "nuts" and they are unique.

The woman then told me the ritual they were going to perform would take place at totality, and was meant to channel power to these fallen angels. In turn they would get favors like financial success, good health, and protection from their enemies.

While talking with the members it was discovered that among them were lawyers, educators, a doctor, a corporate vice president, and other successful individuals. There were six men in red and six women in white. One member of the group lit a fire in the caldera, then all went to their positions in the ritual area and I went back to my telescopes.

At the time of mid-eclipse, I could hear the group chanting and the leader, the high priestess, talking while the others responded. To me it sounded reminiscent of a Catholic priest giving mass with church attendees answering the words of the prayer. They seemed to be speaking in a combination of Latin and English.

At the exact time of totality, the moon turned a deep red. The high priestess then threw something into the fire, causing a brilliant blue flash and a mushroom cloud of white smoke. As she did this, the others fell to the ground and all started yelling very loudly as if in ecstasy. Except for the high priestess, who continued standing, they all stayed on the ground for the duration of totality as she continued to chant words in Latin.

When a white sliver of the moon reappeared, she gave the signal and they all got up from the ground, hugged each other, and began loading up their cars. The burning embers in the caldera were extinguished with water and all thirteen of them hung around and took turns looking through my telescopes at the moon. After about an hour of lunar observation, the high priestess invited me to attend their meetings and learn more about the "secret knowledge" they were able to obtain.

Despite every member of this group being very well educated, they still held the belief that during a total eclipse the moon could transfer some type of power to not only them but also to allegedly incorporeal beings who they deem are in some type of partnership with the members of the coven.

I did in fact attend a number of their parties and meetings over a period of two years as an interested observer and learned a great deal that has helped me with my investigations of the paranormal. At the mansion home of the high priestess there was a remarkable library of occult books written mostly in Latin and Sanskrit from the sixteenth and seventeenth centuries. It's clear this group has existed for a very long time and knowledge of the mystical arts has been passed down for at least four centuries. However, that's another story.

As for the blue explosion and the white cloud of smoke, there was really no magic in that part of the performance, since it was nothing more than one part of finely-powdered zinc mixed with one part of sulfur, a mixture used by stage magicians and chemistry teachers for over a century to thrill their audiences and students.

The next several nights found me at the observatory assisting one of the astronomers to track asteroids. At about two o'clock in the morning, we were waiting for the computer to analyze a number of images, so I mentioned the coven and the lunar eclipse ritual. He laughed and replied they probably were a bunch of crazy kids who were high on drugs and rock and roll devil music. There was no response on my part.

Eclipse Chaser

A friend who passed away about forty years ago was an eclipse chaser. An eclipse chaser is a person who travels the world with the sole purpose of photographing a total eclipse of the sun wherever and whenever it might take place. His travels led him to just about every continent on the planet, and as a result of his efforts, he had a wall full of framed pictures of every eclipse he witnessed.

The color photographs were incredible and, due to the constantly changing corona of the sun, each eclipse appeared different. He loved astronomy and traveling the globe. Hunting solar eclipses and UFOs was his passion in life. He was fortunate to be very wealthy and spent most of his time traveling and pursuing his many interests.

After returning home from an African eclipse, he mentioned that during totality three disklike objects appeared in the sky about ten degrees (20 full moons in angular distance) from the sun. The objects were bright silver in color and stood out in the darkened eclipsed sky. Their apparent size was very large, about the size of a dime held at arms length. It was witnessed by several hundred people present and he was able to snap four color images. The UFOs then shot straight up and then vanished after totality, which was about five minutes long.

He showed me the pictures and it was very difficult to believe that they were real. They looked like your classic flying saucers and appeared to be metallic in nature. From a photographic point of view, they were very sharp images.

He then cautiously mentioned that at the time of the sighting there was a buzzing in his head that no one else seemed to hear. Several weeks later this person called me and said he had made contact with aliens and they wanted something from him, but he was not sure what it was.

We didn't talk for about a month and when he finally called he told me he was diagnosed with bone cancer. I was shocked because he was only about thirty and kept himself in perfect physical condition. He was sure the aliens had something to do with his sickness and was too scared to answer any more of my questions. Four months later he passed away and all his material, including his eclipse pictures, were destroyed by his parents. This took place in 1976 and to this day many aspects of his death remain a mystery to everyone who knew this brilliant young man.

UFOs and Eclipses of the Sun and Moon

Following a total lunar eclipse that took place on November 8, 2008, quite a few UFO reports were sent to me and many other researchers. This eclipse was well publicized and the number of people watching the sky at night was considerably greater than any other time. Since most of the populace is not familiar with the celestial sphere, common artificial or natural objects are often mistaken as UFOs. After reading at least seventy-two reports, it was obvious the majority of them were simple misidentifications of stars, planets, and one of the thousands of satellites in orbit around Earth.

A total lunar eclipse is very mysterious looking, especially when the disk of the moon turns red. While observing an event like this, the mind is altered. Events and objects that are normally looked upon as not being strange suddenly appear mysterious to the observer. People love a mystery and during an eclipse is the best time to create one.

At totality during a solar eclipse, the sky becomes darkened enough to see bright stars and planets. The planet Venus is usually visible during this time and novice eclipse watchers tend to report a bright, silver object that makes small circles in the sky.[148] This movement is caused by a phenomenon known as autokinetic motion and is inside the human brain, not up in the sky.[149] My conclusion on this matter is there is not an increase of UFO sightings during a lunar or solar eclipse. However, this may not be true for other types of paranormal phenomena.

Ghost Hunting During a Total Lunar Eclipse

During the lunar eclipse of November, 2008, I was invited by two paranormal researchers to join them on an investigation at a local home

---

148   Although most reports during a solar eclipse are Venus, the objects photographed by my friend definitely were not.

149   Autokinetic motion effect is a phenomenon of human visual perception in which a stationary, small point of light in an otherwise dark or featureless environment appears to move.

that had experienced episodes of poltergeist activity over the previous several years. These two "ghost hunters" are good guys, but a little too influenced by the *Ghost Hunters* show on cable television. They have always been fans of the show and emulate their heroes to the point where they dress and act like their role models during an investigation. They wanted to do an investigation of this particular home during the lunar eclipse since they believed the chances of documenting paranormal activity would be greater. The owners of the home were fully cooperative and wanted to find out if their home was really haunted. After interviewing the owners of the home and obtaining a long background history of the events that allegedly took place, I personally was not convinced what they described was paranormal in nature. My companions on the other hand thought every incident they mentioned was the result of a ghost or other supernatural force.

Oftentimes ghost hunters will use a digital thermal indicator, which is a device that gives you an accurate measurement of the air temperature within a volume of about 17–23 square centimeters. Most ghost hunters believe that when the temperature drops, some type of invisible entity is drawing energy to use it in some way. Often when paranormal investigators—especially ghost hunters—use this device they get all excited if the temperature drops 2 or 3 degrees. This temperature variation as they move from place to place in the room is quite normal, especially when approaching a poorly insulated window on a chilly night.

As my two fellow investigators walked around the house using a digital thermal device, there was a 5-degree drop in temperature in a matter of seconds. They both got very excited and started bumping their hips together and high-fiving each other, saying how they proved that paranormal events take place during an eclipse. They then pulled out their recorders and tried to contact the "spirit" by asking the same old questions they heard from their television role models: "Who is there? Do you want to talk with us? Give us a sign!"

The ghost hunters were quite disillusioned when I pointed out the reason for the temperature drop was not the result of a ghost or some other type of spirit, but an open window. It seems that due to their excitement they didn't notice (or want to notice) the window was open in the dark room. The cool autumn air caused the reading to drop as they moved closer to the "haunted area." If the lights were on, this person would have caught the mistake, but these errors are rarely corrected and many investigators document a temperature change as a true paranormal event.

Another device that is popular among paranormal researchers, especially my ghost hunter friends, is the EMF meter.

An EMF meter (or EMF detector) is a scientific instrument for measuring electromagnetic fields or the change in an electromagnetic field over time at different locations. There are many different types of EMF meters, but the two most common are the single-axis and tri-axis meters.

Single-axis meters are cheaper than tri-axis meters, but take longer to complete a survey because the device only measures one dimension of the field. Tri-axis instruments have to be tilted and turned on all three axes to obtain a full measurement.

Many paranormal researchers don't know how to use them. Normally they will stand facing in one direction, or axis, and as they move the reading goes higher. When this takes place they think that a ghost is standing in that direction. When they move the meter in a different direction, the reading drops.

During the investigation they did get some interesting readings on the EMF detector, but later I was able to time their readings with the homeowner operating the washing machine. The EMF device is sensitive to the electrometric fields produced in home wiring and all types of electronic equipment and appliances. Sorry guys, not a ghost this time—just the washer going into spin cycle!

My companions would not accept my explanation for the EMF readings and were sure they proved there was a connection between paranormal activity and the eclipsed moon. When you want to believe too much, you lose your objectivity as a researcher-investigator. Take it from me—been there, done that, and had to learn the hard way! Although several noted paranormal investigators will support the theory that strange phenomena take place more frequently during a lunar or solar eclipse, I believe there is no evidence at all.

The Great American Eclipse

The August 21, 2017, total eclipse of the sun was an event that many Americans were waiting for in eager anticipation since the last one visible from the contiguous United States took place on Monday, February 26, 1979. Millions of "eclipse glasses" were being sold across the country, and as the time of the event came closer, they escalated in price.

This solar eclipse was highly publicized and became the most observed in the history of the United States. Millions of people flocked to South Carolina with newly purchased telescopes, cameras, and camping gear as it was in the path of totality. Interviews by nationwide television clearly showed an atmosphere of excitement, and most reported they felt incredibly good with a great deal of energy. I also felt this soon after waking up in the morning. The air seemed charged and it was as if the universe had infused not only energy in my body, but also a feeling of well-being and euphoria in my mind.

I was sponsoring a free observation session for local residents, offering not only filters for eye protection, but also a low power view through a number of telescopes. From my location in the Northeast, only 68 percent of the sun was covered, but that did not stop people from coming to view this great spectacle of nature. Despite some high clouds, there were close to eighty people in attendance.

During the eclipse many reported the same energetic and euphoric feeling. Was there some invisible force being emitted from this rare celestial alignment or was it just excitement induced by the eclipse? Whatever the cause, it was very real and affected everyone present in a positive way. I then remembered a story told to me back in 1993 by my late friend Charlie, last of the great Algonquin medicine men.

According to one of many Algonquin legends about solar eclipses, the sun represented the father of the universe and the moon was the mother. Although they were separated every once in a while they would meet in the daylight sky and consummate their marriage. The energy of their union would spread to the earth and be absorbed by all living things. This invisible force would help heal the sick, make people and animals fertile, cause plants to produce more fruits and vegetables, and give people a feeling of goodness and well-being.

Some might say the belief above is just a myth told to entertain a technologically underdeveloped society and has no scientific foundation, but after witnessing the effects the eclipse had on people, not only in attendance at my event but across the country, it's clear that some power, energy, or force was present.

12

Planetary and Lunar Alignments

Tracking the movements of objects on the celestial sphere was always an important function of priests, astrologers, and (in a more modern time) astronomers. In days of old, carved standing stones were set upright or on a specific angle to line up with the sun, moon, naked-eye planets, and some of the brighter stars. It was believed their positions on the celestial sphere at certain times of the year were important to the welfare of the people.

Although the stars on the celestial sphere kept fixed positions as they moved from east to west, the planets and the moon changed considerably in relation to the stars. If a bright planet went behind or was close to the moon, it was considered to be a sign from a supernatural being. Also, if two or more planets appeared close together in the sky or at specific angles to each other, it was thought to herald a great event or a series of impending important changes for the people of Earth.

These less common and sometimes rare alignments in the night sky are called a conjunction and an occultation. Although the moon frequently occults stars and planets, a planet occulting another planet is a very rare event. This can only take place when a planet that is closer to Earth moves in front of a planet further away. It has happened in recorded history and was always viewed by astrologers and mystics as a sign of an important event that was to change the course of human history.

To civilizations of the past, occultations were wondrous and sometimes fearful events. If by chance an earthquake or a severe storm took place before or after an occultation of Venus or Jupiter by the moon, it was usually seen as the cause of this coincidental natural disaster.

Today, we have lost our fear of these celestial alignments since we now understand why they take place. Although planetary conjunctions and lunar occultations are of little interest to the general populace of the twenty-first century, these celestial events still play an important role in modern astronomy, astrology, and the mystical arts. By the way, if you are into photography, these heavenly configurations make fantastic art photographs suitable for framing.

Occultation

The word "occult" is used to describe something being blocked or covered. An incident that is said to be occult in nature actually refers to an event that temporally covers or blocks our normal reality. A true paranormal event is acknowledged as being occult in nature. Mystics are said to study the occult because they deal with knowledge that is outside our normal reality.

An astronomical occultation takes place when a farther and apparently smaller object on the celestial sphere (as seen from Earth) moves behind an apparently larger and closer one. An example would be a bright naked-eye planet moving in front of a star, or a star or planet being eclipsed by the moon.

Although a planetary–star occultation had little impact on the belief and mythology of prescientific cultures, a lunar occultation involving a dazzling planet like Venus, Jupiter, Saturn, or Mars played an important role in the development of the spiritual beliefs and prophecy of many cultures.

Since the moon orbits Earth from west to east, its apparent motion on the celestial sphere is slower when compared to the stars and planets. This lunar orbital movement allows the moon to move in front of a planet or star, giving the impression that it vanished in the sky.

The most beautiful planetary occultation by the moon that I have observed using my telescope took place on December 26, 1978, at 6:00 a.m. EST. As Venus, which was quite bright at the time, slowly went behind the lunar limb, it seemed to almost freeze on the curve of the crescent moon. At this time Venus looked like a large lit dome on the lunar surface. As the planet slowly vanished behind the moon, I was awarded by seeing the last flicker of reflected light from Venus sparkling through the lower lunar valleys. Then it was gone! The emergence of Venus from the "darkened" side of the moon was truly remarkable and occurred without warning at 8:02 a.m. With the optical assistance of my eight-inch telescope, Venus was still visible in the morning sky until 11:00 a.m., then it was lost in the glare of the sun.

A celestial event like the one described above has taken place numerous times in the past 5,000 years and was witnessed and recorded by many cultures since 2,000 BC. What's really amazing is that the Druids, Greeks, Chinese, and Persian astrologer-astronomers were able to predict a lunar–Venus occultation with considerable accuracy. Ancient civilizations, including the tribes of Africa and the Americas, believed the moon swallowed Venus and then coughed it out on the other side.

In AD 150 astronomer-astrologer Claudius Ptolemy explained the event by simply saying Venus was farther away from Earth, and as a result, it sometimes moves behind the moon. I'm sure many others also figured this out long before the time of Ptolemy, but he seemed to have always gotten credit for discoveries and ideas that today we know were the work of previous Greek philosophers, astrologers, and scientists who lived before his time.

Aztec Myth of the Evening and Morning Star

While living in San Antonio, Texas, I would often attend lectures on Mexicana-Aztec mythology held at the museums and cultural center. San Antonio has a large Mexican American population and many of the people are not only descendants of the Spaniards, but also the Aztecs. Since the Aztecs were avid stargazers, they have many legends of the celestial sphere that have been passed down through the ages.

One Aztec legend involving the moon and Venus was of Tlahuizcal-pantecuhtli, who is the heavenly personification of the "shining dawn star," which is the planet Venus as seen in the morning in the eastern sky. Tlahuizcalpantecuhtli was also a manifestation of Quetzalcoatl and was a guardian of the people against the many evil gods and other deities. His brother Xolotl was the planet Venus as the evening star when seen in the western sky.

The Aztec legend says when the evening or morning star was in the sky, the power coming from these gods kept all evil supernatural beings at bay and stripped them of their power. However, when one of the two were not in the sky, evil was allowed to roam freely and the Aztec priests had to pray or sacrifice to other gods to keep the land safe, but this protection against these evil forces was not guaranteed.

The situation became even worse when Venus (the two gods mentioned above) was occulted by the moon during the evening or morning. At this time their ability to protect the earth was completely neutralized and evil spirits and dark gods were unstoppable. The most powerful of these dark deities stored the tenfold power increase at this time to use in the future to destroy the evening and morning star and the people of the earth.

According to legend, the evil gods and their servants were able to achieve considerable extra power during an occultation by the death of human beings. Mexican historians suspect there might have been secret Aztec cults that offered human sacrifice during an occultation of

Venus by the moon to these evil gods in exchange for power and other favors. The scary thing is that the presenter at the lecture mentioned to the audience that at least one of these cults might still exist in Mexico.

When Venus emerged from behind the moon and was once again brilliant and dominant in the sky, the evil gods and their minions would become incapacitated until the next cycle called for human sacrifice, which was equivalent to every 52 years on our calendar.

Just like the dire prophecies of many religions, the Aztecs believed a horde of evil always lies in the darkness waiting to once again achieve power great enough to destroy their adversaries and rule the universe.

It's clear from the history of the Roman Catholic Church that such dark prophecies were used during the Middle Ages and Renaissance to control the people of Europe and keep them loyal to the church. This is a strategy that was widely utilized by many priests and religious leaders of every faith in human history, and it is still being used today.

Planetary Conjunctions

The planets of our solar system all revolve around the sun, and since the inner planets have a smaller orbit than the outer planets, their positions in relation to each other is constantly changing. These changing planetary configurations are something stargazers have noted since 3000 BC.

A conjunction takes place when two or more planets are apparently close together in the sky as viewed from the Earth's surface. When you also include the moon in the scenario it adds beauty and marvel to the spectacle. The most common historical deception of a planetary-lunar conjunction as a symbol is the crescent moon with a bright stellar object that many identify with the planet Venus.

The origin of the symbol of the crescent moon in conjunction with a bright starlike object is difficult to trace. Ancient depictions of the pictogram always show the crescent with horns pointing upward and an eight-ray star placed inside the crescent. In the first century BC, it was a Byzantium symbol associated with its patron goddesses Selene,

Artemis, and Hecate, and during the Roman Empire it was used as a depiction of the moon goddesses Luna and Diana.

In the mid-twentieth century, the symbol came to be interpreted as the representation of Islam. The New Encyclopedia of Islam states that "in the language of conventional symbols, the crescent and star have become the symbols of Islam as much as the cross is the symbol of Christianity." However, Islamic publications emphasize that the crescent and star is rejected by many Muslim scholars. "The faith of Islam historically had no symbol, and many refuse to accept it." The flags of many Islamic nations do in fact show the crescent moon with a bright star. Although no one can say for sure if the flags of the Ottoman Empire and the Islamic countries Turkey, Libya, and Pakistan represent a conjunction of the moon and Venus, the similarity cannot be denied.

The former Proctor & Gamble logo was a crescent moon in conjunction with thirteen stars. For years the company was accused by Christian fanatics of supporting occult beliefs, saying the horned crescent moon and the number thirteen on their logo represented Satan. Finally, one day the company's board of directors just got fed up with the bad publicity and changed their corporation's logo.

Astrology, UFOs, and Planetary Conjunctions

To modern astrologers planets that form a conjunction represent energies that are united. The power of the planets in this celestial alignment is blended together in harmony, thus their influence is increased considerably. When someone's chart is being prepared, the astrologer will check carefully to see what planets were in the sky at the time of birth and what specific angles they formed.

When two or more bright planets are close together in the night sky, it often results in an increase of UFO reports. Witnesses will report two bright objects in the sky that appear night after night and slowly move apart. In 1980 people in Connecticut, New York, and Massachusetts were calling the local police and airports because they saw two UFOs hovering and moving slowly overhead. These UFOs turned out to be a conjunction of the planets Jupiter and Saturn. Although many witnesses to the event accepted the story, there were those who thought the government was covering up and were sure that what they saw could not have been planets because they "never saw stars or planets that close together."

Unfortunately there are UFO investigators who want to believe every report that comes their way is an alien spaceship and will add facts to their reports to make a very explainable sighting like the one above seem unexplainable.

A conjunction of two or more planets will last several days before the angular separation between them as seen from Earth increases. Sometimes two planets move apart and then once again align to form a new conjunction. This has taken place many times involving outer planets like Jupiter and Saturn. This apparent backward motion is caused by Earth passing the two planets in space.

A conjunction of Jupiter and Saturn is thought to be of great importance by mystics and astrologers and is often referred to as a "great conjunction." Great conjunctions are less impressive than eclipses, comets, and novas, nevertheless they have been the focus of celestial omens of salvation and doom by many.

The 1583 conjunction of Jupiter and Saturn was widely believed to herald apocalyptic changes to the world with the fall of kings and countries and the emergence of a new world leader. By 1603 nothing of significance happened to change the world so the public lost interest quickly in the doomsday predication and it was soon forgotten. Sounds a great deal like what we experienced in our time with the dire predications of 2000, 2012, and the Blood Moon Prophecies.

The last Great Conjunction of Jupiter and Saturn took place on May 31, 2000, while the next one will be in late December 2020. Close conjunctions of Jupiter and Saturn, the two largest planets in the solar system, take place about every 20 years.

On December 31, 2012, the planets Mercury, Venus, Jupiter, Mars, Uranus, and Neptune aligned in the morning sky, giving shivers to those who expected the end of the world, but again nothing happened. Many would like to think of this generation as being informed and educated, but we see how easily we succumb to superstition and fear, and in many cases these uncertainties of our existence are connected to the night sky.

Star of Wonder, Star of Light

A grand conjunction of the two planets Jupiter and Saturn that took place on September 25, 7 BC, is now thought by many astronomers to have been responsible for the so-called "Christmas Star" or "Star of Bethlehem." At that time the two planets were less than one degree apart (about two full moons). At first this made sense to me since this celestial alignment coincided with political events at the time of Jesus, so it warranted further investigation.

Using my computer's planetarium program, I went back to that time in history and took a close look at this conjunction. It is difficult to accept that a person even with poor eyesight would see the two planets as one.

The Star of Bethlehem was described as being one bright object. If Jupiter and Saturn were responsible for the manifestation then they would have had to been very close together with Jupiter nearly occulting Saturn. An occultation of these two planets has not taken place in the last 6,000 years and the next one will occur in the year 7541. In my opinion the theory of Saturn and Jupiter being responsible for the Star of Bethlehem can be dismissed.

Astrologers at the time of the birth of Jesus were excellent observers and recorded the conjunction of Jupiter and Saturn as two separate objects in the sky. However, they could have seen the celestial alignment as heralding the birth of a great leader. This conjunction took place in the constellation of Pisces, the fish, which was identified with the country of Judea and then early Christianity; Saturn represented a great teacher and Jupiter kingship. The three Magi, who are now believed to have been astrologers, may have interpreted the event as saying that the king of the Jews who will be a great teacher and leader is born in Judea. During the Middle Ages the Roman Catholic Church condemned astrology as being demonic, so the three Magi were changed to three kings.

Another planetary conjunction that is theorized by astronomers to have been the Star of Bethlehem took place on June 17, 3 BC, and involved Venus and Jupiter, which at the time were apparently close to the star Regulus in the constellation of Leo, the lion. This explanation still has many supporters since the conjunction would have appeared in the east (as stated in the Bible) and it involved two of the brightest planets as seen from Earth. From the three Magi's point of view, the conjunction could have been interpreted as: Jupiter, kingship; Venus, love, compassion, peace, the god of the universe who protects us from evil; Regulus, the star of kings; and Leo, the lion of Judea. In other words; the king of the Jews who will possess great power and compassion and bring peace to the world is born in Judea.

The appearance of this conjunction however does not coincide with political events during the birth of Jesus which are well documented. Once again from the information obtained during my research it is apparent this explanation can also be discounted.

Although the theories above cannot offer a suitable answer to my age-old quest of solving the mystery of the Christmas Star, they do rationalize why mystics of 7 BC and 3 BC could have interpreted the celestial events as signifying something of great importance.

In the world today there are scientists, mystics, astrologers and paranormal investigators who believe they can offer explanations for the Star of Bethlehem, which include an alien spacecraft, a manifestation of God, a paranormal burst of energy from another dimension, a rogue comet, a supernova, a sign from Satan, the list goes on. There are also agnostics who believe the Star of Wonder never existed and it was made up to give Jesus a divine image by connecting him to a sign in the heavens.

From the evidence we can conclude that the manifestation that appeared in the sky around the time of the birth of Jesus Christ cannot be explained with the facts we have today. Perhaps solving this mystery is not such a good idea since it has become a significant part of our culture and has brought a feeling of peace and happiness to countless people over the centuries. The true solution to the riddle of the Star of Bethlehem can only be found in the faith of the true believer.

The Harmonic Convergence

In 1977 I met with a woman who claimed she had extraterrestrial contact with aliens. Some of the experiences she had were positive, however some were quite negative. These alleged contacts were sometimes humanlike aliens that she described as being "incredible beautiful" and sometimes reptilian in nature and not very nice. Although this person told me her name given at birth, she preferred to be called Evening Star, since she believed this was her name in a past incarnation on another planet.

There are quite a number of contactees who go by the name of Evening Star and some of them have approached me over the years to tell me their story. This Eve was from a very wealthy family and her goal in life was to travel the world looking for spiritual enlightenment and to return to her home in the stars.

Although Eve was about thirty years old at the time, she could have passed for an eighteen-year-old and her physical appearance resembled the Nordic-type aliens that she claimed contact with. Eve was a very intelligent and attractive woman who dressed like one of the last hippies of the sixties. She was a financial backer and dedicated follower of Timothy Leary.

Although we only had one meeting, Eve was a talker, and for several hours, she described her experiences with the aliens in vivid detail.

Finally, she mentioned the "Harmonic Convergence," which was going to take place in 1987, and she felt strongly that "space brothers and sisters" from the Pleiades were going to make a dramatic appearance during the event at major psychic energy centers of our planet.

Eve was planning to go globe hopping on and around the Harmonic Convergence to experience the full effect of this "once in a thousand years happening."

My question to her was, "What makes this time so special?"

Her reply was, "Most of the planets will be aligned and the energy will take our planet into a new era of peace as we begin the countdown to the year 2012 when the world as we know it will transform into a new age."

Eve firmly believed (as well as hundreds if not thousands of others) the planets in this special configuration would provide the catalytic energy required to begin the transformation of our world and its people to a higher realm of existence.

The experiences of Evening Star would fill the content of several books, however it is not my objective to present the saga of another contactee whom my late friend and co-investigator Fred Dennis called "Tinker Bell." It is important that we explore the Harmonic Convergence and its connection to a grand alignment of the planets that took place during that time.

The Harmonic Convergence was a globally-coordinated event that brought together people who had an interest in the mystic arts and other New Age beliefs. It took place on August 16–17, 1987, during an alignment of six planets in the solar system. This was no coincidence, since the organizers not only timed the event with the Maya calendar but also the positions of the sun, moon, and six planets forming what they called the "grand trine."

The Harmonic Convergence was supposed to have resulted in a great shift in Earth's energy from warlike to peaceful. The Harmonic

Convergence was also thought to signify the start of the final 25-year countdown to the end of the Mayan calendar in 2012 and the beginning of a new 5,125-year cycle. During the 25-year cleansing period, evils of the modern world such as war, materialism, violence, hate, and negative thoughts would end with the Mayan principle of the birth of the sixth sun on December 21, 2012.

Despite the claims of the organizers as this being a "rare celestial event," astronomers insisted the positions of the six planets during the convergence was not unique, since it had taken place on numerous occasions in the past 2000 years. Many astrologers at the time of the convergence did not consider trines of this type to be anything of significance, so the notion of a shift in world energy was disregarded.

An important part of the Harmonic Convergence was the gathering of true believers at power centers around the globe such as Mount Shasta in California, Mount Fuji in Japan, Sedona in Arizona, Stonehenge, and the Giza pyramid, just to name a few. The belief was that if 144,000 people assembled at these power centers and meditated for peace it would help the arrival of the new era and act like a beacon for the space brothers to land.

So what took place as a result of the Harmonic Convergence? The answer is nothing at all, except a great number of wishful thinkers who got together with kindred spirits and had a great time imagining all kinds of metaphysical experiences while meditating under the "grand trine."

After the Harmonic Convergence, eight people who attended wrote me and claimed they had contact with Nordic-type extraterrestrials several days after the event. The stories of the experiences of these people were interesting, but since all of them came from the western part of the United States, a follow-up investigation could not be accomplished.

Although most people that did attend were disappointed that no spaceships appeared, it seems some had to invent a grand personal revelation to make the happening mean something personally worthwhile and to prove to others the Harmonic Convergence was not just a gigantic waste of time and money. The only ones who can really claim that they benefited from the event were the organizers.

The Jupiter Effect

The Jupiter Effect is a book published in 1974 by author John Gribbin in which he predicted that an alignment of the planets of the solar system, which was to take place during March of 1982, would generate great catastrophic events on planet Earth, including a powerful earthquake of the San Andreas Fault, volcanic eruptions, tidal waves, magnetic storms, and severe weather. Like all books that focus on disaster and doomsday predications, it became a bestseller and the publisher used every facet of the media to promote the idea.

During the 1970s and early 1980s, the book caused quite a sensation and resulted in many television documentaries and copycat publications. Evangelists of independent churches also jumped on the bandwagon to use the Jupiter effect as another platform to predict the end of the world.

Astronomers and astrologers had known for some time that there would be a grand alignment of the planets in 1982 with all nine on one side of the sun but didn't think too much about it. Although astronomers assured the public that the planets in such a configuration would have no effect on the surface of Earth, there was still concern from the populace on a global scale.

In the book the author proposed that the combined gravitational influence of the sun and Jupiter would act as a trigger to initiate a series of global disasters. What the author of *The Jupiter Effect* did not mention is there was an even closer alignment of the planets in the year AD 1128 with no record of any devastating effects on Earth.

When March of 1982 arrived, nothing out of the ordinary took place; the entire month was calm. Toward the final months of 1982,

Gribben published another book called The Jupiter Effect Reconsidered where he stated that the Jupiter effect actually took place in 1980 and was responsible for the eruption of Mount St. Helens. Needless to say the book was not as successful as the first and finally all the hoopla about the Jupiter effect was finally put to rest.

In 1999 Mr. Gribbin admitted that he was sorry to have had anything to do with the Jupiter effect, but he never stated his theory was incorrect, a theory which was more hype than science.

During the planetary alignment–conjunction of March of 1982, the planets were much closer together than the alignment that took place during the 1987 Harmonic Convergence. So why didn't the organizers of the event stage it in 1982 since the "energy" from the planets would have been theoretically much greater? The reason eludes me since the people running the show never responded to numerous inquires sent by me. It might have had something to do with the impact of the publicity that the Jupiter effect was getting and perhaps they thought people might be too afraid to attend. The other reason why the Harmonic Convergence was not held during the time of the Jupiter effect may lie in a dark prophecy that was circulating at the time that centered on the 1982 alignment of the planets.

A Dark Omen

As many of my readers know, over the past forty-plus years I have investigated claims of the paranormal and also was able to move freely in the inner circle of many groups and cults that practice the mystical arts. Although I am not a member of any cult or group (or a follower), I have been allowed to view ceremonies and privileged to gain knowledge and information that has significantly helped me in my research.

There exists a global cult of the "dark mystic arts" that operates in secret, and at least once a year, on February 1, has a large gathering and performs a Black Mass. For the most part they can be called Satan worshippers, but their beliefs are much more detailed and complex to focus their energies on one group of fallen angels. It is not the purpose of this book to explore this group's purpose or activities, but their governing elders did tell me something quite interesting that has a connection to the 1982 planetary alignment.

They believe the 1982 grand planetary configuration was a celestial sign to herald the birth of the Antichrist. This cult believes that the sole purpose of their organization is to prepare the Antichrist for this world with manpower, money, and knowledge. They claim to have already manipulated leaders of the governments of various countries to place him in a religious and political position of power. If this were true, then this supposed superhuman whose coming is foretold in the book of Revelation would be 36 years old at the publication of this book. The cult also believes the following passage from Revelation refers to this alignment as the sign in the sky heralding the birth of their messiah.

A great sign appeared in heaven, a woman clothed with the sun, with the moon under her feet and a crown of twelve stars on her head. She was pregnant and cried out in pain as she was about to give birth. Then another sign appeared in heaven: an enormous red dragon with seven heads and ten horns and seven crowns on its heads. Its tail swept a third of the stars out of the sky and flung them to the earth. The dragon stood in front of the woman who was about to give birth, so that it might devour her child the moment he was born. She gave birth to a son, a male child, who will rule all the nations with an iron scepter. (Revelation: 12)

I personally do not believe this, but it always makes me wonder why a group of intelligent, successful people would dedicate their entire lives to a few passages in several ancient books and be so greatly influenced by a natural celestial alignment, which in my opinion has no supernatural origin or significance.

13

Comet Phobia

No other celestial object has created more fear in the mind of humans than the display of a bright comet appearing in the sky. Comets have always been thought to be harbingers of doom and even in modern times, despite our scientific awareness, the ghostly sight of these rogue objects of our solar system still generate a deep-rooted feeling of apprehension.

Human beings feel secure when they are in a familiar environment that can be controlled. When change takes place, many are overwhelmed by a feeling of insecurity, anxiety, and a deep subconscious fear that can express itself in many different ways.

Comets appear as vaporous apparitions in the night sky, silent and very mysterious. When a comet becomes visible, the sight of it challenges our sense of security, since the night sky, a predictable part of our life, has been altered.

To the ancient Greeks, comets looked like hairy stars; the word comet actually means "hair" in the ancient Grecian language. In the twenty-first century, we still use this word to describe one of nature's most fantastic and bizarre heavenly displays.

Comets were recorded by most global cultures as far back as 467 BC. Chinese astrologers in 270 BC called them "broom stars" and believed their appearance was a ghastly sign that the moon, sun, and earth were in danger. They performed special comet rituals and prayers to the gods of earth and the sky to keep the comet from striking the ground and splitting the planet in two. In Medieval Europe the Roman Catholic Church believed comets were tortured souls who escaped hell and were trying to make their way to heaven, only to be cast down once again.

The Hindu people of the Bronze Age thought comets were the power-rays of great supernatural beings that were very angry with the mortals of Earth. During its appearance the inhabitants of India would bring gifts, gold, precious gems, and food to the temples to appease these beings. According to the legend, the gifts always vanished shortly after the comet was no longer visible in the sky. No doubt the offerings were taken by priests and distributed to a select few.

The ancient Romans believed a comet was a supernatural prophetic sign that meant a great leader would die or be killed. In 44 BC during the funeral games of Julius Caesar, a bright comet was visible in the sky. This sign in the heavens was used by his great nephew and adopted son Octavius to convince the people of Rome and the Senate that Caesar was a god and ascending to the heavens. He also used this celestial apparition to claim the family of Caesar was also of divine lineage, thus securing his place as Augustus Caesar, the first emperor of Rome.

Roman historians have speculated that if not for this comet, Julius Caesar would not have been given a divine position by the Romans and perhaps completely forgotten. Today almost everyone in the world knows the name Julius Caesar, not only from literature, academic books, and movies, but also from many plays that date as far back as AD 100. It's clear that the appearance of the comet in 44 BC changed the future history of the Roman Empire.

During the apparition of a bright comet over Rome, Emperor Nero (AD 37–68) had all his possible successors and enemies killed so the prophecy that stated "a great leader will fall when the comet appears in the heavens" would not come true.

From ancient Greece to the medieval times, comets were seen as the representation of evil, which brought forth natural disasters, sickness, and war. In the "Epic of Gilgamesh," a comet appears in the sky just before a great flood, which devastates the earth.

In AD 684 Halley's Comet passed close by Earth and was so prominent it was even visible during the day. While the comet was in the sky, Europe was overwhelmed by severe storms and finally an outbreak of bubonic plague. The church told the people the comet was an angel of death sent by God to punish the people who did not follow the doctrines of the church.

The Bayeux Tapestry, which commemorates the Norman Conquest of England in 1066, shows a comet in the sky just before the Battle of Hastings. Mystics at the time warned that the appearance of the comet meant that King Harold would lose his kingdom to William, Duke of Normandy; in this case the prophecy came true. This comet was quite bright and must have been a fearful as well as a spectacular sight in the sky. Today, using high-tech computer planetarium programs, we know for sure the great comet of 1066 was actually Halley's Comet!

To prescientific societies the appearance of a comet upset the balance of the heavens and they believed it was something to fear. The only religious cult group that has a positive view of comets comes from a small radical sect of twentieth-century born-again Christians located in New York State. The pastor told his followers that comets were the chariots that angels use to travel from heaven to earth and then back to heaven. The appearance of a comet in the sky means good fortune for all. During the apparition of a bright comet the pastor and his group would go out to a field that has an unobstructed view of the horizon and spend hours praying to the comet. Their comet prayer sessions and rituals are very similar to a number of cult groups in the Northeast who are definitely not Christians. This belief in the positive aspects of a comet is 180 degrees from how the rest of the superstitious world perceived them.[150]

Science Comes to the Rescue

For thousands of years people of most European countries believed comets were a phenomenon that took place in the atmosphere, and once they appeared, the same comet never returned. In 1578 the Danish astronomer-astrologer Tycho Brahe proposed that comets were farther from Earth than the moon and they were composed of glowing gases. Tycho's theory of comets really wasn't a great epiphany, since more than once he observed a comet moving behind the moon and also noticed that as the comet got closer to the sun it got brighter and its "tail" longer. In the early eighteenth century, Sir Isaac Newton studied the movement of comets and came to the conclusion they travel around the sun in elliptical orbits just like the planets. The only difference is comets had a more eccentric orbit, which would take many of them very far from the sun at aphelion. He reasoned since comets were members of our solar system, the same comet could circle the sun many times and be visible from Earth more than once. Inspired by Newton's theory, Edmond Halley, a professor of math at Cambridge in England, decided to put Newton's theory to the test.

Edmond Halley began a search of historical records for bright comets. He noticed that one particular brilliant comet was reported in 1531, then again in 1607, and finally in 1682 with a time span of 75 to 76 years between apparitions. He concluded it must be the same comet and used Newton's theoretical mathematics to predict this comets return in 1758. Unfortunately, Halley passed away sixteen years before he could see if his prediction came true. Astronomers of the mid-eighteenth century

---

150   Information from my files investigated by this author in 1996 and 1997 with the appearance of comets Hale-Bopp and Hyakutake.

were aware of Newton and Halley's work and were anxious to see if the prediction of the appearance of this bright "periodic comet" would come true. Then in December of 1758 on Christmas Eve, the comet was spotted, proving these strange celestial objects are indeed part of our solar system and the same comet can be seen many times in the course of human history. The "great comet," which we know today as Halley's Comet, appeared as predicted again in 1834, 1910, and finally in 1986. The next predicted apparition of the comet will be July 28, 2061.

Comets like Encke, Tempel, and Halley stay within the confines of the planets and are referred to as short-period comets, while others like Hale-Bopp and Hyakutake take thousands of years to orbit the sun. Comets come from two locations in our solar system; the first is an area just beyond Neptune called the Kuiper belt, the second is a region about ten billion miles from the sun called the Oort cloud. It is estimated that there are billions of comets in the Oort cloud that form a ring around the solar system that, to an approaching deep-space traveler, may appear like a cloud. There are also some comets that have been knocked out of their original orbit and pass Earth's orbital plane more frequently than Halley. Most of these comets are small and quite faint when they are at their closest approach to Earth.

By the end of the eighteenth century, the study and observation of comets became the work and responsibility of the scientist rather than the priest, astrologer, and mystic. Astronomers made the people aware that comets were not the result of supernatural beings, nor are they bad omens, but natural members of our solar system. This new understanding of comets did little to quench the fear of the general populace when one appeared in the sky; this feeling of trepidation is still with us today.

This fear of comets might be justified since if a large comet hit our planet, the results would be devastating and could possibly result in a global extinction event. Even a small comet striking our planet would release energy equivalent to hundreds of nuclear bombs. Not to worry, according to astronomers the chances of this taking place in the lifetime of a twenty-first century human being are astronomical, but it has happened in the past and will again in the future.

Anatomy of a Comet

Comets are composed mostly of water, carbon dioxide (in the form of dry ice), methane, nitrogen, ammonia ice mixed with smaller amounts of dust, and low-density rock. In the early twentieth century, astronomer Dr. Fred Whipple [151] described a comet as being like a "dirty snowball."

While teaching sixth-grade astronomy, comets were always an important part of the curriculum. To give my students a better understanding of comets, we would build them in class. It's quite easy to construct a hands-on laboratory representation of a comet by mixing sand with water to make a mixture wet enough where the sand can be made into a small ball. Next take a small rock and mold the sand around it. Then make a snow (or crushed ice) and sand mixture and wrap it around the sand ball. Finally, you take just snow and pack it around the sand and snow mixture and gently form it into a sphere. You now have a comet.

The main parts of the comet are the nucleus, coma, and tails.[152] The nucleus can range in size from 1 to 40 kilometers. The comet with the largest recorded nucleus was Hale-Bopp (1995), a whopping 40 kilometers (25 miles). If a comet with a nucleus this size ever hit Earth, it would be the greatest catastrophe in human history.

---

151   Fred Whipple (November 5, 1906–August 30, 2004) was an American astronomer at the Harvard College Observatory. During his career he discovered several asteroids and comets and came up with the "dirty snowball" theory to describe the composition of comets. Dr. Whipple was known as the foremost expert on comets in the field of astronomy.

152   The nucleus is composed of rock, ice, and dust. The coma is a surface of ice with an ice cloud around it. The dust tail is composed of tiny sand-like particles and gas, while the plasma tail is ionized (charged) gases. Sometimes the tails are referred to together, as one.

As a comet approaches the orbit of Mars, the sun begins to heat it, causing the ices to sublimate.[153] This can create geysers on the surface of the comet. The mixture of ice crystals and dust blow away from the comet nucleus due to the solar wind,[154] creating the dust and plasma tails. The dust tail is what we normally see when we view comets from Earth. The plasma tail is difficult to see but shows up in time-lapse photography and digital enhancement very well. The tail of the comet always points away from the sun. When a comet swings around the sun and is leaving the inner solar system, it appears to chase its tail.

The tail of a comet, which is composed mostly of dust particles, is left behind, and if our planet should pass through it as it orbits the sun, a meteor shower takes place. There are fifteen bright meteor showers a year and many have been identified with the debris leftover from the tails of known comets.

Each time a comet orbits the sun it loses a percentage of its mass. If it has a short period and frequents the inner solar system, it will eventually break up and disintegrate or lose all its ice to become a small rocky asteroid-like object. Theoretically, a short periodic comet like Halley will be less spectacular each time it is visible in the sky.

Comets played an important role in the formation of the solar system and it is believed that a great deal of the water we have on Earth came from comet impacts billions of years ago. There is also some speculation that organic material necessary for the formation of life may have arrived here during this time of impact, since carbon-based molecules have been found in comets.

---

153   A change in state from a solid to a gas.

154   A stream of particles emitting off the sun that has considerable pressure. It has been responsible for satellites falling from orbit and was one of the reasons why the space station Skylab fell to Earth in the mid-seventies.

Astrology and Comets

When astrologers observe a comet while preparing a chart, they notice its physical characteristics and location on the celestial sphere to determine the scale of its influence. In some cases the color of a comet is noted. If the visual color is similar to a planet's, astrologers consider that that comet might have a similar effect in the sign it appears as the planet would. Astrologers also consider the element of the zodiacal sign in which a comet appears and passes. If a comet passes through a water sign, astrologers believe it might indicate floods, hurricanes, tidal waves, or the oceans in general and perhaps something associated with sea life. A comet passing through a fire sign could mean wars, forest fires, and droughts.

Astrologers of ancient and modern times believe that every kingdom, country, or empire was represented by a sign of the zodiac. For example, Leo was associated with Judea; Aries, England and Israel; Taurus, Ireland and Greece; Gemini, Morocco; Cancer, Scotland, United States, and Belgium. When a comet appeared in the sign of a particular country, it was thought to be a warning that the nation would suffer disasters, war, or plague.

When a vivid comet is near a naked-eye planet or a prominent star, it is thought to impinge on its influence. For example a comet passing Mercury may have a dire effect on transportation. Bridges may collapse, roads wash out, and so on. Astrologers will also consider the direction in which the comet points, since it is believed disaster will follow in that particular bearing. For example if the comet is pointing to a sign of the zodiac represented by Russia, this country may experience a set of disasters and other ill fates in the near future.

Whether or not astrologers can predict dire earthly happenings by the visual appearance and location of a comet on the celestial sphere is a matter of debate. One thing is certain: wars and other terrible things have taken place when a comet appears in the sky. We have to ask ourselves if it is the comet causing this or our own actions using the comet as an excuse to achieve a particular political goal.

The important thing we see here is how the sight of a comet in the sky can affect the judgment, thoughts, and actions of human beings. I have always marveled how the path of history was directed by leaders and monarchs who took the advice of astrologers to make political decisions or go to war. Although the majority of political leaders today claim no connection to astrology, in the 1980s there were a number of stories going around that President and Mrs. Reagan consulted astrologers on a regular basis.[155]

Comet Mind Games

Comets were often used by priests, mystics, religious leaders, and con men to control the way the populace would think. Sometimes their appearance was used to frighten or just make money. It's difficult to prove these actions from ancient apparitions of bright comets, but there are four famous comets that appeared in the twentieth century that brought out the best and worst in human behavior that are very well documented.

Comet Halley

As we learned, comets have been viewed since ancient times as being the bringers of doom and disaster. The appearance of Comet Halley in 1910 was no exception. One would think that twentieth-century people in a scientific society would view the arrival of the comet differently, but that was not the case. Early that year, just before the comet was visible, British newspapers carried a story that the comet was a sign Germany was going to start a terrible war. Four years later World War I began. French and Spanish publications also blamed the approaching comet for severe weather and floods that were taking place in Europe.

---

155   Steven V. Roberts, *New York Times,* May 4, 1988.

In February of 1910, Yerkes Observatory, using a relatively new technique at the time called spectroscopic analysis, had detected cyanogen gas in the comet's tail.[156] They also released orbital data for the comet and reported our planet was going to pass through Halley's tail.[157]

The *New York Times* released the story with a quote from French astronomer Camille Flammarion of the Paris Observatory that stated the gas from Halley's tail "could impregnate the atmosphere and possibly snuff out all life on the planet." The story in the *New York Times* made the public fearful and people were running to fire and police stations asking what they could do to protect themselves and their families.

In response to the media harping on doomsday, famed American astronomer Percival Lowell explained that the gases making up Halley's tail were "so rarefied as to be thinner than any vacuum and no threat to life." Lowell assured the public there was no danger from the tail of Halley and it would pass with no ill effects to planet Earth or its inhabitants.

Despite the reassuring comments from Lowell and other astronomers that there was no danger, the people of the United States were still fearful and decided to take precautions. This opened up the opportunity for con artists and others to exploit the fear in people for profit.

A month before the due date of Halley's Comet, dozens of vendors appeared on the streets selling items of "protection" against the gases of the comet. Con artist vendors offered "anti-comet pills," which when taken would protect the person from the comet's poison gas. The so-called anti-comet pills contained only starch and sugar. People were buying hundreds of gas masks and pigeons; crafty salesman told people the pigeon would die before a person because it would take much less gas to kill it; when the bird dies, it's time to put on the gas mask.

---

156   Cyanogen is a colorless, toxic gas with a strong, foul odor.

157   "Yerkes Observatory Finds Cyanogen in Spectrum of Halley's Comet." *New York Times*, February 8, 1910.

People across North America and the United States began building safe rooms by blocking the windows so no air could get in. Some even dug giant pits in their yard with covers that were water- and air-tight. There were those who believed it was the end of the human race, so for weeks groups of people would have comet parties on rooftops and toast to the arriving comet.

After Halley's Comet passed by Earth in May, the *Chicago Tribune* headline read "We're Still Here." Halley was a spectacular sight and was so bright it could be seen in the daytime. The great comet passed without incidence and the only ill effect it had was that many felt foolish after being manipulated by their fear and take their hard-earned money.

If you ever visit the New York Museum of Natural History, you may find a section that is dedicated to the 1910 apparition of Comet Halley. They still display the newspaper stories, gas masks, and a bottle of the infamous "anti-comet pills," unopened.[158]

In 1986 when Comet Halley once again made its journey into the inner solar system, it was far from Earth and barely visible in the sky. During this recent apparition I gave a presentation on the comet for the Autubon Nature Center in Greenwich, Connecticut, and was quite surprised when hundreds of people showed up to view the comet through ten telescopes set up outside by the Astronomical Society of Greenwich. Although many, including myself, were disappointed in Halley's performance this time around, I can boast to my grandchildren about seeing the famous comet—a once-in-a-lifetime event.

One last interesting note: the renowned writer Mark Twain (Samuel Clemens) often stated that he was born with the comet and would leave with the comet. Twain was born in 1835 when the comet appeared in the sky and died in 1910 as Halley was swinging around the sun and leaving the inner solar system. My friend and mentor astronomer Dr. J. Allen Hynek also told me several times, "Just like Mark Twain, I was

---

158   From the Halley's Comet display, New York Museum of Natural History.

born with the comet and will leave with it." Dr. Hynek was born in 1910 and passed away in 1986.

Comet Kohoutek

Shortly after the discovery of Comet Kohouteck in March of 1973, astronomers calculated the trajectory of its orbit and came to the conclusion it was an object from the Oort cloud with a large nucleus and an orbital period of 75,000 years. Since it was first seen at a great distance from the sun and was an infrequent visitor to the inner solar system, they concluded Comet Kohouteck would become one of the brightest comets ever recorded.

There was a great deal of coverage by the media who christened it "the comet of the century." Amateur astronomers from every part of the world began modifying their telescopes and buying extra equipment in preparation for the arrival of this amazing comet. Kohoutek was the subject of the news almost every night, with each story providing basic comet information and interviews with astronomers and the general population.

Although even the most seasoned astronomers were excited, there was definitely some trepidation in many people, especially in New York City. It wasn't long before the doomsday predications started up again with groups of people walking the streets of NYC dressed in sackcloth with signs saying "The end is coming; the comet is God's messenger of punishment for the human race." Artwork appeared in local newspapers and graffiti on New York City walls showing the comet with a demon-like head ripping the world apart with ghostly hands. The media seemed to be giving more attention to the doomsday fanatics than the astronomers who tried to assure the population that the comet posed no threat to Earth.

In 1973 David Berg, founder of a religious cult called the Children of God, convinced his followers the arrival of Comet Kohoutek foretold a catastrophic doomsday event in the United States. In response to his warning, members of the Children of God fled to existing communes to await the end that never came.[159]

In December of 1973, Comet Kohoutek arrived at perihelion and was nowhere as bright as predicted. Once again there were no great catastrophes in the world as a result of the comet and another doomsday was cancelled. The media seemed quite annoyed with the astronomers who predicted it would be a spectacular sight in the night sky. It was in fact the media, not the astronomers, who hyped up the people with comet fever. In an obvious move to save face, the major television news media began calling Kohoutek "the flop of the century."

After a detailed telescopic study, astronomers concluded that Kohoutek was not a comet from the Oort cloud but actually a Kuiper-belt object, which would account for its apparent rocky makeup and lack of icy material and outgassing. I remember observing the comet with a small reflecting telescope in a field near my apartment. In my opinion it was a fairly bright comet with a long tail and an amazing sight.

Comet Shoemaker-Levy 9

In mid-July of 1994, more than twenty fragments of Comet Shoemaker-Levy 9 collided with the planet Jupiter. This was the first time astronomers observed an object in the solar system colliding with a planet. The Hubble Space Telescope took dozens of spectacular pictures as the comet's pieces crashed into Jupiter's southern hemisphere. The impacts created massive explosions in the upper atmosphere of the giant planet that were thousands of miles high. With the aid of a telescope on Earth over 300 million miles away, the exploding comet bits resembled large, dark "scars" in Jupiter's atmosphere.

---

159   James Chancellor, *Life in the Family: An Oral History of the Children of God* (New York: University of Syracuse Press, 2000).

At the time of collision, I was operating the 12½-inch reflecting telescope at the Bowman Observatory in Greenwich, Connecticut, and, along with the Astronomical Society of Greenwich,[160] hosting a public night. Hundreds of people over a period of four hours lined up to view the aftermath of the impact of Comet Shoemaker-Levy 9 on Jupiter. One could clearly see several dark blotches half the size of Earth in the planet's atmosphere. I explained to our many guests that the explosions they were seeing were equivalent to thousands of our atomic bombs. If the comet pieces hit Earth, it would have been an extinction event for all life on this planet.

Many of our guests at the observatory that night were worried "radiation" from the explosions would reach Earth, change our weather, and cause other "terrible things." I assured everyone that Earth was in no danger.

Human beings perceive the sky as something static and predictable, yet here was an event that showed our solar system and our universe dynamically changing. Comets and their actions in the solar system have always added to the fear and anxiety of the human species, a species that is already insecure with the instability of the world in which they live.

Comet Hale-Bopp

On July 23, 1995, Alan Hale of New Mexico and Thomas Bopp of Arizona telescopically observed an unusually bright comet just beyond the orbit of Jupiter. After a detailed analysis of images obtained using the Hubble Space Telescope, NASA came to the conclusion the new comet's intense brightness was due to the exceptionally large size of its nucleus, which was estimated to be 25 miles in diameter.

---

160   The Astronomical Society of Greenwich, Connecticut is based at the Bruce Museum and has an open membership.

As the comet reached perihelion, Hale-Bopp was so bright that it was easily visible in the bright, light-polluted skies of major cities. Judging by the increase in the sales of telescopes, binoculars, and other optical instruments, Hale-Bopp may have been the most-viewed comet in recorded history. The comet was visible for an amazing 18 months and will not visit the inner solar system again for another 2,475 years.

During Hale-Bopp's apparition I spent a considerable amount of time at the observatory observing and photographing the comet, and despite dozens of people who stopped by because they saw the dome open, a great deal of important work was accomplished. What was unique about this comet was that there seemed to be no fear from the public and no public displays announcing the end of the world—or so I thought!

As Hale-Bopp approached the inner solar system, there was a great deal of buzz in the UFO community that NASA saw a huge alien spaceship behind the comet in several images from the Hubble Space Telescope. Although NASA denied this, it provided fuel for the government conspiracy fanatics.

A starship hiding behind a comet and using its tail to scatter enemy sensors was an idea first proposed by science fiction writers and used in popular space opera television programs including *Star Trek*, *Star Trek: Enterprise*, *Star Trek: Deep Space 9*, and *Battlestar Galactica*. After several months the hidden spaceship rumors died out in the UFO community, but it was used by the leader of a cult who convinced his followers that the comet and the ship behind it was the "gateway to heaven."

Comet Hale-Bopp, UFOs, and Heaven's Gate

In the early seventies, a book called *The Late, Great Planet Earth* by Hal Lindsey[161] was recommended to me by a psychologist friend of mine. From the title it seemed another book written by a religious fanatic

---

161   *The Late, Great Planet Earth* (1970) was the first Christian prophecy book to be picked up by a major publisher. It sold 28 million copies by 1990.

forecasting the end of our time. I purchased the book and finished it in one night and was quite impressed. The author used the book of Revelation, the prophecies of Nostradamus, and other chapters in the Bible to forecast a dire future for the human race.

My next move was to purchase the King James Bible to begin my own study of the book of Revelation and to check Mr. Lindsey's biblical interpretations.

What intrigued me the most was that the book interpreted celestial events as being a sign to the human race from Jesus Christ and God forecasting the end of our world. At the time, it all made sense to me and the meanings behind the symbolism in the book seem to support the ideas of Mr. Lindsey, but then again, I was very young and naive at the time.

The book of Revelation is allegedly a prophecy about the end of our civilization, the rise of the Antichrist, and the return of Jesus Christ.[162] When I was a child in Sunday school, they only allowed us to read and study certain sections of the Bible; the book of Revelation was forbidden.

What interests me the most in Revelation was chapter 11, which is sometimes called "The Two Witnesses." In a nutshell, it says just before the rise of the Antichrist two prophets will appear and warn mankind that the day of the Lord is coming and God is not happy with the human race. Paraphrased, the chapter from Revelation appears below.

> I will appoint my two witnesses, and they will prophesy for 1,260
> days (3.45 years), clothed in sackcloth. They are the two olive
> trees and the two guiding lights, and they stand before the Lord
> of the earth. If anyone tries to harm them, fire comes from their
> mouths and devours their enemies. They have power to shut

---

162 There are scholars and priests of the Catholic Church that believe Roman Emperor Nero was the Antichrist and the number 666 is a code name for him. In Hebrew numerology, 666 decodes as Nero. In Catholicism there are radical groups that believe Nero will return to earth in the twenty-first century as the Antichrist. One such priest who belongs to this group is Father John, whom I have had many conversations with.

up the heavens so that it will not rain during the time they are prophesying; and they have power to turn the waters into blood and to strike the earth with every kind of plague as often as they want. Now when they have finished their testimony, the beast that comes up from the Abyss will attack them, and overpower and kill them. Their bodies will lie in the public square of the great city which is symbolically called Sodom and Egypt.

For three and a half days people will gaze on their bodies and refuse them burial. The people and nations they tormented will gloat over them and will celebrate by sending each other gifts, because these two prophets had tormented those who live on the earth are dead. After the three and a half days the breath of life from God entered them, and they stood on their feet, and terror struck those who saw them. Then there was a loud voice from heaven saying to them, Come Hither and they went up to heaven in a cloud[163], while their enemies looked on in terror. At that very hour there was a severe earthquake and a tenth of the city collapsed. Seven thousand people were killed in the earthquake, and the survivors were horrified and gave glory to the God.

Sometime around 1976 two individuals who claimed to be the prophets in Revelation started getting a considerable amount of publicity. They simply called themselves "Bo and Peep," later their real names were revealed as being Marshall Applewhite and Bonnie Nettles.

This was a little strange to me since in biblical history the prophets had always been men. This is not to say that there hasn't been a prophet who was a woman—there probably was—but still, when the Bible was written and finally accepted by the Romans as the official religion of the

---

163   Once again a cloud is mentioned as a vehicle to heaven.

empire, it was a male-dominated society and the importance of women in early Christianity was mostly ignored or played down.

Applewhite and Nettles claimed they were extraterrestrials and were here to save the chosen few because the earth is going to be cleansed. I kept track of their activities and was able to get my hands on some of their literature, which was quite bizarre.

When Nettles died of cancer in 1985, it challenged Applewhite's belief that they were of divine origin, and his followers began to question his teachings. Somehow he was able to convince them that Nettles was not dead but waiting for them in a higher body to act as a guide when they leave the earth before the great cosmic rapture.

To me the teachings of Bo and Peep were not that of prophets, but schizophrenics with megalomaniac delusions of grandeur. My conclusion was the "Two" were really two very unstable individuals and not prophets sent by God, aliens, or any other type of supernatural beings. The matter was put to rest, and the information was stored in my "dead end" files. Twenty years later Marshal Applewhite's actions would once again be brought to my attention.

During the first week of March of 1997, I received a call from a man and woman who wanted information on Hale-Bopp and UFOs. They told me they belong to a group in California that believed the end of the world was coming and a giant spacecraft was behind the comet and heading to Earth to rescue those who were chosen.

They contacted me because of my interest in not only astronomy, but also my research of the UFO phenomenon. They refused to give me their names and it was obvious the call was being made from a public pay phone. They asked me if there was a spaceship behind comet Hale-Bopp. I told them that the spaceship hiding behind Hale-Bopp was a rumor going around shortly after the comet was discovered, but in my opinion it didn't exist.

I then mentioned my work photographing Hale-Bopp at the Bowman Observatory and told them there was no evidence in any of the images of a UFO, alien spacecraft, or anything else that looked remotely strange.

I asked about their "group" and was told it was called "Heaven's Gate," which at the time meant nothing to me. Had they mentioned their cult leader was Marshall Applewhite, I would have been able to put two and two together. The couple quickly said goodbye and hung up and that was the last I heard from them.

On March 28 the news carried a story about a religious California cult that committed mass suicide thinking their spirits would board a UFO that was behind comet Hale-Bopp. After getting additional information it was obvious the man and woman who called were members of the Applewhite cult Heaven's Gate.

It seems early in 1997 Applewhite began talking about suicide and told his followers "it was the only way to evacuate this Earth." Applewhite heard rumors earlier that a spacecraft was trailing Comet Hale-Bopp, hiding from our view behind the comets coma and tail. Applewhite convinced his 38 followers to commit suicide so that their souls could board the alien spacecraft where Bonnie Nettles would be waiting for them and guide the faithful to a higher plane of existence.

All thirty-eight Heaven's Gate members, plus group leader Applewhite, were found dead in the mansion they rented in San Diego, California, on March 26, 1997. Among the dead was Thomas Nichols, brother of actress Nichelle Nichols, who is best known for her role as Starship Enterprise's communications officer, Lt. Uhura, in the original *Star Trek* television series.

Just before the end of March, I was visited by two members of the FBI who asked me questions about the phone call from the man and woman who were apparently members of Heaven's Gate and were among those found dead.

The two Heaven's Gate members did in fact call me from a pay phone, so the FBI must have been monitoring Applewhite and his followers for some time and most likely tapping nearby pay phones. When I asked the agents how they got my name, they simply said, "It was on record that a call was made from a phone the deceased used to your number." I cooperated fully; they took a report and never contacted me again.

In the days to follow, I would get calls from a number of major television and radio stations wanting to interview me about the Heaven's Gate mass suicide and the alien spaceship that they believed was coming to get them. I refused them all. It seems information at the FBI and other law enforcement agencies is not as secure as they believe.

Tunguska Impact: Comet, Asteroid, or Alien Spacecraft

Doomsday as the result of a comet or asteroid is not just privileged to the realm of religious fanatics. Professional scientists and the media are also responsible for implanting this seed of fear. Almost every educational astronomy documentary available to the public has a segment on the possibility of an impact by a comet or an asteroid and the devastating effects on our world and human civilization. Hollywood's most profitable movies explore the topic of the end of the world, and one of their favorite vehicles for doomsday is a comet or asteroid striking Earth in the near future.

It is estimated that an object at least 150 feet in diameter will strike our planet once every 6000 years or so and an asteroid or comet large enough to cause mass extinction will happen every 25–60 million years. Astronomers tell us it has happened before and will occur again; it's just a matter of time.

On June 30, 1908, something hit the earth in Tunguska, Siberia. Some say it was an asteroid or a small comet, some believe it was a small black hole, while still others say it was an extraterrestrial spacecraft powered by nuclear fusion. Although no one knows for sure what hit the Earth that morning in 1908, we do know it was a real event and the aftermath of the explosion can still be seen over 100 years later.

The first Russian scientific expedition to the blast area did not take place until 1927, when scientist Leonid Kulik convinced his government that the impact was due to a meteorite and there could be vast amounts of iron and other metals that could be recovered.

When Kulik and his team arrived at a village 80 miles from ground zero, the locals were reluctant to talk to him about the explosion, since they believed it was the result of the god Ogdy,[164] who in his anger crushed the trees and killed thousands of animals.

When the expedition finally reached the site, they were shocked to find that hundreds of square miles of secluded forest had been ripped apart, and a million trees were on the ground stripped of their branches, lying in a number of circular patterns. Kulik reasoned the pattern of the trees pointed away from the center of the blast. Later that day when the team arrived at ground zero expecting to find a huge crater, there was nothing. The trees were still upright, but their branches and bark were stripped away.

Dr. Kulik wrote in his diary that the trees in the center of the blast looked like "a forest of telegraph poles." The explosion was recorded on seismometers in Europe and the United States and for several days the night sky glowed so bright that people over a thousand miles away could read at night.[165]

Today the debate still goes on as to the cause of the Tunguska event. Scientists at NASA believe it may have been a small asteroid about 150 feet across that exploded before it hit the ground, releasing the energy equivalent to almost 500 Hiroshima atomic bombs.

In the PBS science series *Cosmos*, Dr. Carl Sagan speculates the Tunguska blast was caused by a piece of Comet Encke breaking off and striking the planet. This small, short-period comet was close to our planet at the time.[166]

Preliminary analysis of soil samples obtained at the blast site in 2009 showed that the explosion may have been caused by a huge piece

---

164   The highest god of thunder and lightning in Siberian myth.

165   Rupert Furneaux, *The Tunguska Event: The Great Siberian Catastrophe of 1908* (New York: Nordon Publications, 1977).

166   L. Kresak, "The Tunguska object: A fragment of Comet Encke?" *Bulletin of the Astronomical Institute of Czechoslovakia*, vol. 29, 1978.

of ice that shattered on impact. This finding would seem to support the theory that a small comet or a piece of one caused the cataclysmic explosion. In contrast, a 2013 analysis of fragments from the Tunguska site by a joint United States and European scientific team found evidence consistent with an iron meteorite.[167]

One thing is for sure: if the object was delayed by about two hours, it would have hit near Moscow and millions of people would have died. If the impact took place in the late fifties, sixties, or seventies, the asteroid or comet would have appeared like a missile dropping down from the sky to destroy Moscow. The Soviet Union could have believed it was an atomic attack by the United States and fired their missiles in retaliation. In turn, the USA would have launched its ICBMs; the result would have been the end of human civilization as we know it.

Think about it. An event from space that was nothing more than a cosmic accident could have triggered a primitive impulse of aggression in the paranoid people of Earth during the Cold War, leading to self-destruction. Even today with all our technology, we would not be able to detect a small asteroid or comet on course for collision until it was too late. Every year astronomers discover dozens of small celestial bodies that cross the orbits of the inner planets, and some of these are a danger to Earth.[168]

---

167   "A mystery solved: Space shuttle shows 1908 Tunguska explosion was caused by comet." *Cornell Chronicle* (Ithaca: Cornell University Press: 2009).

168   These objects have been labeled PHO, which stands for potentially hazardous objects. They refer to asteroids that cross the orbit of Earth and could strike our planet.

14

When Science and Myth Meet

Modern-day scientists label astrology and all aspects of the paranormal as pseudoscience. If you try to discuss astrology or UFOs with professional and most amateur astronomers, they snicker and walk away. There was a time when all areas of the pseudosciences were accepted as being real throughout the civilized world by the greatest intellectual minds of the age. In modern times historians, spiritualists, and mythologists insist the legends of long ago were based on fact, but scientists of today say the legends of paranormal experiences of people long ago are just fairy tales.

In some cases, an event that was called "supernatural" was actually science that was not understood at the time. Examples of this are lightning, thunder, floods, severe storms, disease, earthquakes, meteor showers, meteorites, and astronomical phenomena on the celestial sphere, just to name a few.

However, every once in a while, science and mythology become one. Our ancestors witnessed many things that they could not explain and certainly didn't have the vocabulary to express in writing. In the past fifty years, stories that were once considered to be nothing more than legends were discovered to be fact. It makes me wonder to what extent knowledge has been lost due to the fact myths are considered fairy tales by the established science community of the twentieth and twenty-first century. Albert Einstein once said, "The only thing that interferes with my learning is my education."

We have discovered that many legends were indeed based on factual events; one good example is the Trojan War, which was thought at one time to be just a fictional story made up by a wandering Greek who made up tall tales for a living. We know today that Troy did exist and most likely the heroes who fought in it on both the Trojan and Greek sides were real people.

One myth that was thought to be impossible for centuries by science was the claim that "stars or stones" can fall from the sky. Tales of shooting and falling stars go back to the days of ancient Greece, and although many cultures explained it as a gift or sign from the gods, the scientists of the eighteenth century thought such tales were superstitious nonsense told to a group of uneducated people by the local shaman or priest to frighten or entertain them. The earliest record that we have of the fall of a meteorite is from 465 BC, described by Plutarch[169] in his epic *Life of Lysander*.

> There were those who said that the stars of the twins appeared on each side of Lysander's ship, when he first set out against the Athenians. Others thought that a stone that fell from heaven was an omen of his overthrow. The stone did indeed fall from the sky and it was large in size. The people who found it hold the star stone in great veneration, and show it to this day. It is said that Anaxagoras had foretold that one of those bodies, which are fixed to the sphere of heaven, would one day be loosened by some

---

169   Plutarch (AD 4–120) was a Greek biographer and essayist.

shock and fall to the earth, for he taught that the stars are not in the same place where they were originally formed. Since they are a stony substance and heavy, the light they give is caused only by the reflection of the ether; and that they are carried along, and kept in their movements, by the rapid motion of the heavens which hinders them from falling.[170]

Star Stones

On a stormy night at the beginning of the nineteenth century, a French farmer looked out of his window and witnessed a fiery object fall from the sky and crash with a boom into his plowed land. The next morning, he went out to the field and found a dark stone about five pounds in weight sitting in a small depression. He then picked up the stone and took it to Paris and presented the object to the scientists at the Institute of Science. When he was asked by the scientists where he got the strange-looking stone, he replied, "It fell from the sky."

The scientists all started to laugh and labeled him an unstable individual who must drink a great deal, since according to what they were taught, it was impossible for rocks to fall from the sky. They explained to the farmer what he was claiming was not possible and he probably dug it up earlier while plowing and the lightning and thunder from the storm was the cause of sky fire and boom he heard.

The rock was kept in the Paris museum for almost 100 years in a forgotten storage area until scientists of the twentieth century found it while sifting through the museum's basement and identified the mystery rock as a stony-iron meteorite.

This story always makes me wonder how many other discoveries were (and are) being laughed at by scientists and filed away just because

---

170   E. T. Theodossiou, P. G. Niarchos, V. N. Manimanis, and W. Orchiston, "The fall of a meteorite at Aegos Potami in 467/6 BC," *Journal of Astronomical History and Heritage* 5, no. 2 (2002).

they don't fit into what the established scientific community considers possible. I'm sure that the farmer felt quite silly when he left the museum, and because of his experience it may have stopped many people from reporting comparable occurrences to the local authorities.

A similar story comes from about 1820 when scientists and medical doctors of the United States began an open line of communication with the Native American population. The scientists and doctors from a number of universities in the United States met with Native American medicine men and shamans from a number of tribes with the purpose of investigating claims of "natural cures" or medicine that could be used by the medical profession of the United States.

The story goes on to say that during one meeting, a medicine man emptied his medicine pouch on to the table and there were a number of strange looking stones. The doctors asked what they were and the medicine man replied that they had great power for healing. The doctors then asked where the medicine man found them, and he replied, "They are star stones that fell from the sky." The doctors all began to laugh and ensured the medicine man that it was impossible, since "stones cannot fall from the sky." Well, the laugh was on the doctors because in the late nineteenth century the so-called "star stones" of the medicine men were analyzed and they turned out to be meteorites, and some of them very rare ones.

It was not until 1835 that scientists began to take a serious look at the claim that rocks could fall from the sky. However, Aristotle[171] is credited with proposing the idea of "falling stones from the heavens" and that some of them could even land on the earth and be recovered.[172]

---

171   Aristotle was an ancient Greek philosopher and scientist who lived from 384–322 BC.

172   We do know that the ancient Greeks did observe meteorites fall from the sky and in rare cases they were recovered. In some cultures the iron in the meteorite was used to make the first steel swords. Such swords were believed to have magical powers.

Since the Bronze Age fiery objects were observed streaking across the night sky and were called "shooting stars" since that's what our ancestors believed they were. In modern times we know they are not shooting or falling stars but meteors, although many still refer to them as such.

It was once believed that meteors were a weather phenomenon of the upper atmosphere.[173] Since the end of the nineteenth century, we have known "shooting stars" or meteors to be space debris that range in size from a grain of sand to over a hundred feet.

If an object is large enough to survive the great heat caused by friction as it enters the atmosphere and reaches the ground, it is called a meteorite. There are three basic types of meteorites. They are stones, stony-irons, and iron-nickels. The observation and recovery of a meteorite has always played an important part in the mythology of every culture since the beginning of recorded history.

The Magic Sword

During the Bronze Age, armor, swords, and other weapons were made of the alloy bronze. An alloy is a mixture of two or more metals, in this case copper and tin. Thousands of years ago most cultures had difficulties extracting iron from rock since the metal was often mixed with impurities and difficult to separate. Yet, iron and crude steel swords were present but very rare.

An iron-nickel contains mostly these two elements, iron and nickel, with very little impurities. There are legends from several cultures, including the Norse, Greeks, and Chinese, of people witnessing a "star fall from the sky" and actually recovering it. There have been cases where the meteorite was melted down in a furnace and used to make a sword.

---

173   The word meteor has its origin in Greek as meaning "the atmosphere of Earth."
      Since shooting stars were thought to be a weather event, they were called "meteors."
      A scientist who studies the atmosphere and weather is called a meteorologist;
      however, they don't necessarily study meteors unless there is a personal interest.

When used in battle, the sword would break other weapons and pierce through the strongest bronze armor. Since the material fell from heaven and was harder than any known metal, the sword was believed to be magic and have great power.

Later when mankind learned to harness the iron from the earth to make steel, the story of the magic swords slowly faded into legend. For centuries it was believed that steel was originally denied to mankind by the gods of the sky until one day during a great war in heaven, the secret of making steel fell to earth. Was this legend, which is lost in antiquity, really a great meteor shower where multiple meteorites were recovered in Europe and Asia? Is this what they meant when the ancients said that steel was a gift or stolen from the gods?

According to legends spanning the globe that date back over three thousand years, there were more than six magic swords mentioned in myths that possessed power from the heavens and were stronger than any other metals or alloys available at the time. Although many of these magic weapons may be nothing more than myths, it is possible that a small number did exist and were steel made from the iron and nickel of a recovered meteorite.

When a sword, knife, or other type of blade was forged from a recovered meteorite, it was seen as a gift from their god. Such swords were owned by kings and great warriors. The alleged magical properties of meteorites were believed to be in the swords of Attila the Hun, Arthur's Excalibur, and the fabled sword of the Olympian gods given to mortals to protect them from renegade deities called the "God Killer." [174] A version of this weapon appears in the recent movie *Wonder Woman*.

---

174   Originally known as the "Sword of Harpe" used by Perseus to slay the demigod gorgon Medusa.

The Chiba Institute of Technology[175] has a Katana on display forged from the pieces of a Gibeon meteorite[176] by the great sword smith Yoshindo Yoshiwara. It is called "The Sword from Heaven." The Qur'an mentions that a powerful sword from heaven was given to the Prophet Muhammad. The blade could cut through any material and was unbreakable. It is thought the sword was forged from the iron and nickel recovered from a meteorite.

The Night the Stars Fell like Rain

On the night of April 24, 1995, something took place that amazed and even frightened earthbound observers in North America. At approximately 8–8:30 p.m., the sky became ablaze with streaks of light. Although the day had been quite cloudy the sky cleared up just in time to give the inhabitants of planet Earth a light show that will be talked about for years.

Most of the populace looked up to the sky to see hundreds of shooting stars that lasted for about two hours. Many residents of Connecticut and Long Island were so startled they called police and fire stations to report an exploded plane; some said they saw missiles falling from the sky; and some even called 911 to report an alien invasion. There were those who witnessed the meteors who ran to their church to pray because they believed the manifestation was a sign from God saying the end of the world was near, since "stars falling from heaven" is mentioned in the Bible heralding the end of the world and the second coming of Jesus Christ.[177]

The amazing celestial display was in reality a phenomenal burst of meteors that astronomers believe was a late appearance of an annular

---

175   Chiba Institute of Technology is a private university in Narashino, Chiba Prefecture, Japan. The school was founded in 1942 in Machida.

176   A meteorite with a high iron content.

177   Revelation 6:13.

meteor shower called the Lyrids. The Lyrid shower is normally a very unimpressive display, and at its best only 20 meteors an hour can be seen. However, during the short time of this "late display" of the shower, several hundred meteors an hour were reported by people throughout the United States.

Although the Lyrids are not usually so spectacular, they are one of the oldest showers that have been recorded in history with observations that date back to at least 3500 years ago by many cultures throughout the world. According to Chinese astronomical records, a similar Lyrid meteor shower was described by astrologer-astronomers in 300 BC as the night "the stars fell like rain."

The Lyrid shower is associated with the debris left by the tail of a comet called Thatcher, which was first identified in 1861. Astronomers also speculate that debris left over from the tail of Comet Halley might have also contributed to the shower during times of great intensity. The Lyrid meteor shower can normally be seen anytime after midnight between April 22 and 24 when the constellation of Lyra is high above the horizon in the North-Northeast.

It is almost impossible to predict how spectacular a meteor shower will be. The tiny sand-like particles, left over by the tail of a comet, continue to orbit the sun well after the comet has left the inner solar system. This debris is not evenly distributed, and if our planet passes through a dense field of particles, we will see a spectacular meteor display. Although this event was a rare manifestation for this shower, besides the 1995 display in the last 184 years it has happened four other times, in 1982, 1945, 1922, and 1833.

This phenomenal celestial display has shown us just how much our subconscious fears are controlled by witnessing unexpected events on the celestial sphere. I was allowed to read and listen to about thirty of the many reports made to the Connecticut local and state police and it was clear the people calling in were fearful that something terrible was happening.

Legend of the Guest Stars

In the year 1006 astrologers throughout the civilized world observed what they called a "Guest Star" in the sky, which apparently became sixteen times brighter than the planet Venus. The Persian scholar Sina wrote that the new star was visible for months and kept on changing color and throwing out "sparks." The guest star was said to have magical healing powers both physical and mental on those who gazed into its light for a long period of time.

In 1054 Chinese, Japanese, and Persian astrologers reported a new star in the constellation of Taurus and noted that for weeks it became the brightest star in the sky before slowly fading. Chinese astrologers believed the new stars appearance was a sign that great changes in the destiny of China were about to take place.

Despite a considerable amount of documentation, astronomers of the nineteenth century believed the stories of guest stars were just legends, since both the Chinese and Persians attached mystical significance to their appearance.

Today we know that the guest stars of 1006 and 1054 were exploding massive stars called supernovas. When modern astronomers turn their telescopes to the location that the Persians and Chinese marked on their star maps, large nebulous clouds are seen—the aftermath of great stellar detonations.

We see here that, in this case, not only were the legends true but they provided the scientists of today with important details about the life cycle of a star. If the legends were ignored and modern astronomers took the attitude of the nineteenth-century scientists, then significant information would have been lost.

A Family Feud

The modern science of astronomy actually emerged from the ancient art of astrology. At the end of the seventeenth century, astrology and astronomy split into two factions. The word "astrology" means "study of the stars," while astronomy can be defined as "the observation and cataloging of the stars."

According to a public information statement by the American Astronomical Society, "Astronomy is a science that studies everything outside of the earth's atmosphere, such as planets, stars, asteroids, galaxies; and the properties and relationships of those celestial bodies. Astronomers base their studies on research and observation. Astrology, on the other hand, is the belief that the positioning of the stars and planets affect the way events occur on earth." [178]

It's not surprising that a professional astronomy association would give astrology a brief sentence when comparing the two disciplines. The same comparative descriptive treatment can be found in the publications from many astrological associations where astronomy is given one sentence and astrology several paragraphs.

Having met and worked with both astrologers and astronomers, from my experience it's clear that astronomers know very little about astrology and most astrologers know very little about theoretical astronomy.

If you visit an observatory and call the astronomer an astrologer by mistake, they are usually insulted and will correct you on the spot. This is also true for amateur astronomers who volunteer their time at professional or educational observatories and planetariums. However, if you call an astrologer an astronomer, you probably will not get a response.

Astronomers consider astrology nothing more than a superstitious pseudoscience that has no foundation in reality and is built on the gullibility of the uneducated. What they will not admit is that scientists whom they consider the pioneers and forefathers of modern astronomy were all astrologers and prepared charts for royalty and the wealthy for a living. This includes Galileo, Tycho Brahe, and Johannes Kepler.

---

178   American Astronomical Society, "What's the difference between astronomy and astrology?" last updated February 26, 2016, accessed May 2015, https://aas.org/faq/whats-difference-between-astronomy-and-astrology.

There is also evidence that Isaac Newton, who today is still called a demigod of science, was interested in astrology, alchemy, and the mystic arts. Authors of astrological topics of the twentieth century present and claim that Newton was secretly a devoted student of astrology. When mathematician Edmond Halley once spoke negatively on the subject of astrology, religion, and alchemy, Newton is said to have spoken angrily to him with the remark, "Sir, I have studied the matter. You have not!"[179]

The fact that Halley and Newton often quarreled on theological matters is confirmed by another remark recorded by John Conduitt, who in turn heard it from his wife (and Newton's niece) Catherine Conduitt. However, these altercations were never so intense as to cause a split between these two great scientists who were also close friends.[180]

In 1690 when Newton saw astrology being frowned upon by the new scientific order and the church, it is possible he kept his interests secret. Scientific historians consider Newton the last "real scientist" that had a belief in the paranormal who finally realized astrology and alchemy and the mystic arts were a sham and went on to "true science." But did he?

It's apparent that during the late seventeenth century many astronomers turned away from astrology since the church in Rome was against it. The Catechism[181] of the Catholic Church maintains to this day that divination, including predictive astrology, is incompatible with Catholic beliefs.

All forms of divination are to be rejected: recourse to Satan or demons, conjuring up the dead or other practices falsely supposed to unveil the future. Consulting horoscopes, astrology, palm reading, interpretation of omens, readings by psychics, the phenomena

---

179   M. Gauquelin, *The Cosmic Clocks: From Astrology to a Modern Science* (London: Peter Owen, 1969); D. Parker & J. Parker, *A History of Astrology* (London: André Deutsch Ltd., 1983).

180   B. Cohen, "Isaac Newton—An Advocate of Astrology?" *Isis* (Oxford: University of Oxford Press, 1941).

181   A summary of the teachings and laws of the Catholic religion used for instruction.

of clairvoyance and recourse to mediums all conceal a desire for power over time, history, and, in the last analysis, other human beings, as well as a wish to appease hidden powers. They contradict the honor, respect, and loving fear that we owe to God alone.[182]

In the twenty-first century it is against the law in many states for psychics and astrologers to be paid for predicting the future. The astrologers I have known do not predict, but they do give advice and counseling to their clients. Astrology is very much alive today and has a large following. A great number of newspapers still have a horoscope section that is read frequently by people from all walks of life. Although in many publications horoscopes are close to the comics section, it does not sway many from taking them seriously.

Astrologers believe the positions of planets and other celestial objects have a direct effect on living creatures on the earth. Astronomers will laugh at this and call it ridiculous, yet they seem to want to believe in improbable things like dark matter and dark energy, which like the claims of astrologers cannot be proven. Only recently are theoretical physicists considering the existence of other dimensions, parallel realities and the streams of particles and energy emitting from them into our universe. Yet students of the mystic arts have been talking about this same multiverse scenario for hundreds of centuries, but today's scientists are claiming it's their idea.

The universe is a sea of particles, energy, and other forces of which we can only get a glimpse. We the inhabitants of planet Earth sometimes forget we are part of it all and connected to all these forces. Since electrical impulses are present in the human nervous system, it's difficult to believe these universal forces do not affect us in some way. Perhaps the alignments of the planets and other celestial bodies can direct or focus some of this energy and change it in some way. For scientists to claim

---

182   Catholic Church, *Catechism of the Catholic Church*, Section 3.

they can separate fantasy from reality by using the scientific method is dangerously arrogant. I have always found it amazing that curiosity continues to exist after a formal education. In some it does not.

All life on our tiny world is an integral part of the multiverse, no less than the planets, comets, stars, and galaxies right down to the smallest particles that make up matter. All living creatures in the multiverse are affected by the balance of the cosmos. This is the reason why when we look up at the night sky, feelings of peace, wonder, and sometimes apprehension are generated by the human mind and spirit. There is a deep-rooted subconscious thought imbedded in not only our mind but also in our soul to reconnect with our place of origin.

15

Mysterious Worlds

Thousands of years ago it was thought the celestial sphere was not a place a mere human could journey; it was believed to be the realm of the gods, and passage to the heavens was forbidden. To the masses of antiquity, the moon, sun, planets, and stars were glowing disks—points of light that were not solid ground like the earth. Except in some extreme cases, this belief halted our species from dreaming of transcending to the stars.

The compelling drive for exploration and discovery is an insatiable urge human beings possess, and since the heavens were unreachable, this instinctual drive for discovery was satisfied by focusing on the material world around them. This was a time when the earth was mostly unexplored and the only guides that seafaring civilizations had were crude maps that were not very accurate.

Throughout the Bronze Age, a long sea journey was not only perilous but filled with many unknowns that often brought fear to the mariners of long ago. Yet, humans are an inquisitive species and this compelling curiosity to explore and discover outweighed the fear of the unknown.

Often those who returned from a long voyage would tell tales of strange lands, unusual people, sea serpents, and other monsters they encountered in their adventures. Stories of giants, dragons, and people who could transform into beasts were common. There were even stories of encounters with godlike beings who either helped or harmed the brave explorers.

An example of this would be the classic tale of the great Odysseus and his adventures after leaving Troy. Odysseus and his crew were swept by great storms (which were blamed on the gods) to mysterious islands where they encountered bizarre people, a Cyclops, and other monsters and demigods. There is also the story of St. Brendan the Navigator who sailed across the Atlantic to North America sometime in the fifth century AD with a crew of eighteen. During his journey they encountered sea monsters, angelic beings, flying machines, and what could be viewed as a submarine ship from an unknown technological civilization. Finally, there is the story of the Viking explorer Thorfinn who in AD 1010 apparently sailed to North America and traveled up the Hudson River to the area that we know today as the Catskill Mountains. Here the brave explorers encountered "elves" and did battle with a tribe of Native Americans who could transform into animals at night.

The tales of uncharted lands and encounters with the paranormal continued until the late nineteenth century with stories of prehistoric monsters living in a warm giant crater at the North Pole and legends of a fog-shrouded island in the South Pacific where there exists people lost in time and giant creatures. It is these legends or tall tales that inspired *The Lost World* by Sir Arthur Conan Doyle,[183] the movies *Unknown Island* and *The Land Unknown,* and "Skull Island," from which the original *King Kong* movie is based.

Whether or not any of the exciting tales that sailors brought home about their adventures at sea were true or not, they did set the stage for

---

183 Sir Arthur Conan Doyle (1859–1930) was a British writer best known for his character Sherlock Holmes. Doyle was a great believer in spiritualism and one of the first paranormal researchers.

legends that are still with us today in the form of novels, motion pictures, and video games.

Today, using modern technology, the entire planet has been mapped and explored. If things such as sea monsters, giants, dragons, mysterious islands, and other strange creatures of time and space did exist, they seem to have vanished.

Since the surface of planet Earth no longer holds any great mysteries, there are no more exciting tales of encounters with exotic creatures while sailing the seven seas. As a result we as a culture may have lost an important part of our mythology. However, the human race has a new sea to explore, the cosmic ocean.

Since the late seventeenth century when astronomers discovered that the planets are not just points of light but real places like the earth, many have dreamed of navigating the stars in fantastic ships propelled by the ether of space. Also, when Galileo first turned his telescope and looked at the moon, he realized it was not a flat disk but a large three-dimensional world with mountains, valleys, craters, and dark areas he believed were oceans. When Galileo's ideas were finally accepted it opened up a new set of mysteries for the human race and a vast new area to explore.

Today, people still look up at the night sky and wonder what mysteries lie out among the planets and stars. The solar system, galaxy, and entire universe is our new frontier, which we are determined to explore.

In 2000 BC the early Europeans and Asians may have stood on the shore of their homeland and looked out toward the vast Atlantic and Pacific Oceans and wondered what is out there. In more modern times the inhabitants of planet Earth now look up at the night sky and, like our ancestors, also wonder what is out there.

Just like those brave explorers who sailed the seas in ships of wood, someday in the near future courageous men and women will sail the vastness of space in ships made of new alloys and once again return with fantastic stories that will excite the human race, create new legends, and elevate our minds to a new level of consciousness.

Since in this moment of time we do not have the capability to navigate the stars, scientists, engineers, and amateurs have been using radio to send or hopefully receive a message from somewhere in the multiverse. A symbolic message in a bottle that the people of Earth have thrown into the cosmic ocean hoping that someone out there is listening and will respond.

A Message in a Bottle

At the turn of the twentieth century, the possibility of life on Mars was a great fascination, and the Red Planet was considered to be the most mysterious planet in the solar system. According to the literature at the time, the majority of people believed Mars to be inhabited. They thought if Mars had intelligent life-forms, then many of the other planets of the solar system must also be populated, and some may have a technological civilization equal, lesser, or greater than humans on Earth.

In 1910 Madame Ann Goguet Guzman, a wealthy Parisian who had a great interest in astronomy and extraterrestrial life, established the "Guzman Prize," out of honor for her son Pierre Guzman.[184] The Guzman Prize was a contest that stated the first person to establish interplanetary communication would be awarded 100,000 francs, with one stipulation: Mars was excluded since the Guzman family believed communicating with the Red Planet would be too easy.

In the hope of winning the prize and being the first to establish extraterrestrial communication, thousands from all over the world began buying or building radios, which was a brand new technology at the time. Professional scientists and engineers also joined in the quest, but the task would be more difficult than anyone imagined.

In the hope of enticing Venusians or other aliens to land on Earth, one person had the idea of painting the sand in the Mojave Dessert with

---

184   Frank H. Winter, "The Strange Case of Madame Guzman and the Mars Mystique," *Griffith Observer*, 1984.

black lettering that read, "Hello from the people of Earth. Please visit us soon." Although some claimed they made alien contact there was no proof and the family of Madam Guzman kept their money.[185]

The Guzman Prize was still available in the twentieth century, but the monetary awards were given to those who made great advances in science and medicine. In 1969 it was awarded to the astronauts of Apollo 11 after their historic moon landing.

Science fiction writers of the 1950s speculated that by the beginning of the twenty-first century we would have colonies on the moon and Mars. They were also sure we would be traveling to other solar systems in great starships and frequently encountering alien beings, some friendly and some not. As of the writing of this book, human beings are still grounded on our planet, and despite great advances in technology, we have put the manned space program on hold to focus our resources on other earthly things.

In the 1950s astronomers had no knowledge of extrasolar planets and most of the multiverse was unknown to us. Close celestial bodies like the planets Mars and Venus were shrouded in mystery, and their nature was left to the imaginations of science fiction writers.

Scientists knew the planet Venus was covered with clouds and its atmosphere contained carbon dioxide. This led many to imagine its surface was a tropical jungle with prehistoric-like beasts. Astronomers could see the surface of Mars and noted what some thought to be signs of intelligent beings. These observations spawned an entire generation of Martian invasions and Red Planet exploration themes in literature and movies.[186]

---

185   William Ley. *Rockets, Missiles, and Space Travel,* (New York: Viking Press, 1958).

186   Today there are many who believe there is or was once intelligent life on Mars. There are quite a few unexplainable images captured by several space probes. Many of these have made it to the internet, but be warned, the majority have been faked.

During the early 1960s astronomers confirmed that Venus, Mars, and the outer planets are inhospitable to human life. Despite this new knowledge humans continued to pollute the earth, and the threat of nuclear war was an everyday fear. The scientists of that decade made it very clear to the world leaders and politicians that if we poison our planet with radiation and toxic chemicals, there is no other place to go. Yet, their warnings fell on deaf ears and the world powers continued to stockpile atomic weapons and pollute the oceans and atmosphere.

As technology improved the hope of finding intelligent life in our solar system faded to the dismay of many and the delight of some who feared an alien invasion. There were religious leaders who stated the scientists were wasting time and money, since they believed God created life on Earth and nowhere else.

As a result of the human desire to explore and look for life in the cosmos, we had to look further than our optical telescopes could see, into deep space—to the edge of the visible universe. In the mid-twentieth century, a new breed of astronomer emerged and found a novel way to explore the visible and invisible universe. This new branch of science became known as "radio astronomy."

In 1960 Dr. Frank Drake of Cornell University began a pioneering project to search for extraterrestrial radio signals called Project Ozma. Project Ozma was named after the princess Ozma, ruler of the fictional land of Oz. Dr. Drake was inspired by the novel *The Marvelous Land of Oz* since the author L. Frank Baum claimed radio communication with Oz to get the information to write a series of books.[187]

Although Dr. Drake did not believe Baum's claims, he thought it was a good name for the project, since in reality he was going to attempt to receive radio signals from beings from an unknown, distant, exotic land. Dr. Drake and his staff used a radio telescope 85 feet in diameter located in Virginia and chose a number of nearby stars that they

---

187   Some say he was joking, but others took him seriously.

thought could possibility have planets. One of the many problems they encountered was that among trillions of radio frequencies, which one do you listen to?

The radio astronomers picked a microwave frequency of 1.420 giga-hertz, which is the natural electromagnetic emissions of neutral hydro-gen [188] in the galaxy. Drake rationalized that if an extraterrestrial society was trying to send a message they would use this frequency because it is the universal signature emission of our galaxy. Project Ozma and Ozma II continued into 1976, but no signals were received that were verified as being intelligent in origin.

This is not surprising since technology at this time was quite primi-tive when compared to today. Just like the light of your flashlight, radio transmissions spread out and weaken as they travel farther and farther from the source. Also, space is not a vacuum; electromagnetic waves are absorbed by dust, gas, and other particles between the stars. Another problem is the radio bands they selected are quite noisy with natural radiation and it would have taken a super powerful signal to be recog-nized as being from a technological civilization once it reached Earth.

In 1967 Jocelyn Bell, an astronomy graduate student, noticed a strange signal coming from the radio telescope she was using at the Mullard Radio Observatory in Cambridge. Bell and her advisor Dr. Anthony Hewish initially thought they might have detected a signal from an extraterrestrial civilization.

The signal, a series of short pulses that repeated every 1.34 seconds, seemed too regular and fast to be coming from a natural source. Bell and Hewish in jest called the new source "LGM-1," short for "Little Green Men-1." Although they joked about the discovery with their peers, both Bell and Hewish seriously considered they might have found a radio bea-con from a very advanced extraterrestrial civilization. When they scanned the sky and found more of the LGM sources with different periods, they

---

188   A hydrogen atom containing one proton and one electron.

began to realize it was a newly discovered natural radio emission that was emitting from a dying stellar object called a neutron star.

Neutron stars were first predicted to exist in 1933, but not proven until the discovery of the LGM signal. These extremely dense stellar objects are the collapsed remnants of massive stars after a supernova. The rapid rotation produces a beam of radiation that sweeps around as the star spins, much like the beacon in a light house. Neutron stars that send out bursts of electromagnetic radiation were then named "pulsars." Although pulsars are no longer identified by the letters LGM, the discovery of a new one always creates excitement among astronomers.[189]

There are many astronomers who are interested in the possibility of extraterrestrial life. In the sixties and seventies, fifteen radio transmissions were been sent from Earth and beamed in the direction of stars that may possibly have planets with a civilization possessing a technology capable of receiving the signals. So far no one has answered our call, but the search continues with the SETI program and various other projects astronomers have in the planning stage.

Tesla's Extraterrestrial Radio Signals

Ever since the development of radio and television, people have reported picking up unknown sounds and voices on their radio receivers and unidentified images on their television sets. The first person credited with receiving mysterious radio signals was the great scientist Nikola Tesla. In 1899, Tesla was sure that the signals he received on his experimental receiver came from outer space, but did they?

This claim was incredible for his time and the scientific community called him a liar, dreamer, or just plain insane. This reaction was not surprising, since after Tesla had his fallout with Thomas Edison, he had very little support from his peers. Despite the attacks on his character,

---

189   If you would like to hear a number of pulsars recorded by astronomers from their radio telescopes, please go to https://www.youtube.com/watch?v=gb0P6x_xDEU.

he stuck to his belief that what he received was not of terrestrial origin. In the long run, the claim that he picked up signals from outer space discredited his reputation in the scientific world.

On February 19, 1901, *Colliers Weekly* published a story by Tesla entitled "Talking with the Planets." The story starts with a comment by the editor stating his great respect for Tesla and his achievements, then goes on to the main article that was written by Tesla himself.

It is accepted by many today that Nikola Tesla was the first one to build a radio and experiment listening in on a number of different frequencies. In the article Tesla was claiming something fantastic that even the most open-minded people at the turn of the century had trouble believing.

While working in his laboratory alone at night, Tesla claimed to have heard a series of rhythmic tones on his radio receiver that repeated itself in a predictable pattern. Once he realized the signal might be under intelligent control, it terrified him. Being familiar with natural electromagnetic disturbances, he ruled out the cipher as being produced by electrical phenomena on Earth or in the atmosphere. Tesla was sure that he had received a signal from outer space and it might have come from a nearby planet like Venus or Mars. It wasn't long after he began talking about his discovery that the entire scientific world came down on him like a ton of bricks.

In 1932 Tesla applied for the Guzman Prize, since he was convinced his signals were extraterrestrial in origin and from an alien intelligence with a technology more advanced than man. His request was quickly turned down by the governing board of the Paris Academy of Science, who at the time was responsible for overseeing the award.

Tesla's belief in psychic phenomena, spiritualism, and his fascination with the possibility of life on Mars was used as fuel by the scientific community to ridicule him, and no "reputable" scientist at the time took his claims seriously. However, in the summer of 1920, another genius, a man considered a solid scientist and engineer with no meta-physical viewpoints, was reaching the same conclusions. That person was Guglielmo Marconi, a Nobel Prize winner and inventor of the wireless telegraph.

Marconi and the "Signals from Mars"

At the time of Tesla's incredible announcement that he received signals from another world, Marconi was developing radio as a means of communication, sending the letter "V" in Morse code to his assistants over a 50-mile (80-kilometer) distance.

In 1920 Marconi announced to the scientific community that he had received mysterious signals on his radio which he was certain were produced by artificial means. After hours of listening to the signal, Marconi noticed something incredible. Within the cipher, there was a recurrence of the Morse "V" and "S," which he had been transmitting to his assistants back in 1899.

In an article published on January 29, 1920, in the *New York Times*, Marconi was quoted as saying that he believed the mysterious signals, or some of them, originated outside our planet from a close-by world like Mars. Despite considerable publicity regarding Marconi's "signals from Mars," not one person made the connection with Tesla's claim about receiving interplanetary signals twenty years earlier. This was most likely because his claim was ignored and discredited by the media and the scientific community.

Both Tesla and Marconi believed the signals they received may have come from the planet Mars, but their claims were largely disregarded by the scientific community until 1924. Even though Marconi was a well-respected scientist and awarded a Nobel Prize he was ridiculed by the scientific world after the publication of the *New York Times* story and later refused to talk about the strange signals he received. There are rumors that linger in scientific circles to this day that Marconi secretly continued investigating the origin of the signals and actually established communication with intelligent beings from another reality.[190]

Unusual Signals Continue

Strange signals continued to be received on radio throughout the first half of the twentieth century, particularly on the long wave band. In the fall of 1927, two scientists from the United States, Drs. Taylor and Young, took the claim of mysterious radio signals received by Marconi and Tesla seriously enough to attempt receiving and identifying their source.

During their time as graduate students, Taylor and Young had met Marconi and worked with him for a short time. They knew for a fact, beyond a shadow of doubt, that Marconi was not a person to let his imagination run away with him and that he was always conservative when making a statement concerning a new controversial discovery. It was their opinion that whatever Marconi heard on his radio receiver must have excited him enough to go out on a limb making the claim that he believed the mysterious signals were not from planet Earth but originated on some unknown mysterious world.

After two years of self-funded research, Drs. Taylor and Young were sure they had identified a signal originating from a distance 6,000 miles from the surface of Earth. When they compared these signals to the descriptions of what Marconi received, both scientists felt there was a close similarity between them.

By the end of 1928 after reading a paper published by Young and Taylor in the magazine *Science*, a number of other scientists and engineers also got interested. They included Dr. Jurgen Hals of Philips's Eindhoven laboratories in Holland and Professor Carl Stormer of Oslo.

On October 28, 1929, after two years of research, Hals and Stormer confirmed that they had noted anomalous signals almost every morning

---

190   "Did Marconi Receive the First Extraterrestrial Radio Signals?" *Science* 56, (March 1931).

of "short duration" in the long wave band. To this day these signals remain unidentified, but it is speculated by twenty-first century atmospheric physicists that they somehow were connected with natural emissions created in the magnetic field of Earth.

It is now believed by most twenty-first century scientists that both Tesla and Marconi's "strange signals" was energy shifting through the magnetosphere of Earth. Today unusual sounds are still heard on radio receivers from this area of space and have been called "whistlers, hissers, risers, and drifters" [191] by atmospheric physicists. Although no one can explain for certainty how these strange sounds are created, scientists from the National Oceanic and Atmospheric Administration (NOAA) are sure they are naturally formed.

In his paper published in *Scientific American* in September of 1964, Dr. Theodore Rupplett admits that such transmissions emanating from the magnetosphere of Earth do appear to be artificial in nature and it's easy to understand why Marconi believed they might be extraterrestrial in origin.

Were the signals received by Marconi and Tesla natural emissions from the magnetosphere, a signal from an extraterrestrial civilization, or stranger still, human beings from a parallel reality? I guess we will never know, since there are no recordings of the mysterious sounds they both heard coming from their devices.

One of the projects that I am currently working on is very long wave (VLF) reception of the magnetosphere during times of magnetic storms. Using my telescope to keep track of solar activity and monitoring the NOAA website, a rough estimate can be obtained to predict the time of suitable atmospheric activity. If modern theories in quantum

---

191   If you would like to hear some of these sounds, you can watch "VLF Whistlers" at https://www.youtube.com/watch?v=FeuI8AJMIxU (accessed Sept. 9, 2018). A even better one is "Earth and Planets Make Strange, Exquisite Noises | Video Compilation" at https://www.youtube.com/watch?v=fdj8p6c2lew (accessed Sept. 9, 2018).

physics are correct and other dimensions and parallel realities do exist, it might be possible to obtain electromagnetic signals from these hidden areas of space at this time.

This may sound like a far-fetched theory, but then again many such ideas sometimes lead to discovery. The invention of radio, television, flight, and space travel are some of many far-fetched ideas that were once thought to be nothing more than a fool's dream.

After hundreds of hours of listening, I did receive a faint transmission that faded in and out and sounded like some form of modulated cipher. A copy of the signal was sent to a friend of mine who is an expert on atmospheric electromagnetic radiation and terrestrial radio phenomena in Italy. After a lengthy investigation, he could not identify it. It was his opinion there is no explanation for the signal and it is a mystery. This is a new area of research that might yield fantastic findings in the future and, like early astronomy, it is open to all.

My current plans are to do a study of mysterious radio and television transmissions that have taken place since the beginning of the twentieth century to the present. This historical research and my current exploration into this phenomenon using a radio telescope might be presented in a future book or publication. The good news is I received a rather large private grant to buy land and equipment and build a large antenna. It is my hope to begin work on this project in 2019 or 2020.

Phantom Planets

Spanning from ancient to modern times, the planets and other members of our solar system have been the subject of mystery and wonder. The belief that planets and other celestial bodies that cannot be seen from Earth exist is a favorite topic of many authors, mystics, and UFO contactees.

In the nineteenth century, astronomers in France, using a large solar telescope, claimed they observed an intramercurial planet crossing the disk of the sun. The French stargazers were so sure of their discovery that they named the new planet "Vulcan." [192]

The observation was never taken seriously by astronomers in Great Britain and the United States. However, since the report came from a well-respected astronomer-mathematician named Urbain Le Verrier, the American scientists decided to look into his claim. After an investigation of unknown duration, they could not verify the existence of Vulcan and gave up the search.

Nothing was reported until 1932, when American astronomers observed three objects that were estimated to be anywhere from 50 to 150 miles in size crossing the solar disk. Since the objects were difficult to observe as a result of the solar glare, accurate measurements were impossible to obtain. Although "Vulcan" has been seen crossing the disk of the sun several times since 1932, all reports of the alleged new planet came from amateur astronomers and were not taken seriously by scientists at major institutions.

The discovery and confirmed observation of intramercurial bodies remain elusive to this day. Astronomers do admit it is theoretically possible a number of large asteroids exist in orbit between the sun and Mercury, but obtaining proof would be difficult.

During the fifties, the 1932 observations of Vulcan made by American astronomers were used by the flying saucer subculture to "prove" that "giant alien spaceships" were in orbit between the sun and Mercury hidden from our telescopes by the solar glare. Throughout the American flying saucer craze, the media had a field day with the claims of

---

192   Vulcan was selected after the Roman god of fire. This is where we get the word "volcano." Also, it is also the name of Mr. Spock's home planet in the science fiction franchise *Star Trek*. Mr. Spock's Vulcan is a hot planet close to its sun. It is possible that Star Trek creator Gene Roddenberry chose the name Vulcan from the observations of French astronomers in the nineteenth century. Roddenberry had a great interest in astronomy and the unsolved mysteries of the solar system.

contactees like George Adamski who believed there were giant alien ships in the inner solar system using Vulcan as a base.

In my files are two individuals who claimed they met aliens that once hailed from a planet in our solar system that was once between Mercury and the sun before it was destroyed. Is it possible that "Vulcan" really did exist at one time, or does it only exist in the fantasies of those who want to believe they are part of something much bigger than their mundane existence on planet Earth?

There are mystics and contactees in the twenty-first century who believe a mysterious planet named Solarium is in the same orbit as Earth, but always on the opposite side of the sun. They also claim Solarium is the home of angelic super beings and a base for the Pleiadians who frequent our planet. They also say Solarium is "cloaked" and even its gravitational influence on the other planets is filtered through other dimensions. Amazing as it sounds there is a considerable number of people who believe this and for decades have sponsored channeling sessions to receive "knowledge and teachings" from the Solarians.

I have attended one of these sessions and found nothing that would convince me this group is in communication with highly involved beings. The followers of Solarium embrace their beliefs with fanatical veracity. In this case we see how the improvable and the vastness and complexities of space can be used to validate the existence of something that can only exist in the mind of the faithful true believer.

For over twenty years there has been a great deal of talk in the UFO and contactee community about a giant planet called Nibiru.[193] Nibiru is one of the phantom planets that astronomers know does not exist, but some conspiracy theorists and contactees say it does and they believe it's heading right for us from the outer reaches of our solar system.

The idea that doomsday was coming after a collision between Earth and Nibiru originated in 1995 from a contactee who claims she can

---

193   Named after the Sumerian god of the night sky.

receive messages from aliens who hail from Zeta Reticuli through an implant in her brain.[194]

Since then well over a hundred internet websites have emerged centering on the prophesied collision of Nibiru and Earth. In these websites are hundreds of pages of alien warnings given to us by "benevolent extraterrestrials" channeled through self-proclaimed modern-day prophets on how humanity can save itself.[195]

The first predication that was made during the last decade of the twentieth century stated that Nibiru was supposed to have a close fly-by or crash into Earth, wiping out 90 percent of the human race shortly after Comet Hale-Bopp left the inner solar system. It is the prediction of the Nibiru doomsday that may have pushed the Heaven's Gate cult leader, Marshall Applewhite, over the edge.

After the comet was no longer visible and doomsday did not keep its appointment, the destruction of Earth was changed to 2012 by the contactees. When 2012 passed without incidence, the predication once again changed to "sometime in the early twenty-first century."

The Nibiru doomsday predication is so ridiculous that you have to wonder how anyone could possibly believe it. Many of the websites sell Nibiru books, tapes with messages channeled from the aliens, and even Nibiru doomsday "survival kits."

---

194   They seem to be the same aliens that Betty and Barney Hill claim abducted them back in the sixties. Betty was shown a map on the ship, which she later drew under hypnosis that showed the star configuration in the Reticulum star system. To this day the map has never been disproven. I knew Betty Hill and met with her several times and she always stuck to her story. The Betty and Barney Hill story is presented in the book *The Interrupted Journey* by John G. Fuller.

195   You can get the latest on the web. The main site that seems to have started the Nibiru scare is Zetatalk.com. The website is actually well done and filled with information about the paranormal, lost civilizations, alien contact, and whatever you're interested in. However, the information above came from my own research and not the website mentioned.

There are three websites where a self-appointed human–alien representative offers to train people to become ambassadors for the Galactic Brotherhood to help spread the "truth" and promises contact with aliens after they pay a rather steep fee and complete the training.

In 2011 while I was still teaching, several parents of children in my sixth grade class contacted me, since their child accessed one of the Nibiru doomsday websites and was terrified after reading it. I was asked to talk with them in private, explaining there was no truth in the matter and the world was not going to end in 2012. I ended up addressing the entire middle school in the auditorium to ensure our students that doomsday would not occur in December of 2012 and there is no phantom-rogue planet on a collision course with Earth.

In response to the public concern, astronomers have openly stated for years that if there was a giant planet heading for Earth, they would know about it. There are still many who think NASA is covering it up to avoid a worldwide panic. Although we know there are a number of dwarf planets beyond the orbit of Pluto, nothing that fits the description of Nibiru has been confirmed.

There is a theory among some scientists that a large planet is in fact lurking somewhere at a great distance from the sun, but it would be no threat to Earth. There is a small group of astronomers who are constantly imaging the celestial sphere, looking for new planets beyond Pluto. Astronomers have noted that the orbits of Neptune and the dwarf planets are being affected by the gravitational attraction of something they can't see. Some professional astronomers think it's the elusive Planet X, while others call it Planet 9, while still other scientists are calling it a waste of time.

Regardless of whether Nibiru is real or not, the idea that something mysterious is lurking in the darkest reaches of our solar system has influenced the thinking of humans billions of miles away on a tiny planet called Earth. In response to its possible existence, the phantom planet Nibiru has resulted in the creation of cults and provided fuel for conspiracy theorists, but mostly it generated fear, especially in our children.

In December 2015 astronomers detected a single fast-moving object at a considerable distance from the sun. They named it "Gna" after the Norse messenger goddess. The first impression was that Gna was a dwarf planet with a diameter of about 400 miles. However, if it were a rogue planet not gravitationally bound to the sun and as far away as 4000 AU, it could be much larger.

The discovery was never confirmed and the scientific community's response was extremely skeptical. Follow-up investigations have proven negative since the mysterious object can no longer be detected. Could the ghostly object known as Gna be one of the phantom planets known as Nibiru, X, or 9? I guess we will never know, because there has been no further information since its questionable discovery.

In *Star Trek: Into Darkness*, the crew of the enterprise is sent to survey an inhabited world named Nibiru. They end up saving the planet and Captain Kirk is later chastised by Starfleet for violating the Prime Directive of non-interference with a developing species. In this case it's obvious where the writers of the film got the name for the hypothetical planet.

The unusual gravitational perturbation of the outer and dwarf planets is something that has been noticed for quite some time. Astronomers have not yet discovered the reason for this anomalous effect. The search for a mysterious Planet X as the culprit continues into the twenty-first century. In the late twentieth century, several scientists put forward a theory to explain the strange motions of Neptune and the Plutoids, a conjecture so frightening the world can only hope is wrong.

Nemesis: the Death Star

In 1984 paleontologists David Raup and Jack Sepkoski claimed that they had identified a pattern of mass extinctions on Earth over the last 250 million years. By analyzing the geologic fossil record, they discovered the average time interval between extinction events was 26 million years.

A team of astronomers working independently also discovered a similar pattern and proposed a theory that states the sun may have an undetected companion star in a highly elliptical orbit that periodically disturbs comets in the Oort cloud, causing them to be pushed into the inner solar system and impact the planets, resulting in mass extinctions on Earth. Their theory became known as the "Nemesis" or the "Death Star" hypothesis.

Nemesis is a hypothetical red or brown dwarf companion star to our sun orbiting at an average distance of about 1.25 light-years. As of the publication of this book, astronomers using the Infrared Astronomical Satellite (IRAS) failed to discover Nemesis. If Nemesis is out there, it has eluded detection so far. Perhaps it is much smaller and fainter than previously thought.

In the early nineties, a high school earth science workbook had a lesson on the Nemesis mystery. As of the beginning of the twenty-first century, this chapter has been removed since many educators think doomsday and speculation should not be taught in school.

Nemesis Update, August 2017

Astronomers were once convinced that stars like our sun are born from a nebulous cloud by themselves. The theory was the cloud that formed our sun and the planets was small and did not contain enough matter to produce more than one star. First proposed in the late twentieth century, this hypothesis was used to rule out the existence of Nemesis.

Recent findings by theoretical physicists at the University of California at Berkeley and radio astronomers from the Smithsonian Astrophysical Observatory at Harvard University suggest our sun was born with a companion, most likely a red dwarf star.

The new claim is based on a radio survey that discovered that all sunlike stars are born with at least one companion. Astronomers now believe that Nemesis does exist, and although it hasn't been discovered, the Death Star is believed to orbit our sun at a distance 17–20 times farther from the sun than the planet Neptune.

This new information gives the theory of periodic mass extinctions more credibility since it is thought that the gravitational attraction of Nemesis at its closest approach may have pushed a rain of comets and asteroid-like objects into the realm of planets in our solar system.

Although the inner planets are small targets, a great number of objects increases the chances of impact with Earth. The asteroid that hit Earth 65 million years ago and caused the extinction of the dinosaurs could have been the result of Nemesis. Astronomers are once again planning a search for the sister of our sun, the deadly Death Star.[196]

The Black Hole

Another theory explaining the gravitational disruptions we see in the outer solar system is that they may be due to a black hole slowly pulling our sun and planets toward it. Whether Planet X, Nemesis, Nibiru, or a black hole is responsible, teams of astronomers from every major country are working together, utilizing the latest technology, to solve the mystery of gravitational variance in the outer solar system.

My generation was brought up during the Cold War when nuclear doomsday seemed to be a reality. We had atomic bomb drills at school and air raid sirens were often tested. While those of us who grew up in the fifties and sixties are numb to today's doomsday scenarios, children of the twenty-first century seem more sensitive to such fears. In response, their parents and grandparents have done what they can to shield them from all the end of the world scenarios presented on television and the internet. Shrewd business people have discovered that doomsday stories improve television ratings and sell merchandise.

---

196   For more information, see http://news.berkeley.edu/2017/06/13/new-evidence that-all-stars-are-born-in-pairs.

The children of my generation feared the end of the world would come from Russian missiles, while young people today look up to the sky and wonder if doomsday will come from somewhere in the dark vastness of space.

Recommended Reading

Baum, Richard, and William Sheehan. *In Search of Planet Vulcan: The Ghost in Newton's Clockwork Machine*. New York: Plenum Press, 1977.

Campbell, Joseph. *The Power of Myth*. Potter/TenSpeed/Harmony, 1988.

Fuller, John G. *The Interrupted Journey*. London: Souvenir Press Ltd, 1970.

Hamilton, Edith. *Mythology*. Boston: Little, Brown and Company, 1942.

Hawkins, Stephen. *The Universe in Short*. New York: Bantam Press, 2001.

Hynek, J. Allen. *The UFO Experience*. New York: Ballantine Books, 1974.

Hynek, J. Allen, Philip Imbrogno, and Bob Pratt. *Night Siege: The Hudson Valley UFO Sightings*. St. Paul: Llewellyn Worldwide, 1998.

Imbrogno, Philip J., and Marianne Horrigan. *Celtic Mysteries: Windows to Another Dimension in America's Northeast*. New York: Cosimo Publishing, 2008.

Joseph, Frank. *Unearthing Ancient America*. Franklin: Career Press, 2009.

Keel, John. *Operation Trojan Horse*. Lilburn: IllumNet Press, 1996.

Michell, John, and Robert J. Rickard. *Phenomena: A Book of Wonders*. New York: Knopf Doubleday Publishing Group, 1977.

Sagan, Carl. *Cosmos*. New York: Random House, 1980.

———*The Cosmic Connection*. New York: Random House, 1976

Sanderson, Ivan T. *Uninvited Visitors: A Biologist Looks at UFOs*. New York: Crowles Education Corporation, 1967.

Sitchin, Zecharia. *Genesis Revisited*. New York: Avon Publishing, 1990.

Skinner, Charles. *Myths and Legends of Our Land*. Philadelphia: J. B. Lippincott Press, 1896.

Westfall, Richard. *A Biography of Isaac Newton*. Cambridge: Cambridge University Press, 1980.

Bibliography

Although most of the material used in this book comes from my own investigation and research files, the following resources were used to supplement information. Over the past forty years I have collected detailed reports of many types of paranormal events. From 1982–2011 my astronomy column appeared on a weekly and monthly basis in thirteen Connecticut newspapers. The listing of resource material below can also be used as a reference for other researchers and will make an excellent source for those who want to study selected topics of this book in greater detail.

Adamski, George, and Leslie Desmond. *Flying Saucers Have Landed.* London: W. Laurie, 1952.

Ancient Aliens. Seasons 1, 3, and 5. Narrated by Robert Clotworthy. The History Channel. Originally released April 20, 2010.

Balch, Robert, and David Taylor. "Heaven's Gate: Implications for the Study of Commitment to New Religions." *Encyclopedic Sourcebook of UFO Religions.* Amherst: Prometheus, 2003.

Bonnefoy, Yves. *Roman and European Mythologies.* Translated by Wendy Doniger. Chicago: University of Chicago Press, 1992.

Bonwick, James. *Irish Druids and Old Irish Religions*. New York: Dorset Press, 1986.

"Comet of the Century." *TIME*, June 4, 1973.

Constable, Trevor James. *The Cosmic Pulse of Life: The Revolutionary Biological Power Behind UFOs*. Garberville: Borderland Publishing, 1990.

Cowling, Thomas George. *Isaac Newton and Astrology*. Leeds: Leeds University Press, 1977.

Eddy, John A. "The Maunder Minimum." *Science*, June 1976.

Encyclopedia Britannica: Academic Edition 2009, "Sun Worship."

Encyclopedia Britannica: Academic Edition 2014.

Fontenrose, Joseph. *Orion: The Myth of the Hunter and the Huntress*. Berkeley: University of California Press, 1981.

Freely, John. *Celestial Revolutionary: Copernicus, the Man and His Universe*. New York: Free Press, 1941.

"Harmonic Convergence." *Washington Post*. August 22, 1987

Homer, Charles. *Studies in the History of Medieval Science*. New York: Frederick Ungar Publishing, 1967.

James, Edward, and Patrick Grim. *Philosophy of Science and the Occult*. Albany: State University of New York Press, 1982.

King James Bible. Nashville: Holman Bible Publishers, 1973.

Korff, Kal K. *Spaceships of the Pleiades: The Billy Meier Story*. Amherst: Prometheus Books, 1977.

Lang, Kenneth R. *The Sun from Space*. Berlin: Springer Science+Business Media, 2008.

Leverington, David. *Babylon to Voyager and Beyond: A History of Planetary Astronomy*. Cambridge: Cambridge University Press, 2003.

"Man and Myth: A Conversation with Joseph Campbell." *Psychology Today*, 1971.

Manilius, Marcus. *Astronomica*. Translation by G. P. Goold. Cambridge: Harvard University Press, 1977.

Molnar, Michael R. *The Star of Bethlehem: The Legacy of the Magi*. New Brunswick: Rutgers University Press, 1999.

Morison, Samuel Eliot. *Admiral of the Ocean Sea: The Life of Christopher Columbus*. New York: Time Publishing Inc., 1962.

Nicholson, Henry B. *Handbook of Middle American Indians*. Austin: University of Texas Press, 1971.

Proctor, Richard A. "Leverrier and the Discovery of Neptune." *New York Times*, September 30, 1877.

Ridgeway, William. *Solar Myths, Tree Spirits, and Totems*. Cambridge: Cambridge University Press, 1915.

Rose, Mark. "When Giants Roamed the Earth." *Archaeology*, November–December 2005.

Sagan, Carl. *Cosmos*. New York: Random House, 1980.

Schaaf, Fred. *The Brightest Stars: Discovering the Universe through the Sky's Most Brilliant Stars*. Hoboken: John Wiley & Sons, 2008.

"Search for Vulcan." *Scientific American*, November 25, 1876.

Smith, William. *A Dictionary of Greek and Roman Antiquities*. Collier Publishing, 1878.

Temple, Robert. *The Sirius Mystery*. New York: St. Martin's Press, 1976.

Glossary of Astronomical Terms

Absolute Magnitude: The brightness of a celestial object when measured at a distance of 32 light-years from Earth.

Albedo: The total percent of light reflected by a planet.

Annular Eclipse: A solar eclipse in which the moon covers all but a bright ring around the circumference of the sun.

Aphelion: When a planet or comet is farthest away from the sun.

Apogee: The point where our moon is at the greatest distance from Earth's center.

Apparition: When a comet is visible in the sky.

Archeoastronomy: Branch of archaeology and astronomy that studies how prehistoric civilizations observed the celestial sphere to establish cycles of the year using megaliths and other stone structures.

Asteroids: Thousands of smaller bodies or planetoids that orbit around the sun. They range in size from 1.6 miles to 480 miles. Most orbit between Mars and Jupiter.

Astronomical Unit: A unit of distance that is equal to the mean distance of Earth from the sun, or 93 million miles.

Aurora: Radiant emission from the upper atmosphere that occurs intermittently over the middle and high altitudes of both hemispheres. They appear in the form of luminous bands or streamers. Auroras are caused by the constant bombardment of the atmosphere by charged particles from the sun, which then are attracted by earth's magnetic lines of force.

Axis: The point in the central part of a sphere in which it rotates.

Binary Star: A star system composed of two stars that orbit a common center.

Black Hole: A massive object formed at the beginning of the universe or by a gravitational collapse of the core of a massive star exploding as a supernova. The gravitational field is so strong that even light cannot escape.

Bolide: A large, brilliant meteor that explodes.

Brown Dwarf: A cool, dark star too small to initiate nuclear reactions that generate heat and light by the pressure of gravity.

Celestial Sphere: An imaginary spherical dome formed by the sky.

Circumpolar: Circumpolar stars are permanently above the horizon from a given observing point on Earth; that is to say, they never set.

Comet: A celestial body moving about the sun consisting of a central mass surrounded by an envelope of dust and gas that may form a tail that streams away from the sun.

Conjunction: Two or more celestial objects that appear close together in the sky.

Core: The central region of a planet, star, and galaxy.

Cosmology: The branch of astronomy that deals with the general structure and evolution of the universe.

Dark Energy: Energy we cannot detect but we see its effects on matter in the universe.

Dark Matter: A term used to describe matter in the universe that cannot be seen, but can be detected by its gravitational effects on other bodies.

Eclipse: The total or partial blocking of one celestial body by another.

Eclipsing Binary: A binary star with an orbital plane oriented so that one star passes in front of the other.

Ecliptic: The path the sun, moon, and planets take across the celestial sphere.

Ellipse: An oval shape. Kepler discovered the orbits of planets are elliptical in shape and not circular.

Elongation: The angular separation of a planet and the sun.

Ephemeris: Table that identifies the positions of astronomical objects at any given time.

Exobiology: The study, origin, development, and distribution of life-forms that may exist outside of Earth.

Extra Solar: Beyond the sun.

Gas Giant: Planets made primarily of gas; these include Jupiter, Saturn, Uranus, and Neptune.

Gravity: The attractive force that all objects exert on one another; the greater an object's mass, the stronger its gravitational pull.

Greenhouse Effect: An increase in temperature on a planets surface when incoming solar radiation is passed but outgoing thermal radiation is blocked by the atmosphere. Carbon dioxide, methane, and water vapor are three of the major gases responsible for this effect.

Habitable Zone: Zone around a star in which a planet can maintain liquid water on its surface.

Heliacal Rising: The period of time when an object, such as a star, is briefly seen in the eastern sky before dawn and is no longer hidden from the glare of the sun.

Inferior Conjunction: The configuration of an inner planet like Mercury and Venus when it lies between the sun and Earth.

Infrared: A form of light with slightly lower energy than visible light but with greater energy than radio waves. Infrared waves can be felt on your skin as heat.

Interplanetary: Space between the planets.

Interstellar: Space between the stars belonging to the same galaxy.

Ion: An electrically charged atom due to the loss or gain of one or more electrons.

Ionosphere: An atmospheric layer of Earth with a high concentration of ions and free electrons. These ions, which originate from the sun, can cause the ionosphere to act like a mirror reflecting radio waves. This can result in a phenomenon called "skip," which allows radio operators to communicate with another station around the curve of the earth thousands of miles away.

Kuiper Belt: A region in the outer solar system beyond Neptune's orbit that contains millions of small, icy bodies. Pluto is the most well-known Kuiper Belt Object.

Libration: A small twisting in the moon's motion that allows Earth-based observers to see slightly more than half the moon's surface.

Light Pollution: Light, typically from artificial sources, that reaches the night sky, obscuring the view of faint astronomical objects.

Light-year: The distance light travels in one year, equivalent to approximately 5.9 trillion miles (9.5 trillion km).

Limb: Edge of a celestial object.

Long Period Comet: Comets that have orbital periods greater than 200 years.

Luminosity: The amount of light that an object radiates.

Lunar Month: The time of one complete revolution of the moon around Earth, 29.5 days.

Lunation: The time from new moon to new moon, 29.5 days.

Magnetosphere: The region around a planet where its magnetic field traps charged particles from our sun's solar wind.

Magnitude: The measurement of an object's brightness; the lower the number, the brighter the object. For example the moon has a magnitude of about -12 while Venus is -4. Most naked-eye stars range from +1 to +4. The faintest stars you can see in a dark sky are about +5.

Mare: Dark and smooth area on the surface of the moon or on a planet usually formed by melted rock or other volcanic actions.

Meteor Showers: Period of meteor activity that occurs when Earth collides with many meteoroids; an individual shower happens at the same time each year and radiates from one central point in the sky. These particles are the size of a grain of sand and are the remains of the tail of a comet.

Meteorite: Rock from space that survives as it passes through the earth's atmosphere and falls to the ground. Most are made of rock, but some contain large amounts of iron and nickel.

Meteoroid: Small rock that orbits the sun.

Morning Star: Venus, when it appears in the morning sky just before sunrise.

Nebula: A cloud of interstellar gas and dust composed of hydrogen and helium with trace elements.

North-South Celestial Pole: The point in the sky to which Earth's geographical North or South Pole points.

Nova: An explosion on the surface of a white dwarf star that is accreting matter from a nearby companion star, which causes the star to temporarily brighten by a factor of several hundred to several thousand times.

Nuclear Fusion: The process by which two atomic nuclei combine to form a heavier atomic nucleus; this is the energy source of most stars.

Occultation: The passage of one object in front of a smaller one.

Open Cluster: System containing a few dozen to a few thousand stars that formed from the same nebulous cloud and are not close together.

Opposition: When an outer planet like Mars or Jupiter is directly across Earth. At this time the planet is at its closest point and visible all night.

Orbit: Curved path, usually elliptical in shape, that an object follows around a larger object with more mass and greater gravity.

Orbital Period: The length of time it takes one body to orbit another.

Out Gassing: Release of gas from rocky body, especially a comet.

Perigee: When the moon is closest to earth.

Perihelion: Position of an object, or body, when it is closest to the sun.

Planet: A gaseous or rocky body that orbits a star.

Plasma: Gas heated to a state until it contains ions and free floating electrons.

Pulsar: A rotating neutron star that radiates regular synchronous pulses of electromagnetic radiation.

Red Dwarf: A small, cooler star with a low mass and is less luminous than the sun.

Red Giant: Cool star that has expanded up to a hundred times the diameter of the sun and is at the end of its life.

Red Supergiant: A star with a lower temperature nearing the end of its life. This type of star usually expands from a hundred to a thousand times the diameter of the sun.

Retrograde: Objects that move or appear be moving in the opposite direction when compared to other bodies on the celestial sphere or in the solar system orbiting the sun or a planet.

Revolution: Orbital motion of a body around a common center of mass or another body.

Short Period Comet: A comet that orbits the sun in less than 175 years.

Solar Eclipse: When the moon passes between the earth and the sun and covers the solar disk.

Solar Wind: Stream of charged particles coming from the sun primarily consisting of protons and electrons.

Solstice: Two points on the celestial sphere where the vertical ray of the sun striking Earth is farthest north or south of the equator. This marks the first day of summer and winter for the Northern Hemisphere.

Speed of Light: The speed of light through a vacuum is 186,000 miles per second, or 300,000 km per second.

Superior Conjunction: When an inner planet such as Venus is on the far side of the sun as seen from Earth.

Supernova: A massive star that explodes. A single supernova can outshine every star in the galaxy in which it belongs.

Terminator: Boundary of a planet or moon separating the lighted from the unlit sides.

Terrestrial Planet: Planets with solid rock surfaces, which includes Mercury, Venus, Earth, and Venus.

Trans-Neptunian Object: Object in our solar system lying beyond the orbit of Neptune.

Transit: Passage of a smaller body in front of a larger body. An example would be the planet Mercury crossing the solar disk as seen from Earth.

Umbra: Area of complete darkness in a shadow.

Variable Star: Star that varies in brightness and energy output.

Vernal Equinox: Time of the year when the vertical ray of the sun crosses celestial equator toward the north, usually around March 21.

Visible Light: Wavelengths in the electromagnetic spectrum that the human eye can see.

White Dwarf: Dense remains of a star similar to our sun that has collapsed to the size of Earth.

Zenith: Point on the celestial sphere directly above an observer.

Zodiac: Constellations that are on or close to the ecliptic.

Zodiacal light: Cone of light caused by small particles of reflected sunlight that can be observed above the horizon near the ecliptic before sunrise or after sunset.

Index